AIB Sub-Saharan Africa (SSA) Series

Series Editors

Ifedapo Adeleye
Lagos Business School
Lagos, Nigeria

Lyal White
Gordon Institute of Business Science
Johannesburg, South Africa

Aim of the Series

Sub-Saharan Africa has recently been cited as the 'next frontier for growth,' and academics across business disciplines are increasingly focusing on this specific territory of study. **The AIB Sub-Saharan Africa (SSA)** series addresses topical issues concerning this emerging market. With contributions from leading scholars in the field comprising of Africans in the diaspora, non-African scholars with a keen interest in the region and African scholars and consultants who reside in the region, the series is uniquely multi-disciplinary in nature with contributions from the core business disciplines including strategy, entrepreneurship, marketing, international business, human resources management. Other interesting areas include political economy, economic geography, development economics, and international economics.

More information about this series at
http://www.springer.com/series/14762

Ifedapo Adeleye • Lyal White • Nathaniel Boso
Editors

Africa-to-Africa Internationalization

Key Issues and Outcomes

palgrave
macmillan

Editors
Ifedapo Adeleye
Lagos Business School
Lagos, Nigeria

Nathaniel Boso
Leeds University Business School
Leeds, West Yorkshire, United Kingdom

Lyal White
Gordon Institute of Business Science
Johannesburg, South Africa

AIB Sub-Saharan Africa (SSA) Series
ISBN 978-3-319-30691-9 ISBN 978-3-319-30692-6 (eBook)
DOI 10.1007/978-3-319-30692-6

Library of Congress Control Number: 2016949781

Printed on acid-free paper

This Palgrave Macmillan imprint is published by Springer Nature
The registered company is Springer International Publishing AG Switzerland

Preface

The Academy of International Business-Sub Saharan Africa (AIB-SSA) Book Series features a collection of impactful research papers and teaching cases aligned to the theme of the annual conference of the AIB-SSA chapter. The 2015 conference of the chapter, which was successfully hosted by Gordon Institute of Business Science (GIBS), South Africa, from August 26 to 28, had the theme "Africa Direct Investment: Trends, Prospects, Challenges and Policy Issues." The conference attracted over 90 delegates from 20 countries of the Sub-Saharan Africa region and around the world. Over 25 doctoral candidates and early career faculty participated in the Journal of International Business Studies (JIBS) Paper Development Workshop led by Prof. Elizabeth Rose of the University of Otago, New Zealand, and Prof. Robert Grosse of American University, Sharjah, UAE.

Building on keynote addresses and presentations at the 2015 conference, this volume provides research papers and teaching cases that highlight an emerging trend in Foreign Direct Investment (FDI) to Africa: the increase in trade and investment between African countries. This is an area that has received little coverage as attention has focused on FDI from traditional sources (Western economies) and, of late, the BRIC economics of Brazil, Russia, India and China economies (especially China). This volume aims to draw attention to this trend, defining the agenda and providing guidance on directions for future research.

The coverage is extensive sector-, geography-, and discipline-wise. Contributions cover the key economies in all the sub-regions of Sub-Saharan Africa—Nigeria, South Africa, Kenya, Ghana, Uganda, and Mozambique—as well as the key industries—extractive, financial services, telecommunications, brewing, and hospitality. The chapters in this volume cover multiple academic disciplines and managerial functions, including strategy and entrepreneurship, marketing and brand management, economics, and political economy.

The volume contains not only empirical and conceptual research papers but also a collection of teaching case studies. These cases help to illustrate the practical issues and challenges organizations face when they embark on Africa-to-Africa internationalization. Hence, the volume serves as a "bridge" publication, providing both theoretical and real-life insights on an important phenomenon in the African context. All the chapters are written by scholars and executives with practical and extensive professional experience conducting international business in Africa.

The AIB-SSA chapter—in line with its commitment to advancing International business (IB) research, teaching, and practice in Africa—will continue to organize annual conferences and capacity-building activities. We hope that this second volume in the Palgrave Macmillan AIB-SSA Book Series will help readers better understand the complexities and challenges of doing international business in Africa. Titles in the AIB Sub-Saharan Africa Book Series include:

Ifedapo Adeleye, Kevin Ibeh, Abel Kinoti and Lyal White (Editors)
The Changing Dynamics of International Business in Africa

Ifedapo Adeleye, Lyal White and Nathaniel Boso (Editors)
Africa-to-Africa Internationalization: Key Issues, Challenges and Outcomes

Ifedapo Adeleye, Lagos, Nigeria
Lyal White, Johannesburg, South Africa
Nathaniel Boso, Leeds, UK

Acknowledgements

We would like to express our sincere thanks and appreciation to all those who contributed to this volume and to the conference. Many thanks also to the following institutions for the immense contribution of their faculty to the 2015 conference and to this book: GIBS (Nicola Kleyn, Lyal White, Adrian Saville, and Helena Barnard), China Europe International Business School (CEIBS) (Annette Nijs and Mathew Tsamenyi), and Lagos Business School (Chris Ogbechie, Olawale Ajai, and Ifedapo Adeleye).

Many thanks to our conference sponsors—the Tony Elumelu Africapitalism Institute (Platinum Sponsor), PYXERA Global (Gold Sponsor), GIBS Centre for Dynamic Markets and Lagos Business School (Silver Sponsors), and Emerald Group Publishing (Bronze Sponsor)—for their immense support. We are especially grateful to Mr. David Rice of the Tony Elumelu Africapitalism Institute and Dr. Jurie van Niekerk of PYXERA Global for contributing to the insightful scholar-meets-practice sessions.

Many individuals supported the inaugural conference as PDW and symposia/special topic session organizers, track chairs, session chairs, and reviewers; their contribution in raising the quality of the papers and cases selected for this volume is much appreciated. We especially thank Professors Elizabeth Rose, Africa Ariño, Robert Grosse, Amon Chizema, Kenneth Amaeshi, and Nathaniel Boso.

Special thanks to the Palgrave Macmillan team for extending their special partnership with the AIB to the SSA chapter. We are grateful to Liz Barlow and Maddie Holder for their efficient and professional handling of the production of this volume.

Finally, we thank the contributors to this second volume of the SSA book series for their efforts to increase our understanding of Africa-to-Africa internationalization. Their commitment to this project made the editors' work easier, and without them we sure wouldn't have this insightful book.

Contents

Notes on the Editors and Contributors

Ifedapo Adeleye is Senior Lecturer in Strategy and Management and Director of Custom Executive Education at Lagos Business School, Nigeria. Dr. Adeleye's research engagements are largely practice-driven and revolve around three critical areas of management: strategy practice and execution, performance and reward management, and international business and comparative management. Dapo has produced over 50 journal articles, book chapters, conference papers, and teaching cases, mainly in international outlets. He is currently engaged in research and case development projects investigating the internationalization of African firms and the challenges of doing business in Africa. Dr. Adeleye received his PhD in Business Administration from Manchester Business School, UK.

Adjei Emmanuel Kofi is a doctoral student in Corporate Strategy and a lecturer in the Department of Marketing and Corporate Strategy, Kwame Nkrumah University of Science and Technology, Kumasi, Ghana. He has an MBA in International Business and a postgraduate diploma in Business Administration from the Kwame Nkrumah University of Science and Technology. He also has a bachelor's degree in Management Studies from the University of Cape Coast, Ghana. He has research interests in marketing, cross-cultural studies, human resource management, corporate strategy, international business, and entrepreneurship. He has rich experience in the area of project management, international business, and management of SMEs.

Ebimo Amungo lectures at the at the Nigerian Turkish Nile University, Abuja, and he is an approved tutor for Edinburgh Business School's Marketing and

Organizational Behavior courses in Nigeria. Amungo has an eclectic background in private and public sector organizations, having worked as a freelance reporter for the British Broadcasting Corporation and as a newspaper publisher and government media spokesman. His journey into academia began with his graduation from Edinburgh Business School, Heriot-Watt University, UK, with a Doctor of Business Administration degree. Amungo's research interests include internationalization of African firms, strategic management in the African context, and the role of context in international business research. Dr. Amungo is the Managing Partner of Amungo Consulting, a management consultancy.

José Barreira is a practicing entrepreneur, specializing in the areas of investment and manufacturing, and a part-time lecturer in entrepreneurship at the Graduate School of Business Administration at the University of the Witwatersrand, Johannesburg, South Africa. Dr. Barreira has published and co-authored a number of papers in accredited journals and is an external examiner of master's dissertations and doctoral theses for a number of universities. He completed his PhD in Entrepreneurship at the University of Pretoria, South Africa.

Claire Beswick heads up the Case Centre at the University of the Witwatersrand Graduate School of Business Administration, having joined the institution as a case writer in September 2001. She has more than 20 years' experience in research and writing, including as a researcher at the South African Institute of Race Relations, as a journalist, and now at the WBS Case Centre. In her position as head of the Case Centre, Claire has written a wide range of cases herself and overseen the writing of most of the cases that are currently in the collection.

Nathaniel Boso is Associate Professor of Marketing at Leeds University Business School, UK. His research interests include international entrepreneurship and innovation management. His research has won multiple awards, including Best Empirical Paper Award at the 25th USASBE Annual Conference and nomination for the 2014 AIB Haynes Prize for the Most Promising Scholar Award. His works have been published in leading scholarly journals, such as the *Journal of Business Venturing,* the *Journal of Product Innovation Management,* and the *Journal of International Marketing*. Dr. Boso sits on the editorial review boards of *International Marketing Review* as an Associate Editor and of *European Journal of Marketing* as a reviewer. He is also a specialist educator in Structural Equation Modelling (using LISREL) and has consulted with multiple companies across Africa. He received his PhD from Loughborough University, UK.

Amanda Bowen is the Case Centre Operations Coordinator at Wits Business School, South Africa. She has been writing and editing case studies for the WBS Case Centre since 2009. Dr. Bowen comes from a work background of retail management and English language teaching. Amanda holds an MA degree with a specialty in TESOL and a D Litt et Phil degree in English. She has written case studies on a range of business topics, including education, organizational design and development, marketing, and sustainability.

Dianna Games is the author of the book *Business in Africa: Corporate Insights* (Penguin South Africa, 2012; reprinted 2013) and has contributed to chapters of a number of other published books, including, recently, *The Changing Dynamics of International Business in Africa* (Palgrave Macmillan, 2015) and *Africans Investing in Africa* (Palgrave Macmillan, 2015). She has also had academic research papers on African issues published. Dianna is a regular contributor to the media and a columnist on Africa for *Business Day* newspaper in South Africa. As the honorary CEO of the South Africa-Nigeria Chamber of Commerce in Johannesburg, formed in 2005, she has played a leading role in facilitating business and investment between Africa's two biggest markets. Dianna is also a Fellow of the Centre for Dynamic Markets and the Gordon Institute of Business Science (GIBS), one of Africa's leading business schools.

Nkemdilim Iheanachor is an International Strategy doctoral student at Lagos Business School, Nigeria. He has a bachelor's degree in Electrical/Electronic Engineering and an MBA from the Lagos Business School. He has had prior experience in banking as a Relationship Manager in the Multilateral, Conglomerates and Private Banking Group of Zenith Bank; as an Investment Banker involved in project finance, mergers and acquisitions, and financial advisory; and as a Consultant involved in advisory engagements for state governments, large multinationals, and local corporates. Nkemdilim has extensively consulted for companies in the area of corporate strategy development, competitive strategy development, and blue ocean strategy development.

Charles Godfrey Mbalyohere is an academic with The Open University, UK, where he earned a PhD and a Master of Research degree in Strategic Management as well as an MBA. His roots, though, are in engineering, having attained an MSc in Food Technology from the University of Applied Sciences, Berlin. Following engagements in the food industry, he got into international management consulting, working with Deloitte for a few years. He was also an associate lecturer with The Open University for several years in the MBA program in continental Europe. Reflecting his diverse interests, he is currently the President of a development NGO in Uganda and among the diaspora. His research interests stretch across pro-market reforms, corporate political strategy, MNC internationalization, entrepreneurship, emerging institutionalization, and emerging market multinationals.

Chris Ogbechie is Senior Fellow in Strategic Management and Director of the FirstBank Sustainability Centre at Lagos Business School, Nigeria. He obtained a first-class honors degree in Mechanical Engineering and an MBA from the University of Manchester and a PhD from Brunel University, UK. He has extensive experience in international business, derived from his work as a marketing/sales executive at Nestlé in Nigeria, Singapore, Malaysia, and Switzerland, and from his consulting work with Nigerian, Ghanaian, and Kenyan firms. Ogbechie has published widely in international journals and has developed several teaching cases, some of which have received international awards.

Stephanie Townsend is a research associate and case writer for the Case Centre of the University of the Witwatersrand Graduate School of Business Administration (WBS). She has researched and written more than 30 cases in the last 11 years that cover a broad range of subject areas, including marketing, information and communications, micro-insurance, and the cellular industry. She began her career at the Centre for Scientific and Technical Information at the Council for Scientific Research in Pretoria and joined the Case Centre upon completion of her master's degree in journalism at the University of Stellenbosch.

Lyal White is the Director of the Centre for Dynamic Markets (CDM) at the Gordon Institute of Business Science (GIBS), where he is also an Associate Professor of Political Economy and International Business in Africa, Asia and Latin America. Prof. White has held various senior research positions in the past and was a Visiting Scholar at the Center for Latin American Studies (CLAS) at the University of California, Berkley. Committed to enhancing cultural understanding and building commercial and political ties between Africa and the world, Prof. White is of the firm belief that a combination of strong institutional and cultural understanding will harness development and long-term prosperity. Prof. White completed his PhD in Political Studies at the University of Cape Town, South Africa. He has published extensively, most recently as co-editor of *The Changing Dynamics of International Business in Africa* (Palgrave Macmillan, 2015) and chapter contributor to *Africans Investing in Africa* (Palgrave Macmillan, 2015).

List of Figures

List of Tables

Part I

Exploring the Africa-to-Africa Internationalization Concept

1

Africa-to-Africa Internationalization: Emerging Trends and Key Issues

Nathaniel Boso, Ifedapo Adeleye, and Lyal White

The Changing Dynamics of International Business in Africa (Adeleye et al. 2015a, b), the inaugural volume of the Academy of International Business Sub-Saharan Africa Chapter Book Series, provides multidisciplinary insights on inward foreign direct investment (FDI) to Africa, outward FDI from Africa, and intra-regional FDI in Africa. Highlighting the emerging trends, key issues, complexities and challenges of doing business in the Sub-Saharan Africa region, the book deliberately covers a wide range of topical issues. As the editors observe, one phenomenon remains understudied in the international business literature: the marked increase in intra-African trade and investment, or Africa-to-Africa internationalization.

N. Boso (✉)
University of Leeds, West Yorkshire, UK
e-mail: N.Boso@leeds.ac.uk

I. Adeleye
Lagos Business School, Ajah, Lagos, Nigeria

L. White
Centre for Dynamic Markets, Gordon Institute of Business Sciences,
Illovo, Johannesburg, South Africa

I. Adeleye et al. (eds.), *Africa-to-Africa Internationalization*, AIB Sub-Saharan Africa (SSA) Series, DOI 10.1007/978-3-319-30692-6_1

> *While much attention in the international business literature has focused on the rise of FDI from BRIC countries into Africa, the literature on intra-African and outward FDI from the region is scant. This is surprising, given the marked increase in the internationalization activities of African firms in the last decade or so: South African multinationals such as MTN, SABMiller, Standard Bank, Telkom, Dimension Data, Massmart, Nampak and ShopRite now have a presence in at least a dozen African countries, as do Nigerian firms such as Dangote and UBA … Togo-based Ecobank has established a significant footprint across the region, with operations in 33 countries. This phenomenal increase in the internationalization activities of African enterprises provides an interesting opportunity to explore the patterns, strategies, barriers and outcomes of the 'Africa-to-Africa Internationalization'*. Adeleye et al. (2015a, b): 5–6

This volume therefore seeks to address this major gap in the literature. *Africa-to-Africa Internationalization: Key Issues and Outcomes* examines the key issues, challenges and prospects of intra-African FDI and provides guidance on avenues for future research. The goal is to increase our understanding of Africa-to-Africa internationalization and, ultimately, to stimulate research about this important but under-researched topic. This introductory chapter provides an extensive overview of Africa-to-Africa internationalization and is organized into three main sections. In the first section, we provide contextual information on Africa's position in the global economy. The second section focuses on the internationalization of African firms, examining current trends, key issues and challenges. In the third section, we highlight the five thematic areas and issues covered in this volume: the rise of pan-African banks, corporate political activity in the context of business regionalization, internationalizing in the digital era, internationalizing in a VUCA region (a region characterized by volatility, uncertainty, complexity and ambiguity), and building proudly African businesses and brands.

Background: Africa in the Global Economy

The global economy is witnessing rapid growth in the economies of developing nations, to the extent that the conventional wisdom that major international business and investment activities are undertaken primarily by multinational enterprises originating from developed economies has come under scrutiny (Sun and Lee 2013). In particular, the global economy has witnessed an increasing number of excellent business models and innovations from the developing world, such that multinationals originating from the developing world are now able to compete with rivals from developed economies (Luo et al. 2011). Meanwhile, as the developing economies of Africa, Asia, Eastern Europe and Latin America continue to outgrow developed economies, as economic prosperity spreads across multiple developing economies, and as these countries continue to be viewed as attractive locations for global investments (UNCTAD 2012), developed economy multinationals, such as Microsoft, General Electric and Cisco, have begun to look to such markets to strengthen their growth trajectories (Khanna and Palepu 2010). While success stories continue to be told about the big emerging markets of Asia (e.g. China and India) and Latin America (e.g. Brazil and Chile) and the transition economies of the former Soviet Union and Eastern Europe, success stories of emerging markets in Africa (e.g. Kenya, Nigeria and South Africa) are seldom the topic of discussion in international business research and policy debates. Indeed, Africa is often in the news for negative reasons: stories of extreme and challenging conditions, including civil wars, revolts, famines, diseases and corruption, often attract headlines in the global press.

At international business and trade forums, discussions tend to coalesce around the idea that Africa is isolated and disconnected from global business and trade activities. Arguments have been put forward that while other continents, particularly Europe, have removed most barriers to international trade, resulting in free movement of goods, services and people, the African continent is still burdened with heavily militarized national borders that hamper free movement of goods, services and people from within and outside the continent. It is also argued that free trade is impossible in Africa because Africa does not have much to offer the world by way of trade links: shipping routes, air networks and internet connections (for both communication and for commerce) to the global economy are underdeveloped. For example, businesses in Africa are required to deal with multiple and incoherent sets of national contract laws, adding billions a year to transaction costs for businesses. Less than 1 % of African consumers shop online within an African border, and most African country markets are barred from online business transactions by severe internet security problems. Inbound financial transactions to Africa are saddled with multifaceted transfer problems, making it increasingly unsafe for multinational enterprises to do business with Africa cost effectively. Land and property ownership is a massive problem: traditional chiefs and kingships claim informal hereditary rights to landownership, making legal land acquisition in Africa by investors a big risk. While Africa also suffers from the notion of rich-country protectionism by the West, Africa's own domestic policies on customs, tariffs and foreign investment lack transparency and consistency, and poor port and road infrastructure limits timely flow of merchandize goods. Africa's high land transportation costs limit cross-border transactions. Barriers to crossing borders within Africa also restrict intra-African business, thus limiting Africa's participation in the global economy. As can be seen in Fig. 1.1, Africa's contribution to the global economy seems to be negligible compared to other regions.

The Global Flow of Foreign Direct Investment

As the world continues to struggle to recover from the impact of the 2008 financial crisis, and as many nations and regions continue to experience low economic growth, the flow of FDI globally has struggled to return to the growth rates experienced prior to 2008. From 2001 to 2007, global foreign direct investment inflows grew by a compounded annual growth rate (CAGR) of 18.3 %. However, from a post-2008 high of $1.58 trillion in 2011, global FDI inflows have declined by 21 % to $1.23 trillion in 2014. The fall in global FDI inflows has been influenced by a number of economic and political factors. These include the recent economic contraction in the major emerging markets of Brazil and Russia, lacklustre economic growth in the European Union, slowing economic growth in China, and ongoing geopolitical tension in various parts of the world compounded by a crash in oil prices that blew open a hole in the budgets of many oil-producing nations.

One key trend that has emerged from an examination of global FDI flows from 2008 to 2014 is the fact that developing countries, led by Asia and Africa, are now the major recipients of FDI. From 2011 to 2014,

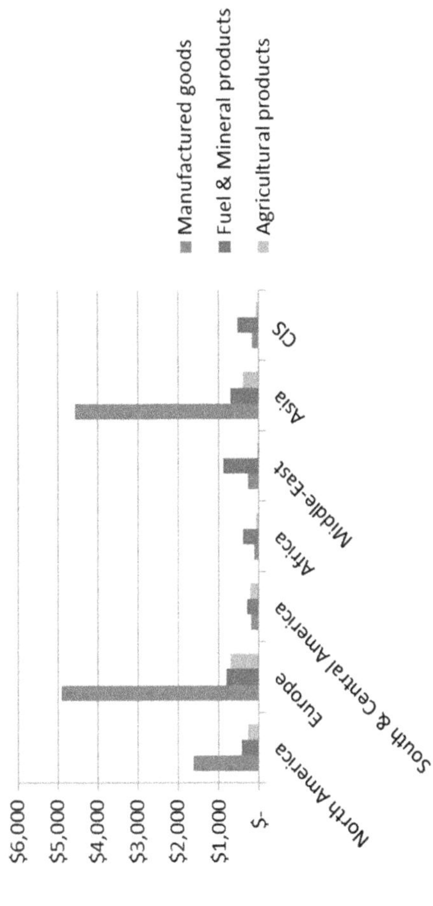

Fig. 1.1 World Merchandize Exports by Region, 2013 (US$ billions). *Source*: WTO International Trade Statistics, 2014

developing countries have seen their share of FDI increase from $639 billion to $681 billion, a 6.6 % increase. Over the same period, global FDI to developed countries fell drastically by 39 %, from $828 billion in 2011 to $498 billion in 2014. Faster economic growth coupled with improved macroeconomic management practices, high domestic demand, a relatively more stable political environment in developing economies, and increased government liberalization policies have improved investing prospects in many parts of the developing world, a trend that many investors seeking higher returns have sought to explore. While Asia continues to attract the largest share of global FDI, accounting for over 40 % of global FDI inflows, Africa's share of this global FDI flow is increasing, a trend that has contributed to post-crisis average growth that is 2 percentage points above that of the world economy.

Foreign Direct Investment to Africa: Overview and the Growth of Intra-African FDI

Since 2005, Africa has experienced significant growth in FDI, from $14 billion in 2005 to $54 billion in 2014. This represents an 18.4 % increase on a CAGR basis, making Africa one of the world's fastest-growing regions for foreign investment. Key factors that have contributed to the growth of FDI into Africa are the rise in commodity prices, increased government liberalization in certain sectors of the economy, including finance and telecommunications, and slow global economic growth in other regions of the world. These factors have made the faster-growing economies of Africa more attractive to investors, particularly emerging market investors. In recent times, however, following the dramatic decline in global commodity prices, FDI into Africa has declined slightly, from $56 billion to $54 billion in 2014. Egypt, Ghana, Nigeria, South Africa, and central African countries like Ethiopia have emerged as the major destination for FDI.

FDI inflows into Africa have traditionally been dominated by developed countries, with Western Europe and the United States providing substantial FDI in terms of capital invested and the number of projects engaged in. However, while Europe and North America have been the major sources of FDI funds, their share of the number of FDI-related products has stagnated.

Table 1.1 Major Sources of FDI Projects to Africa

Region	Share of projects in 2005 (%)	Share of projects in 2014 (%)
Western Europe	39.0	36.8
Africa	7.9	19.2
Asia-Pacific	17.5	15.7
North America	24.6	14.7
Middle East	8.0	9.1
Rest of Europe	1.3	3.7

Source: Ernst & Young Africa Attractiveness Survey, 2015

Intra-African investors are increasingly becoming a major source of FDI (as measured by the number of projects, see Table 1.1). In 2005, Africa's share of total FDI projects announced on the continent amounted to approximately 7.9 %. By 2014, FDI projects originating from Africa had increased to about 19 %, led by transnational corporations from Nigeria, Kenya and South Africa. For many countries, particularly land-locked or non-oil-exporting countries, intra-African FDI remains a significant source of foreign capital. The increasing trend in intra-African FDI is in line with many African governments' effort at improving regional ties by encouraging trade within Africa. Intra-African projects have been concentrated in manufacturing and services, particularly financial and telecommunications services. In contrast to external FDI flows, only 3 % of intra-African FDI projects were in the extractive industries during the period from 2009 to 2013. Intra-African trade, while small, is growing and is seen as a major source of expansion for many African corporations seeking to increase their presence outside of their home countries.

Intra-African FDI flows have taken an interesting and promising course in recent years. According to *World Investment Report* (2014), the observed increase in FDI to Africa is being sustained by growth in intra-African flows. Importantly, FDI inflows to Africa have risen by 4 % to $57 billion, an increase driven by international and regional market-seeking and infrastructure investments. In the period leading up to 2014, expectations for sustained growth of an emerging middle class attracted FDI in consumer-oriented industries, including food, information technology, tourism, finance and retail. The overall increase has been driven by the eastern and southern African sub-regions, while others have been experiencing falling investments. In southern Africa, flows have almost doubled to $13 billion, mainly due to record-high flows to South Africa and Mozambique.

In both countries, infrastructure has been the main attraction, with investments in the gas sector in Mozambique also playing a role. In East Africa, FDI has increased by 15 % to $6.2 billion as a result of rising flows to Ethiopia and Kenya. Kenya is becoming a favoured business hub, not only for oil and gas exploration but also for manufacturing and transport. Ethiopian industrial strategy may have attracted Asian capital to develop its manufacturing base. FDI flows to North Africa decreased by 7 % in 2014 to $15 billion. Central and West Africa saw inflows decline to $8 billion and $14 billion, respectively, partly due to political and security uncertainties brought about by the Boko Haram insurgency.

Intra-African investments are also increasing, led by South African, Kenyan and Nigerian transnational corporations (TNCs). Between 2009 and 2013, for example, the share of announced cross-border greenfield investment projects originating from within

Africa increased to 18 % from less than 10 % in the preceding period. For many smaller African countries that are often land-locked or non-oil-exporting, intra-regional FDI is a significant source of foreign capital. Increasing intra-African FDI is in line with leaders' efforts towards deeper regional integration. However, for most sub-regional groupings, intra-group FDI represents only a small share of intra-African flows. Only in two regional economic communities (REC) initiatives has intra-group FDI constituted a significant part of intra-African investments. In particular, East African Community (EAC) and South African Development Community (SADC) have respectively recorded 50 % and 90 % jumps in sub-regional FDI flow, largely due to investments in neighbouring countries by the dominant outward-investing economies in these RECs, Kenya and South Africa. RECs have thus so far been less effective for the promotion of intra-regional investment than a wider African economic cooperation initiative could be.

Intra-African projects are concentrated in manufacturing and services. Only 3 % of the value of announced intra-regional greenfield projects is in the extractive industries, compared with 24 % for extra-regional greenfield projects (2009–2013). Intra-regional investment could contribute to the build-up of regional value chains. However, African global value chain (GVC) participation is still mostly limited to downstream incorporation of raw materials for export to developed countries.

Internationalization of African Firms: Current Trends, Key Issues and Challenges

Although Africa's participation in international business and trade seems to be discouraging and still largely concentrated in the extractive sector, evidence is emerging to show that many parts of Africa are progressively overcoming the institutional and infrastructural conditions that undermine the ability of African firms to contribute meaningfully to the global economy. The outcome of these transformations has been the rapid emergence of African multinationals. Indeed, evidence suggests that the speed, scope and scale at which African firms have been investing in Africa and the global economy in the last decade have been phenomenal (Ngwu et al. 2015; Rolfe et al. 2015; McNamee et al. 2015; Krüger and Strauss 2015). In the financial services industry alone, over 70 pan-African banks have emerged, with eight of them having operations in at least ten countries. Many of these regional banks have not only increased their geographic footprint in Africa and neighbouring continents, but they have also become dominant international players (Beck et al. 2014). For instance, Ecobank, Standard Bank and First National Bank (FNB) individually hold over 30 % of banking assets in nine countries across Africa. Beyond banking, African multinationals have emerged in several sectors, from retail to telecommunications, manufacturing, energy, agribusiness, aviation and technology, with firms like MTN, SABMiller, Telkom, Dimension Data, Massmart, Nampak, ShopRite and Dangote now having a presence in at least a dozen African countries (Adeleye et al. 2015a, b; Ibeh 2015). Others, like Oando, Glo, Interswitch, Computer Warehouse Group, Nakumatt, Smile and Sasol, have expanded to several African countries, positioning themselves as serious market challengers in their host economies.

Given the impressive performance of African multinationals on the global stage in recent times, the Boston Consulting Group has identified 40 African global challengers: 18 from southern Africa, 17 from northern Africa, 3 from western Africa and 2 from southeastern Africa. These African challengers fall into five categories. First, *Big Local Players* are African multinationals with 90 % of assets and sales derived from their domestic market but who continue to record an impressive and gradually increasing amount of international activity. A good example is Societe Nationale d'Investissement Group, the largest Moroccan industrial, financial and services conglomerate, which has focused on building leadership and value creation in business activities in Morocco, the Maghreb region and across the African continent. Second, *Exporters* are firms that have a vast majority of their sales coming from exporting operations but whose assets are largely local. These firms tend to be mining and oil companies. Representative of these large African exporters is Sonangol, a parastatal business that oversees petroleum and natural gas production and export in Angola. A third group is *Regional Players*. These African firms have at least 10 % of their assets located outside of their home country but within Africa. Maroc Telecom, the main Moroccan telecommunications operator, with operations in Mauritania, Burkina Faso, Mali and Gabon, is one of these regional players. Ecobank, a pan-African banking conglomerate headquartered in Togo and with banking operations in 36 African countries, is a typical regional player in the financial services sector. In the retail sector, ShopRite Group of Companies, a South African retail giant, is Africa's largest food retailer, operating 1751 corporate and 360 franchise outlets in 15 Africa countries and recently expanding its operations to the Indian Ocean Islands.

A fourth group, the *Multi-Continental Players,* have at least 10 % of their assets outside of Africa. Many were originally regional players but have recently expanded overseas. Orascom Telecom, based in Egypt, is a typical example, as the company has operations in Bangladesh, Europe, the Middle East and Pakistan. South Africa's Aspen Pharma, the largest generic drug maker in the southern hemisphere, has expanded beyond Africa. The company's operations now span 47 countries, including South Africa, Kenya, Nigeria, Tanzania and Uganda, and, outside Africa, Australia, Hong Kong, Malaysia, Philippines, Taiwan, Japan, Ireland, United Arab Emirates, Germany, France, the Netherlands, Mauritius, Brazil, Mexico, Venezuela and the United States. The company announced major acquisitions in 2013, which have taken its operations to emerging markets in the Commonwealth of Independent States, comprised of Russia and the former Soviet republics, as well as to Central and Eastern Europe.

Finally, a fifth group, *Global Players*, comprise three African multinationals with more than half of their assets outside of the continent. Anglo

American, a multinational mining company located in South Africa and with offices in the United Kingdom, is the world's largest producer of platinum, accounting for about 40 % of world outputs. SABMiller, the world's second-largest brewer measured by revenues (after Anheuser-Busch InBev), has operations in 80 countries spread across the world. As of 2009, the company's brands include Fosters, Grolsch, Miller, Peroni and Pilsner, enabling the company to sell more than 21 billion litres of beverages in 2009 alone. Old Mutual, established in 1845 in South Africa and now headquartered in London, is an international investment, savings, insurance and banking group with more than 16 million customers and $419 billion assets under its management.

Another aspect of internationalization of African firms is intra-African investment. In this arena, South Africa has played a leading role, with more than 80 companies listed on the Johannesburg Stock Exchange and operating in Africa across a very diverse range of sectors: mining (AngloGold Ashanti and Gold Fields), retail (Massmart, Pick n Pay, ShopRite, Woolworths, Tiger Brands), telecommunications (MTN, Vodacom) and banking (Standard Bank, FNB), to name but a few.

Current trends reveal a picture of a unique variety of factors propelling African firms to internationalize their operations. These include reliance on networking and inter-organizational cooperation, the tendency to serve regional African markets, the dominance of the service sector, and a rising number of early-stage and minority entrepreneurs. The continent is now witnessing a rising number of business networks comprising private-private partnerships and private-public partnerships intertwined with large business hubs to execute large infrastructural and technology projects across Africa and beyond. For example, Sasol Limited, an integrated energy and chemical processing company headquartered in Johannesburg, South Africa, has been leading the parade to develop and commercialize synthetic fuel technologies, liquid fuels, chemicals and electricity across the world. The company operates large regional hubs in southern Africa, North America and Eurasia, enabling the company to supply its products and services in 37 countries, including Africa, the Americas, Europe, Asia, the Far East and Australasia (Sasol Investor Report 2014; Donnelly 2008). The Sonangol Group, in partnership with the Angolan government, has pioneered one of the largest acquisitions in and beyond Africa, with 30 Sonangol subsidiaries and overseas facilities, including major shareholding in the Portuguese energy company Galp Energia. Outside Africa, the company also maintains footprints in Hong Kong (China) and Houston (USA), among other locations, through inter-firm collaborations (e.g. acquisitions and mergers).

Furthermore, there is a tendency for African firms to serve regional African markets, often believing that knowledge about customers, competitors and regional market institutional norms, values and rules of engagement are similar to conditions at home. Thus, a major driver of internationalization is the low cost of searching for knowledge of situational conditions in regional African markets. The concentration of Sonangol's operating activities in southern Africa, while linked to the nature of its core operating business activity, is a demonstration of the regionalization of African businesses. African retail giants such as ShopRite and Boxer from South Africa and Nakumatt and Tuskys from Kenya have followed a similar regionalization process in their gradual expansion to other African markets. This emerging behavioural characteristic of African firms' internationalization is consistent with established internationalization theory (i.e. the Uppsala model) that asserts that firms tend to focus on their home market first and slowly expand to neighbouring markets to take advantage of low psychic distance before venturing into more psychically distanced markets. However, evidence is also emerging to show rapid internationalization of African firms. For example, many internet-based firms located in Africa are taking advantage of the gradual connectivity of African markets to launch operations in multiple African markets simultaneously soon after inception. For example, M-Pesa, a mobile phone-based money transfer, financing and microfinancing service, originally launched in 2007 in Kenya and Tanzania by Vodafone for Safaricom and Vodacom, internationalized rapidly to distant markets such as South Africa, Afghanistan, India and, recently, Eastern Europe (Visa Africa Integration Index 2014).

Another characteristic of the trend in internationalization of African firms is the dominance of the service sector, particularly banking, telecommunications and retail businesses, and the gradual demise of traditional agricultural and extractive sectors. In contrast to the conventional notion that traditional extractive industries are the driver of Africa's international business and trade, the major drivers of recent internationalization efforts of African firms include expanding non-traditional sectors (particularly African private equity, services and manufacturing), fuelled by growing middle-class consumer markets.

A related driver of contemporary international business transformation in Africa is the rise of early-stage entrepreneurs in the continent, especially in Nigeria and Zambia, ranked in the top ten in the world (see The Africa Report 2015). An interesting phenomenon is that many African nations are now performing well in the Personal Freedom, Economy, and Entrepreneurship & Opportunity sub-indices, fuelling an increasing number of minority (e.g. women and youth) contributions to international business activities on the continent. In particular, female entrepreneurs, who have traditionally been constrained by a variety of factors, including social prejudice, poor access to education, limited access to finance, and exclusion from business networks, are now leading major African conglomerates. For example, Siza Mzimela, the first female chief executive officer (CEO) of South African Airways, is also the first woman in Africa to launch her own regional airline. Also at the forefront of African firms' internationalization have been other African women business leaders, including Maria Ramos, head of former ABSA Group (now Barclays Africa Group), South Africa's largest bank; Nombulelo Moholi, the CEO of South Africa's Telkom Limited; Eva Muraya, the CEO of Brand Strategy and Design company in Kenya; Isabel Dos Santos, the Angolan millionaire businesswoman with majority shares in Angolan cement company Ciminvest and the Banco Angolano de Investimentos; and Hajia Bola Shagaya, the CEO of Bolmus Group International and a board member of Unity Bank in Nigeria.

Given the rising number of African firms internationalizing their operations, Africa has recently been depicted in the global press as being at the receiving end of burgeoning international business and politics (Schwarz and Yellin 2013). For example, a recent Ernst and Young business attractiveness survey concluded: 'While skeptics still abound … a critical mass of African economies have grown at high and sustained rates; so much so that, despite the impact of the ongoing global economic situation, the size of the African economy has more than tripled since

2000. The outlook also appears positive, with many parts of the region forecast to continue experiencing relatively high growth rates and a number of African economies predicted to remain among the fastest growing in the world for the foreseeable future' (Ernst and Young 2013: 4). Given this growth trajectory and the associated competitive pressures that come with it, many African governments are also becoming increasingly oriented towards international markets, aiming to support the internationalization efforts of their home country firms to gain much-needed foreign exchange returns.

Although the increased involvement of multinational enterprises and the opening up of manufacturing and service sectors to international business in Africa are strongly welcomed as ways of broadening the competitiveness of African markets, the increasing opening up of the African market also comes with some notable challenges and issues. Specifically, there are growing concerns that Africa is actually not benefiting from its recent engagement with the global economy. Questions have been raised with respect to whether multinational firms (African and non-African) can be trusted to engage in fair business activities in Africa (see Tull 2006; Woods 2008). Questions have also been asked about how much of this international business activity has truly originated in Africa and whether African firms are ready to handle the influx of foreign multinationals hurrying to Africa to take advantage of emerging opportunities (Bräutigam and Xiaoyang 2011).

The increasing internationalization of African markets has also drawn attention to the issue of Africa's inadequate infrastructure, undersupply of skilled labour, and underdeveloped market-supporting institutions (e.g. commercial courts and supply chain systems). Estimates suggest that Africa still has one of the highest investment costs relative to its levels of income and productivity and in comparison to other countries in the developing world. In addition, research shows that Africa's industries are sparse, and indigenous, minority and foreign investors are fractured along ethnic lines (World Bank 2011). It has been noted that great differences exist in the productivity levels of large and small firms in Africa. These high indirect costs and business environment bottlenecks have a tendency to hold back the performance of African firms relative to their counterparts from other parts of the world. Africa produces a large pool of university graduates, yet much of this skilled force has been lost to former colonial powers and other Western economies that are perceived as greener pastures, making access to skilled workers a headache for emerging multinational enterprises in Africa.

Despite the challenges, Africa is experiencing rapid economic reforms characterized by massive and multifaceted transformation of its institutional environment, including changes in social structures, governmental involvement in economic transactions, and the nature of enterprise ownership (Williamson 2009). Many African countries have made significant progress in recent years to stabilize their political and economic systems, including rising privatization and simplification of laws and regulations. Most industrial sectors are experiencing rapid structural changes, including the opening of their economies to foreign direct investments (Goedhuys and Sleuwaegen 2010; Chironga et al. 2011). Indeed, some African governments are making deliberate efforts to attract African professionals residing in the diaspora to return home. For example, in 2002 a project was initiated by technology firms, non-profit organizations and United Nations agencies to reverse the loss of professional skills from Africa (Mutume 2003). These transformations and initiatives have brought substantial opportunities for African firms to leverage their capabilities for growth. The dynamics have also shaped the managerial assumptions and decision-making processes of many internationalizing African firms, including decisions regarding how entrepreneurial opportunities are pursued and how customer value is created and delivered in Africa.

All of these developments indicate that there are plentiful avenues for scholarly research into the dynamics and challenges in Africa and their implications for the global competitiveness of African firms. In particular, international business dynamics and the challenges across Africa provide opportunities for researchers to identify under-recognized and under-researched themes and phenomena in order to develop new theories and extend existing concepts (Whetten 2009). Yet, scholarly efforts to understand how African firms are strategically managed for international competitiveness have only recently begun to take shape. This book series is, therefore, an attempt not only to highlight important international business opportunities and challenges facing internationalizing African firms but also to examine interesting and challenging research opportunities related to African businesses investing in Africa and beyond.

With the increasing speed, scope and scale of intra-African internationalization experienced over the last decade or so, several issues have come to the fore. Will African firms continue investing in the region, expanding their geographic footprint and becoming market leaders (or challengers) on a continent historically dominated by European multinationals and, in recent years, by emerging market multinationals? More importantly for international business scholars, what research opportunities exist on the internationalization of African firms? In the second chapter (of Part I), Adeleye and Boso attempt to address these two issues. First, the authors provide a brief analysis of likely future trends in Africa-to-Africa internationalization, 'predicting' the following four trends: an increase in the scale and scope of geographic expansion of African firms; the expansion of African investments/Africa-focused internationalization by Africa's multi-continental and global players; a reduction in the internationalization age of African firms and the emergence of born regional firms; and the emergence of powerful foreign-owned, pan-African multinationals. These likely future trends (as well as the current trends highlighted in this volume) provide interesting opportunities for international business researchers to examine the internationalization of African firms, contributing to the discourse on emerging and frontier market multinationals. Given the scant extant literature on Africa-to-Africa internationalization, the authors' discussion spans a broad range of topical issues in the international business literature: drivers and motivations for internationalization, location determinants of FDI, speed of the internationalization process, and internationalization and firm performance. Adeleye and Boso's review also provides a summary of the literature in these areas, drawing extensively from studies on emerging market multinationals while providing direction on fruitful research avenues.

Thematic Areas Covered in This Volume

The remainder of this chapter provides a summary of five major themes captured across the chapters presented in Parts II and III of this volume: the rise of pan-African banks (Chap. 3), corporate political activity in the context of business regionalization (Chap. 4), internationalizing in the digital era (Chap. 5), internationalizing in a VUCA region (Chaps. 6, 7 and 8), and building proudly African businesses and brands (Chap. 9). Part III (Chaps. 6, 7, 8 and 9) comprises four cases that illustrate practical issues and challenges firms face when embarking on Africa-to-Africa internationalization.

The Rise of Pan-African Banks

The banking sector has led the way in driving Africa-to-Africa internationalization (Ngwu et al. 2015), with a ten-fold increase in international expansion since 1990 (Boojihawon and Acholonu 2013). These pan-African banks now outnumber the colonial and Western banks that have historically maintained a region-wide presence in Africa. Of the 104 cross-border banks in the region, about two thirds are of African origin (Beck et al. 2014). Banks from the three regional giants—South Africa, Nigeria and Kenya—and Morocco have dominated the group of pan-African banks. South Africa's 'big four' have advanced northwards strongly, with Standard Bank leading the pack with operations in 18 countries. Nedbank has subsidiaries in six markets and is leveraging its alliance with Togo-based Ecobank, the regional lender with operations in 36 African economies. Kenya's Equity Bank has expanded to four countries and has ambitious pan-African expansion plans. Nigeria's UBA now has operations in 19 markets, and Guaranty Trust Bank operates in nine countries. Most banks have internationalized by first expanding to neighbouring countries, then to their sub-region, and then to the entire region. With this rapid internationalization, many African banks now have significant asset share in foreign countries and are considered 'systemically important' operators. Standard Bank, for instance, holds over 10 % of banking assets in nine countries, and there are about ten instances where Ecobank, Standard Bank, BMCE Bank or First National Bank individually hold more than 30 % of banking system assets outside their domestic economies (Beck et al. 2014).

What is driving the internationalization of these pan-African banks? What are the location determinants and motives for internationalization? How can we explain the internationalization pattern and process of these financial institutions? Do these firms follow the same pattern as other internationalizing African firms, or is the pattern similar to those of established or emerging market banks? How do African banks tend to enter new markets? How do pan-African banks overcome the liabilities of foreignness when expanding to other African countries? How do they overcome the liabilities of country of origin, smallness and newness? How do internationalizing banks engage key stakeholders, such as customers and regulators? What ownership advantages do internationalizing African firms have? Do regionally focused African banks perform better than domestically focused banks? (How) Are pan-African banks able to compete with the more established colonial and Western banks (like Barclays, Standard Chartered, BNP Paribas, Société Générale and Citi)? Do pan-African banks tend to target the same corporate or high-value segment as the established multinationals, or do they instead focus on serving retail and base-of-the-pyramid segments?

Empirical evidence, building on extant exploratory studies, is required to increase our understanding of these issues (Ngwu et al. 2015; Boojihawon and Acholonu 2013). The Nigerian banking sector provides an interesting context to explore the issue of Africa-to-Africa bank internationalization. Many Nigerian banks, following the increase in the minimum capital requirement from Naira 2 billion (around US$ 14 million) to Naira 25 billion (around US$ 180 million) in 2005, used part of their newly raised capital to finance international growth. The pattern of internationalization across the banks has been quite similar, as they tend to first expand to neighbouring Ghana and then to the rest of Anglophone West Africa; only a few banks have expanded to Francophone Africa or outside the West Africa region (Ngwu et al. 2015). Beyond the regulator-induced institutional push factor, it is important to understand what other institutional factors and demand pull factors explain the internationalization decisions of Nigerian banks. In Chap. 3, 'Examining the Factors Influencing the International Expansion of Nigerian Banks', Ebimo Amungo attempts to provide an explanation. Evidence from the five case study firms suggests that beyond the banking sector reforms in the mid-2000s, other expansion factors have included a shift in the strategic scope of the banks and a desire to exploit tangible and intangible assets in less developed but profitable banking markets in Sub-Saharan Africa.

Corporate Political Activity in the Context of Business Regionalization

Research suggests that firms develop ties with political authorities (including governmental officials and regulators) to earn regulatory resources and opportunities. While some scholars argue that many firms politically disengage and tend to pursue arms-length relationships with political leaders to avoid accusations of political patronage in the global business arena (e.g. Baron 1995), recent observations indicate that corporate political activity is globally pervasive because it provides firms opportunities to (1) influence the public policy agenda (Oliver and Holzinger 2008), (2) lower operational costs, (3) gain favourable access to resources under the control of state officials (Sheng et al. 2011) and (4) obtain target market legitimacy (Li et al. 2008). Hence, there is a growing suggestion that firms need to develop their corporate political networking competences and capabilities. For example, research shows that Standard & Poor 500 companies spent nearly US$ 1 billion on political contributions in 2010 alone, with 87 % committed to the United States for federal lobbying expenditures on social and environmental policies (Skroupa 2012). In Europe, evidence shows that firms are getting ahead of the competition, spending heavily on hiring former politicians and diplomats to lobby European Union policy makers to enact favourable legislation (Lipton and Hakim 2013). In China, being close to communist party leadership is a major strategic asset for firms seeking favourable treatment from industry regulators (Sheng et al. 2012). In Africa, business conditions tend to experience rampant political shifts, and it is well known that corporate executives continue to bankroll political electoral campaigns in many African democracies (Burgis et al. 2014). It is contended that several Sub-Saharan African leaders are able to hold on to political office, and to even attempt to change constitutional provisions in their favour, because of financing provided by business organizations (Burgis et al. 2014). Bankrolling political leaders is one way firms influence public policy to obtain preferential access to state-controlled resources (Saffu 2003). As a result, it has been contended that firms with excess discretionary capital and executives with good political networking skills have the advantage of paying their way through into the corridors of political power to influence regulations that help reduce a company's operational costs (Schuler et al. 2002).

Why is corporate political activity so pervasive in Africa? First of all, it is important to highlight that corporate political activity is not an Africa-only phenomenon. Li and Zhang (2007) argue that in any developing society where formal institutional frameworks are not well developed, business success is predicated on the idea of 'who you know', to the extent that political (as well as social) connections help substitute for the insufficient formal infrastructure (Sheng et al. 2012; Acquaah 2012). In Africa, factor mobility is severely limited by market inefficiencies and governmental interferences (Acquaah 2012); hence, corporate political activity provides corporations flexible access to resource allocation. In addition, Acquaah (2012) argues that because risk and uncertainty are high in Africa, ties to political leadership help maximize a firm's access to valuable industry information on impending new regulatory changes. It is also noted that increased institutional uncertainty has given rise to increased suspicion and lack of trust among African people, and the richness and usefulness of information are evaluated not on the basis of people's knowledge and competence but on the basis of people's relations (Acquaah 2012). Furthermore, Acquaah (2007) argues that Sub-Saharan Africa is a highly collectivistic region in which the extended family and the broader community wield substantial influence on corporate behaviour. Within Africa's collectivist cultures, community leaders such as local chiefs, kings, religious leaders and extended family heads have the powerful role of decreeing access to local resources and information. In Nigeria, for example, there may be an elected national government, but family heads, chiefs and kings are better recognized as custodians and allocators of resources (including lands). Thus, ties in relation to kinship, village of origin, religion and political party are important aspects of African business life (Khayesi et al. 2014). There is a notion that Africa is still a society of many strong men who wield significant influence, sometimes even more than that wielded by the institutions of state.

With these characteristics in mind, Ajai (2015) argues that the failure of internationalizing firms is linked to the inability of managers to adopt effective corporate political strategies and to manage government relations skilfully in the host country's political environment. However, a case study of corporate political activities appears not to support this proposition: evidence suggests that none of the African countries studied showed adverse political actions taken by the state against any of the companies. Yet, Grobbelaar (2004: 10) finds that 'several of the successful large South African investments in Mozambique could be described as having been politically driven, or at least politically sanctioned ... The success of this combined effort to boost economic interaction is illustrated by the myriad bilateral agreements that have been signed since 1992 by the two governments.' Moreover, Mellahi et al. (2015) suggest that it is important to develop a better understanding of how firms' concerted patterns of actions help improve their performance by managing the institutional or societal contexts within which they compete.

Chapter 4 of this volume, therefore, focuses on the institutional and political environment lessons of Africa-to-Africa investments, helping explicate the bright and dark sides of close ties with political leaders in Africa. To this end, Mbalyohere's paper draws scholarly attention to the idea of how public and private organizations in Africa can partner with each other to create competitive advantage for African businesses to venture into unfamiliar overseas markets, which of course raises the related question of how Africa's political elites and power brokers use their ties to multinational business to advance their own national political goals.

Internationalizing in the Digital Era

It is widely accepted that the arrival of the internet (and the World Wide Web) has provided firms worldwide with opportunities to undertake business, communicate market offerings and exchange information with customers and partners to improve their efficiency and develop new ways of conducting cross-border business transactions. Importantly, as digital platforms evolve for conducting business internationally, providing incredible benefits to firms in terms of cost savings, sharing of information among supply chain members, and expansion of global market bases, firms now have new tools to more rapidly and effectively internationalize their operations. Despite these benefits, there are also associated challenges and barriers to the spread of digital intermediaries, including difficulties in integration of information technology systems across multiple global supply chains, high investment costs required to participate in the digital economy, and the reluctance of business leaders and perhaps policy makers to alter their true and tested methods of managing international business relationships.

However, the last decade has witnessed significant progress in the adoption of digital intermediaries in the conduct of international business. Particularly, the advances in the Web 2.0 platform have propelled many firms worldwide to gravitate towards adoption of e-commerce strategies as a mode of doing business at home and abroad. For the digitalized firms, the internet has become a key driver of their speedy internationalization efforts. In this regard, studies have shown that digitalized global firms now enjoy significant advantages in the global business arena because of their close collaborations with other firms and customers that result in greater market values.

Africa has not been left behind in this contemporary digitalized world: she leads several continents in terms of the degree and speed of adoption of mobile technology as a mode of personal communication and of doing business. It is estimated that Africa is home to more than 350 million mobile phone users, and this number is growing at a faster rate than anywhere on the globe (Etzo and Collender 2010). Across Africa, mobile phones are being used to transfer money, provide health care services, provide information on natural disasters and monitor national elections. This emerging phenomenon is widespread across Africa, to the extent that it is visible in upper-class, middle-class and shanty town communities. Broadband services with increasing penetration are taking over from previously unavailable and expensive analogue services. The emergence of a middle class is fuelling rapid adoption of online services, leading to the creation of a growing e-commerce industry in many African countries. M-Pesa in East Africa, for example, is globally acknowledged as an African innovation that has revolutionized the manner in which money is transferred across national borders. Many financial services institutions are looking at how to use mobile technology to create efficiencies and expand rapidly, and to drive inclusive growth and reduce the barriers to physical borders. Retailers, hospitality services, financial services and educational institutions are increasingly using the digital network of consumers and suppliers to reach multiple market segments across Africa. This, coupled with increasing use of social media platforms, has made the African consumer more and more informed and empowered. Thus, it is now widely accepted that Africa has an opportunity to leapfrog the digital revolution, and African multinationals need to welcome and incorporate this phenomenon in their strategic planning to earn a sustainable competitive edge.

The paper by Adjei in Chap. 5 contributes to this discussion by reporting a survey of a group of consumers of hotel services in Ghana, focusing on explaining Ghanaian consumers' perception of inward internationalization of hotel services through the use of internet marketing. A useful finding from this study is that there is a growing preference for the use of the internet in hotel booking. Interestingly, the study finds that a top priority for customers in Ghana is for hotel services to have websites that have audio-visual features and an effective feedback system. Given the slow internet connectivity problem identified in this study, the author recommends that telecommunication policy makers invest more resources in the communication industry to strengthen the rate of internet connectivity in Africa.

Part III: Cases on Africa-to-Africa Internationalization

Part III of this volume presents case studies of several African firms that have invested in industries other than the natural and extractive industries. Unlike inward foreign direct investment from non-African multinationals which tends to focus on natural resources and extractive industries, it is evident that Africa-to-Africa internationalization operates across a wide range of sectors: financial services, hospitality, telecommunications, manufacturing, information technology, infrastructure, fast-moving consumer goods, retail, and so forth. Another interesting fact is that A2A investment originates from a diversity of home markets. Just fifteen years ago, South African multinational firms like Standard Bank, MTN, Sasol and SABMiller accounted for almost all Africa-to-Africa investments. Today new players, especially from countries like Nigeria and Kenya, have embraced a pan-African investment strategy and are rapidly emerging as household brands across the continent. Consequently, Part III of this volume explores selected examples of African firms that have expanded and actively invested in other markets across the continent. The four cases in this section cover firms across multiple sectors (banking, brewing, telecommunications and oil and gas) and delve into some of the more pertinent issues and experiences the firms have faced, many of which have defined the range of opportunities and challenges encountered along the way. Two broad themes can be identified: internationalizing in a VUCA region and building proudly African challenger businesses and brands.

Internationalizing in a VUCA Region

Africa can be a difficult place to do business, with many economies in the region featuring regularly at the bottom of the World Bank's Ease of Doing Business ranking. Interestingly, there have been many improvements and success stories in recent years, with Sub-Saharan Africa accounting for the largest number of regulatory reforms in 2013 and 2014. An impressive 39 countries have reduced the complexity and cost of regulatory processes, and 36 have strengthened their legal institutions over the last few years (World Bank 2014). In spite of the recent progress (from a relatively low base), some key African markets still rank poorly relative to global peers. In a recent ranking of 189 countries on a scale of 0–100, Nigeria ranked 170th with a score of 47.33, Kenya ranked 136th with a score of 54.98, Mozambique 127th with a score of 56.92, Ghana 70th with a score of 65.24, and South Africa 34th with a score of 71.08 (World Bank 2014).

The business environment in many African countries can be described as being characterized by VUCA: **V**olatility, **U**ncertainty, **C**omplexity and **A**mbiguity. Given that many firms across Africa operate in such challenging environments, with institutional voids and market imperfections, a pertinent question arises: Are African firms better positioned than foreign multinationals to successfully conduct international operations within the region? Even if they are, they still face considerable and varying challenges, from how to enter new markets to choosing the right partners, building a strong employer brand to attract and retain top talent, and crafting strategies for competing successfully against established multinationals and domestic players. The three cases (in Chaps. 6, 7 and 8) illustrate the challenges and dilemmas executives face when expanding within the region. The three firms covered are all South African multinationals (two large global challengers and one micro-multinational enterprise) seeking to compete in challenging economies and sectors in Nigeria, Kenya and Mozambique (three countries that rank relatively poorly on the Ease of Doing Business index). Further, since South Africa is a much more advanced economy (and an easier place to do business) than these three host economies, the issue of whether and how South African firms can compete effectively in these VUCA environments comes to the fore.

The SABMiller case (Chap. 6), developed by Iheanachor and Ogbechie, delves into the key issues of market entry and market share retention in one of the most exciting beer markets in the world. With per capita beer consumption of 10 litres, compared to the global average of 27 litres, and a population of around 185 million people, Nigeria is an attractive market for SABMiller. The South African multinational, the world's second-largest brewer, has entered the competitive Nigerian beer market, which has been dominated for several decades by the European multinationals Nigerian Breweries (a subsidiary of Heineken) and Guinness (a subsidiary of Diageo). Such an entrance is bound to have a disruptive impact on market dynamics, and indeed it has triggered 'the Nigerian Beer Wars'. The case examines the industry structure and the competitive strategy of market incumbents seeking frantically to ward off new competition, while shedding light on where the new entrant might explore fresh opportunities. The case is unique in that it represents a situation where a global African challenger is competing aggressively with non-African global competitors/market incumbents in a foreign country in its home region.

Organizational change, culture, context and a degree of variable geometry in forging strategies in Africa are some of the themes addressed in the Sasol case (Chap. 7) developed by White and Games. As one of South Africa's global companies, petrochemical giant Sasol now has new competition in one of its key markets, Mozambique, after more than a decade of enjoying first-mover advantage in that country. Mozambique is poised to become a significant global player in gas production if recent discoveries are exploited effectively. In countries like Mozambique, it is crucial for strategy to be about much more than the bottom line. Recognizing the importance of local empowerment and overtly acting on it as a core component of building a long-term and sustainable business is crucial. This case study looks at the challenges Sasol has faced in Mozambique as a proxy for other similar markets in Africa, along with the key issues it needs to consider in building its global strategy for the future.

In Chap. 8—'NGN Telecoms' Re-Entry into Kenya: The Power of Perseverance'—Bowen, Townsend, Barreira and Beswick draw attention to the importance of personal and organizational resilience in Africa-to-Africa internationalization. NGN Telecoms is a telecommunications company founded by Calum McCracken, an inveterate entrepreneur. As the chapter title suggests, the importance of perseverance and leadership cannot be overemphasized. Following rapid expansion and growth in South Africa, with the firm capturing 95 % of the telephony value-added services in that market by 2014, NGN considered entering the Kenyan market after previous failed attempts. Lessons learnt from the previous attempts, specifically related to market entry, are key aspects of the discussion in this case, including deeper understanding of the market, their competitors and the approach to be taken—whether to go it alone or take on a local partner. An issue that comes to the fore is that failure can be an opportunity to gain strategic foresight (Amankwah-Amoah and Zhang 2015).

Building Proudly African Challenger Businesses and Brands

Western multinationals have dominated the business landscape in many sectors across Africa for many decades, including Accenture, Barclays, British American Tobacco, Chevron, Citi, Diageo, DHL, Ernst & Young, General Electric, Heineken, Procter & Gamble, PwC, Lafarge, Nestlé, Shell, Standard Chartered, and Total. In recent years, emerging market multinationals, especially from the so-called BRIC countries (Brazil, Russia, India and China) have also invested considerably in the region; Vale, Tata, Airtel and Huawei represent some of the new multinationals competing in Africa. As earlier mentioned, South African multinationals (like Game, ShopRite, Dimension Data, MTN, FNB and SABMiller) have also expanded rapidly in the region in the last decade or so and are by far the largest contributors to intra-African FDI; in some countries they are the major source of foreign direct investment.

Competing with these groups of established multinationals is a new group of challenger firms from countries like Nigeria and Kenya. Most of them are big players in their home markets and have only recently embarked on internationalization. Examples include Dangote, FirstBank, Glo, Guaranty Trust Bank, Interswitch, Oando, UBA, Equity Bank, KCB Bank and Nakumatt. Although many of these firms are relatively small and new to cross-border investments, they are challenging the more established players and building strong brands in their sub-regions and beyond. To compete effectively, they have leveraged the strategic capabilities they developed in their home markets and have also invested heavily in building their corporate brands to help overcome the liabilities of smallness, newness and country of origin. The last chapter in this book focuses on Equity Bank of Kenya, a highly respected and award-winning institution in its home market.

Equity Bank of Kenya has won numerous awards, including the Best Bank in East Africa (Think Business, 2014), Most Innovative Bank in Africa (African Banker Awards, 2012), Best Managed Company in Africa: Banking & Finance Sector (*EuroMoney* Magazine, 2012), Ai 40 Company of the Year (Africa Investor Series Awards, 2010), Microfinance Bank of the Year (African Banker Awards, 2009), African Business of the Year (Commonwealth Businesses Council & Africa Business Awards by *African Business* Magazine, 2009) and Best Performing Company in Africa (Africa Investor Series Awards, 2009). The bank has built a strong reputation by competing through technology and innovation; unlike many global and pan-African banks, Equity has focused on servicing underserved market segments and driving financial inclusion.

In Chap. 9, Ogbechie and Iheanachor write on the internationalization of Equity Bank and the challenges of building a pan-African multinational. After expanding to neighbouring East African markets, the bank announced an ambitious $200-million expansion to Ethiopia, Burundi, the DR Congo, Mozambique, Malawi, Zambia, Zimbabwe, Nigeria, Ghana and Cameroon. One key dilemma facing the firm's executives is whether and how to enter Nigeria's highly competitive banking space. The low market penetration rate, the tendency of large institutions to focus on large corporate and high-net-worth individuals, coupled with Equity's capability to service lower-level market segments suggest that there is an abundance of opportunity for the bank. The case highlights the key strategic issues and considerations in executing Africa-to-Africa internationalization, especially in a high-regulation, high-competition and high-stakes context.

Conclusion

This volume draws attention to the increasing speed, scope and scale at which African firms are investing in Africa. The nine chapters provide evidence and insights on emerging trends and key issues relating to Africa-to-Africa internationalization and how African multinationals are developing strategies to compete and win in an increasingly dynamic, volatile and competitive environment. We hope that this volume will provide useful ideas for further research to advance our understanding of intra-African FDI, especially firm-level internationalization behaviour. We are confident that the four cases presented in this book will stimulate learning and be useful for educating international business students and executives on how to deal with the complexities of Africa-to-Africa internationalization.

References

Acquaah, M. (2007). Managerial social capital, strategic orientation, and organizational performance in an emerging economy. *Strategic Management Journal, 28*, 1235–1255.

Acquaah, M. (2012). Social networking relationships, firm-specific managerial experience and firm performance in a transition economy: A comparative analysis of family owned and nonfamily firms. *Strategic Management Journal, 33*(10), 1215–1228.

Adeleye, I., Ibeh, K., Kinoti, A., & White, L. (2015a). *The changing dynamics of international business in Africa*. Basingstoke: Palgrave Macmillan.

Adeleye, I., White, L., Ibeh, K., & Kinoti, A. (2015b). The changing dynamics of international business in Africa: Emerging trends and key issues. In I. Adeleye, K. Ibeh, A. Kinoti, & L. White (Eds.), *The changing dynamics of international business in Africa* (pp. 1–16). Basingstoke: Palgrave Macmillan.

Amankwah-Amoah, J., & Zhang, H. (2015). 'Tales from the grave': What can we learn from failed international companies? *Foresight, 17*(5), 1–15.

Baron, D. P. (2003). *Business and its environment* (p. 2). Englewood Cliffs, NJ: Prentice Hall.
BCG (2010). *The African challengers: Global competitors emerge from the overlooked Continent*. Johannesburg: BCG.
Beck, T., Fuchs, M., Singer, D., & Witte, M. (2014). *Making cross-border banking work for Africa*. Eschborn, Germany: GIZ.
Boojihawon, D., & Acholonu, K. (2013). Internationalization process of African banks: An exploratory study. *African Journal of Economic and Management Studies, 4*(2), 244–266.
Bräutigam, D., & Xiaoyang, T. (2011). African Shenzhen: China's special economic zones in Africa. *Journal of Modern African Studies, 49*(1), 27–54.
Burgis, T., Sevastopulo, D., & O'Murchu, C. (2014). China in Africa: How Sam Pa became the middleman. *Financial Times*. Retrieved from http://www.ft.com/cms/s/2/308a133a-1db8-11e4-b927-00144feabdc0.html
Chironga, M., Leke, A., Lund, S., & van Wamelen, A., 2011. Cracking the next growth market: Africa. *Harvard Business Review, 89*(5), 117–122.
Daspit, J. J., & Long, R. G. (2014). Mitigating moral hazard in entrepreneurial networks: Examining structural and relational social capital in East Africa. *Entrepreneurship Theory and Practice, 38*(6), 1343–1350.
De Soto, H. (2000). *The mystery of capital: Why capitalism triumphs in the West and fails everywhere else*. New York: Basic Books.
Donnelly, L. (2008). *Sasol the tax cow*. Mail & Guardian. Retrieved May 20, 2014.
Ernst and Young. (2013). *Getting down to business: 2013 attractiveness survey*. Ernst and Young: Emerging Markets Center.
Etzo, S., & Collender, G. (2010). The mobile phone 'revolution'in Africa: Rhetoric or realty? *African Affairs*, adq045.
Goedhuys, M., & Sleuwaegen, L. (2010). High-growth entrepreneurial firms in Africa: A quantile regression approach. *Small Business Economics, 34*, 31–51.
Grimm, M., Gubert, F., Koriko, O., Lay, J., & Nordman, C. J. (2013). Kinship ties and entrepreneurship in Western Africa. *Journal of Small Business & Entrepreneurship, 26*(2), 125–150.
Grobbelaar, N. (2004). *'Every continent needs an America': The experience of South African firms doing business in Mozambique*. Johannesburg: SAIIA.
Hart, S. L. (2005). Innovation, creative destruction and sustainability. *Research-Technology Management, 48*(5), 21–27.
Ibeh, K. I. N., Wilson, J., & Chizema, A. (2012). The Internationalization of African firms, 1995–2011: Review and implications. *Thunderbird International Business Review, 54*(4), 411–428.

Khanna, T., & Rivkin, J. W. (2001). Estimating the performance effects of business groups in emerging markets. *Strategic Management Journal, 22*(1), 45–74.

Khayesi, J. N., George, G., & Antonakis, J. (2014). Kinship in entrepreneur networks: Performance effects of resource assembly in Africa. *Entrepreneurship Theory and Practice, 38*(6), 1323–1342.

KPMG. (2015). Business in Africa: How much has Africa started to invest in its own future?. Retrieved from http://www.blog.kpmgafrica.com/business-in-africa-how-much-has-africa-started-to-invest-in-its-own-future

Lau, C. M., & Bruton, G. D. (2011). Strategic orientations and strategies of high technology ventures in two transition economies. *Journal of World Business, 46*(3), 371–380.

Li, H., & Zhang, Y. (2007). The role of managers political networking and functional experience in new venture performance: Evidence from Chinas transition economy. *Strategic Management Journal, 28*(8), 791.

Li, Y., Zhao, Y., Tan, J., & Liu, Y. (2008). Moderating effects of entrepreneurial orientation on market orientation–performance linkage: Evidence from Chinese small firms. *Journal of Small Business Management, 46*, 113–133.

Lipton, E., & Hakim, D. (2013). Lobbying Bonanza as Firms Try to Influence European Union. *The New York Times*, Retrieved October 18, 2013.

London, T., & Hart, S. (2004). Reinventing strategies for emerging markets: Beyond the transnational model. *Journal of International Business Studies, 35*(5), 350–370.

Luo, Y. (2003). Industrial dynamics and managerial networking in an emerging market: The case of China. *Strategic Management Journal, 24*, 1315–1327.

Luo, Y., Sun, J., & Wang, L. S. (2011). Emerging economy copycats: Capability, environment, and strategy. *Academy of Management Perspectives, 25*, 37–56.

Mellahi, K., Frynas, J. G., Sun, P., & Siegel, D. (2015). A Review of the Nonmarket Strategy Literature Toward a Multi-Theoretical Integration. *Journal of Management*, 0149206315617241.

Mutume, G. (2003). Reversing Africa's 'brain drain': New initiatives tap skills of African expatriates. *From Africa Recovery, 17*(2), 1.

Ngwu, F., Adeleye, I., & Ogbechie, C. (2015). Africa-to-Africa internationalization: Rhetoric, reality and risks of intra-African regional expansion. In S. Nwankwo & K. Ibeh (Eds.), *The Routledge companion to business in Africa* (pp. 9–31). New York: Routledge.

O'Grady, S., & Lane, H. (1996). The psychic distance paradox. *Journal of International Business Studies, 27*(2), 309–333.

Oliver, C., & Holzinger, I. (2008). The effectiveness of strategic political management: A dynamic capabilities framework. *Academy of Management Review, 33*(2), 496–520.

Saffu, Y. (2003). The funding of political parties and election campaigns in Africa. In R. Austin & M. Tjernström (Eds.), *Funding of political parties and election campaigns* (p. 203). Stockholm, Sweden: The International IDEA Handbook Series.

Sasol Investor Reports. (2014). Retrieved from http://www.sasol.co.za/investor-centre/dividend-information/major-shareholders

Saville, A., & White, L. (2013). Realising potential: Connecting Africa. A report prepared for Visa (South Africa). Working Paper.

Schuler, D. A., Rehbein, K., & Cramer, R. D. (2002). Pursuing strategic advantage through political means: A multivariate approach. *Academy of Management Journal, 45*(4), 659–672.

Schwarz, G., & Yellin, J. (2013). Obama in Tanzania, sees Africa as next global economic success. Retrieved from http://www.cnn.com/2013/07/01/world/africa/tanzania-obama/index.html?hpt=wo_c2

Sheng, S., Zhou, K. Z., & Li, J. J. (2012). The effects of business and political ties on firm performance: Evidence from China. *Journal of Marketing, 75*(1), 1–15.

Suder, G. (2015). Regional trade agreements: Non-market strategy in the context of business regionalization. In T. C. Lawton & T. S. Rajwani (Eds.), *The Routledge companion to non-market strategy* (pp. 332–347). New York: Routledge.

Sun, S. L., & Lee, R. P. (2013). Enhancing innovation through international joint venture portfolios: From the emerging firm perspective. *Journal of International Marketing, 21*(3), 1–21.

The Africa Report. (2015). Top 500 companies in Africa. Retrieved from http://www.theafricareport.com/Top-500-Companies/top-500-companies.html

The World Bank. 2011. Ghana Data. Retrieved November 12, 2011, from http://data.worldbank.org/country/ghana

Tull, D. M. (2006). China's engagement in Africa: Scope, significance and consequences. *Journal of Modern African Studies, 44*(3), 459–479.

UNCTAD. (2015). World Investment Report 2015: Reforming international investmentgovernance.Retrievedfromhttp://unctad.org/en/PublicationsLibrary/wir2015_en.pdf

Viswanathan, M., & Rosa, J. A. (2007). Product and market development for subsistence marketplaces: Consumption and entrepreneurship beyond literacy and resource barriers. *Advances in International Management, 20*, 1–17.

Webb, J. W., Ireland, R. D., Hitt, M. A., Kistruck, G. M., & Tihanyi, L. (2011). Where is the opportunity without the customer? An integration of marketing activities, the entrepreneurship process, and institutional theory. *Journal of the Academy of Marketing Science, 39*(4), 537–554.

Whetten, D. A. (2009). An examination of the interface between context and theory applied to the study of Chinese organizations. *Management and Organization Review, 5*(1), 29–55.
Williamson, C. R. (2009). Informal institutions rule: institutional arrangements and economic performance. *Public Choice, 139*(3–4), 371–387.
Woods, N. (2008). Whose aid? Whose influence? China, emerging donors and the silent revolution in development assistance. *International Affairs, 84*(6), 1205–1221.
World Bank (2014). *Doing business 2015: Going beyond efficiency*. Washington, DC: World Bank.
World Bank. (2015). Data: Sub-Saharan Africa. Retrieved from http://data.worldbank.org/region/SSA
World Investment Report. (2005). United Nations, Geneva: http://unctad.org/en/PublicationsLibrary/wir2012_embargoed_en.pdf
Yiu, D. W., Lau, C., & Bruton, G. D. (2007). International venturing by emerging economy firms: The effects of firm capabilities, home country networks, and corporate entrepreneurship. *Journal of International Business Studies, 38*(4), 519–540.

2

Africa-to-Africa Internationalization: Future Trends and Research Avenues

Ifedapo Adeleye and Nathaniel Boso

Introduction

Chapter 1 of this volume discusses current trends in the internationalization of African firms. In taking these current developments into account and looking into the future, an important question arises: Will African firms continue investing in the continent, expanding their geographic footprint and becoming market leaders (or challengers), on a continent historically dominated by European multinationals and in recent years by emerging market multinationals? More importantly for international business (IB) scholars, what research opportunities exist on the internationalization of African firms? In this paper, we attempt to address these two issues. First, we provide a brief analysis of likely future trends in Africa-to-Africa

I. Adeleye (✉)
Lagos Business School, Ajah, Lagos, Nigeria
e-mail: iadeleye@lbs.edu.ng

N. Boso
University of Leeds, West Yorkshire, UK

I. Adeleye et al. (eds.), *Africa-to-Africa Internationalization*, AIB Sub-Saharan Africa (SSA) Series, DOI 10.1007/978-3-319-30692-6_2

internationalization, 'predicting' the following four trends: an increase in the scale and scope of geographic expansion of African firms; the expansion of African investments/Africa-focused internationalization by Africa's multi-continental and global players; emergence of young internationalizing African firms and the emergence of born regional firms; and the advent of powerful foreign-owned, pan-African multinationals. These likely future trends (as well as the current trends highlighted in this volume) provide interesting opportunities for international business researchers to examine the internationalization of African firms and contribute to the discourse on emerging and frontier market multinationals. Given the scant extant literature on Africa-to-Africa internationalization, our discussion spans a broad range of topical issues in the international business literature: drivers and motivations for internationalization, location determinants of foreign direct investment (FDI), speed of the internationalization process, and internationalization and firm performance. Our objective here is to provide a summary of the literature in these areas, drawing extensively from studies on emerging market multinationals, and to draw attention to fruitful research avenues.

Future Trends in Africa-to-Africa (A2A) Internationalization

> *In 10 or 15 years, Nigeria will represent no more than 40 per cent of our turnover. We try to diversify ourselves, both on geographical and sectoral plans.*— Aliko Dangote, President of Dangote Group[1]
>
> *Supermarket retailer Shoprite has shifted its investment focus from South Africa to the rest of Africa. The group plans to invest R1.5 billion* [$100 million] *in opening 30 new stores and strengthening distribution infrastructure in Africa's fastest growing economies, taking its store base on the continent to 200 stores in 2015.*[2]
>
> *Equity Bank* [of Kenya] *plans to expand to ten countries in the next five years at a cost of Sh20 billion* [$200 million].[3]

The push and pull factors that have led to the rapid, unprecedented internationalization of African firms are likely to continue in the near future. Sensing immense market opportunities in the region, many African firms will proactively expand, following the lead of their corporate clients and partners. Drawn by the success of firms that have grown phenomenally through internationalization, many firms will be unable to resist the opportunity to acquire a share of Africa's one billion consumers. Firms in economies or sectors with limited growth potential will be tempted and eventually 'forced' to diversify geographically. Several companies will have easier access to capital and resources, providing them with large war chests for cross-border acquisitions and greenfield investments. For others, interestingly, the mere ambition of becoming a pan-African or international firm will override other apparently important (economic) considerations. Beyond these factors, more regionalization activities are likely to occur as economic integration at the sub-regional and regional levels progresses. The proposed commencement of the African Continental Free Trade Area in 2017 will most certainly trigger greater intra-African trade and investments.

In sum, the marked increase in the internationalization activities of African firms experienced in the last decade is likely to continue in the decade ahead. We describe four trends that are likely to characterize this phenomenon. First, there will be an increase in the scale and scope of the geographic expansion of African firms, resulting in significant 'upward mobility' for firms (based on their foreign assets and sales; see Boston Consulting Group 2010). Most of the movement is likely to be amongst the 'big local players' (recent internationalizers for whom the domestic economy accounts for about 90 per cent of assets and sales) and the 'exporters' (mainly mining and oil companies with considerable exports but most of their assets held locally). Many firms in these two categories have announced ambitious internationalization plans, which when realized will make them 'regional players' (with at least 10 per cent of assets outside their home countries but within Africa) or regional challengers. Many of the newly internationalizing banks (e.g. FirstBank of Nigeria) fall into this category. Most will pursue sub-regional strategies, expanding first to neighbouring countries within their sub-region. Beyond the three regional 'elephants'—Kenya, Nigeria and South Africa—international firms from other large and high-growth African economies, including Ethiopia, Tanzania, Ghana and Zambia, are likely to emerge.

As these regional contenders/challengers rise, many of the (more) established regional players will accelerate their expansion across Africa. For instance, Dangote Group, based in Nigeria, recently announced ambitious plans to expand to 18 African markets, aiming to generate over 60 per cent of its revenues abroad over the next 10 to 15 years. Similarly, Equity Bank, an East African giant, has earmarked US $200 million for expansion plans to enter ten African markets outside East Africa. ShopRite is committing US $100 million to greenfield investments in the region, increasing its number of stores across the 15 countries it operates in. As these and many other African firms strengthen their competitiveness across the continent, there is a likelihood that a surge in cross-border mergers and acquisitions will begin to occur within Africa. In the process, some firms will become 'multi-continental players' (with at least 10 per cent of their assets outside of Africa), and a handful will even grow to compete globally (with more than half of their assets outside of the continent). South African multinationals will continue to dominate the surge, including major players such as SABMiller, Old Mutual, Bidvest, Sasol and MTN.

The second trend we predict is the expansion of African investments/ Africa-focused internationalization by Africa's multi-continental and global players. Driving Africa's post-crisis growth has been an increased inflow of investment funds to the continent, fuelled by repatriation of earnings by African firms (mainly South African firms) that had expanded their operations outside the region (to the Middle East, Europe, and even as far as the Americas and Asia). The trend implies that African firms face a dilemma as to whether to focus on growing their operations in Africa (where they might have a competitive 'home' advantage) or continue operating in more advanced economies (where competition might be more intense and where they might suffer from liabilities of foreignness). In other words, a few firms are likely to either increase the scale and/or scope of their operations in the region or embark on a dramatic reorientation of their internationalization towards Africa. For example, Standard Bank recently changed its vision from being a leading emerging market bank to being 'an African bank where our entire focus is on Africa realizing its potential'. The 'African tiger' (the region's largest bank by assets) has discontinued operations in Brazil, Argentina, Turkey and Russia while expanding the scale of its operations across Africa, with a presence in 20 markets (Grosse 2015). While not all multi-continental and global players will make such a radical strategic move, many will continue to expand their footprint in the region, and increasing revenue contribution from Africa will be a top priority.

A third trend is likely to be the emergence of young internationalizing firms, including born regional firms, in Africa. Many of the leading internationalizers in Africa embarked on internationalization at a relatively young age, compared to established Western multinationals. MTN, for instance, embarked on internationalization in 1998, just four years after it was established. This can be partly explained by the increasing pace of liberalization and globalization Africa has experienced in the last two decades or so. In the future, advancements in information and communication technologies will make it easier for firms to start up international operations at relatively low cost, particularly in sectors that are not highly regulated. In addition, as more executives gain international experience working with emerging and established multinationals, some of them are likely to set up competing pan-African firms to take advantage of market opportunities in the region. Thus, as macroeconomic management across the continent improves, domestic demands for value-added products and services grow, the stability of the political environment currently being experienced across the continent continues, and more minorities (including women and youths) enter into entrepreneurship, it can be expected that many entrepreneurial opportunities across the continent will be exploited in the form of new business start-ups.

A fourth likely trend is the emergence of powerful foreign-owned, pan-African multinationals. With the global attention Africa has received in recent years as an investment destination, many foreign multinationals will set up operations in a particular country as a beachhead into Africa, with some making big-ticket acquisitions of emerging or established regional multinationals. Walmart, the world's largest retailer, recently acquired a majority stake in Massmart, a South Africa-based regional giant with more than 350 stores in South Africa and 12 other Sub-Saharan African countries (see Luiz et al. 2015). In a unique international venture, Latin American telecommunications firm Millicom and the German firm Rocket Internet invested in Jumia, an online retailer focused on the African market. There have been rumours and speculations about other takeover targets, and it is very likely that some of these 'successful' regional multinationals will eventually be acquired by global challengers seeking to explore the African market.

In sum, there are strong indications that the internationalization of African firms will intensify in the decade ahead. Most of the upward mobility will be from two groups: firms making the transition from big local players to (sub-)regional players or challengers, and those growing from (sub-)regional challengers to become regional champions.

Africa-to-Africa Internationalization: Theoretical Perspectives and Research Avenues

> *Further research is needed to gain fuller understanding of the dynamics of firm-level internationalization behaviour across Africa. This is particularly given the economics-oriented, rather than behavioral or strategic management, perspective taken in several of the reviewed studies. International business scholars and research sponsors are, thus, urged to take greater interest in firm-level internationalization research in Africa with a view to improving the overall level of research output and data quality on the region.*—Ibeh et al. (2012: 423)

Given the phenomenal increase in intra-African trade and investments and the growing international attention on Africa as the next regional source of economic growth, it is surprising that research focusing on understanding internationalization behaviour of African firms remains scant. While some attention has been paid to understanding macro, country-level trade and investment activities in Africa, research focusing on theorizing and empirically validating micro, firm-level behaviours of internationalizing African firms is limited, prompting Ibeh et al. (2012) to call for scholarly work on firm-level internationalization behaviour of African firms.

In fact, African markets have been singled out as important emerging markets that are new to the international business discourse and as an opportune area for extending existing international business theories and models (Yiu et al. 2007; London and Hart 2004; Webb et al. 2011). For the past two or so decades, China and other Asian stories have dominated international business research as an alternative to Western economy narratives. For example, there is an acknowledgement that less developed markets of the world create substantial business opportunities for both local and multinational enterprises (Hart 2005), but evidence to that end is predominantly from Asia and, to some extent, the southern hemisphere countries (e.g. Brazil and Chile). Despite the huge development of international business activities of African firms (see the http://www.theafricareport.com/Top-500-Companies/top-500-companies.html for a full list of the 500 top multinationals in Africa), not enough research has so far been done to report on the international business processes in these firms for the purposes of theoretical extension and empirical investigation. There is no doubt that these multinational African firms are doing something unique and important that may help explain variations in international business successes. Certainly, there are challenges in undertaking empirical research in an environment that has for so long been disconnected from the rest of the world and that is logistically difficult to navigate. However, these difficulties themselves call for additional research into the opportunities and challenges of conducting research in Africa. A few studies (e.g. Boso et al. 2013; Ngwu et al. 2015; Masango and Marinova 2014; Boojihawon and Acholonu 2013) have taken the lead to research the internationalization behaviour of African firms. This second volume of the AIB-SSA International Business in Africa Series (as well as the first volume; see Ibeh 2015, Rolfe et al. 2015; Ajai 2015) attempts to fill the gaps in the literature by identifying topical issues related to the international behaviour of African firms, issues that have so far been under-recognized and under-researched.

In drawing scholarly attention to fruitful research avenues on the internationalization of African firms, we focus on issues pertaining to Africa-to-Africa internationalization. To this end, we cover debates and theoretical developments as they relate to issues of relevance and appropriateness to established internationalization theories, set within the context of emerging market multinational enterprises (EMNEs). Given that the dominant theoretical perspectives in the field of international business (such as the internationalization process model and the eclectic paradigm) have largely been developed with advanced economies in mind, the utility of such theories for explaining the internationalization of multinationals from the developing world is being questioned (London and Hart 2004). There is now a burgeoning literature seeking to theorize the internationalization of EMNEs, much of which has focused on Asian (in particular, Chinese and Indian) firms. The central premise of this body of literature is that emerging market multinationals internationalize differently from developed economy multinationals in terms of the drivers, motivation and patterns of cross-border expansion (Mathews 2006). It would be interesting, therefore, for researchers to investigate theoretical frameworks that are more relevant to the internationalization context of African firms. We believe that theorizing from the African context has the potential to contribute to this debate, and especially to contribute to the discourse on EMNE internationalization.

We do not, however, take it for granted that since internationalizing African firms seem to have many similarities with EMNEs in terms of the state of economic development at home, institutional arrangements and firm characteristics, EMNE internationalization theories are definitely more relevant than traditional theories. Several scholars have argued that many of the idiosyncrasies of EMNEs do not warrant the abandonment of established IB theories, as they still retain the capacity to explain the key features of EMNEs' internationalization (Dunning 2006; Narula 2006; Narula 2012; Ramamurti 2012). Moreover, the EMNE literature itself is to a large extent based on large organizations from China and India, hardly representative of all internationalizing firms from emerging and frontier markets. For researchers, therefore, a fundamental question arises: To what extent, if any, are internationalizing African firms different from (or similar to) emerging market multinationals or (similar-aged) advanced economy multinationals?

Hence, we focus on reviewing the literature of both established and emerging market multinationals, not only to see which theories better explain the international expansion of African firms, but also to offer ideas about how researchers investigating the international behaviour of African firms can contribute to the advancement of IB scholarship. Since our focus is on Africa-to-Africa internationalization, we draw insights from the literature on regionalization strategy. In view of the paucity of scholarly research on internationalization in African firms, our discussion spans a wide range of issues in the international business literature: drivers and motivations for internationalization, location determinants of FDI, the speed of the internationalization process, and internationalization and firm performance.

Drivers and Motivations for Internationalization

The issue of what drives firms to expand internationally is at the core of the debate between established IB theories and the burgeoning literature on emerging market multinationals. Traditional theories maintain that firms internationalize gradually as they accumulate resources and capabilities. According to Dunning's (1977) influential work utilizing the OLI (ownership, location and internationalization) or 'eclectic' approach', firms internationalize when they possess specific advantages. First, ownership advantages, derived from possession of firm-specific resources and capabilities that allow firms to overcome the costs of operating abroad, explain why some firms decide to embark on cross-border expansion. Second are location advantages, which address the issue of where a multinational firm decides to invest. Third, the possession of internalization advantages helps explain how a multinational firm decides to operate in a foreign market.

On the basis of the OLI framework, Dunning (1993) identified four key motivations for FDI: resource seeking, market seeking, efficiency seeking and strategic asset seeking. Resource seeking occurs when firms internationalize to secure access to specific resources (for example, raw materials and natural resources) that are not available in their countries or that are cheaper in foreign markets. Market seeking refers to situations in which firms expand internationally to exploit new market opportunities. Efficiency seeking occurs when firms go abroad to 'take advantage of differences in the availability and costs of traditional factor endowments in different countries' and to 'take advantage of the economies of scale and scope, and of differences in consumer tastes and supply capabilities' (Dunning 1993: 60). Finally, strategic asset seeking is displayed when firms internationalize, typically by acquiring the assets of foreign companies, to promote their long-term strategic objectives, which may include global (or regional) competitiveness.

There have, however, been arguments that established IB theories do not satisfactorily explain the behaviour of EMNEs because they tend to internationalize differently from developed economy multinationals (Mathews 2006; Luo and Tung 2007; Parente et al. 2013). One central argument is that EMNEs do not rely on the possession of complex ownership advantages to expand internationally, as proposed by established theoretical frameworks such as the OLI. The increase in south-to-north international investments, especially high-profile acquisitions of developed economy multinationals by Chinese and Indian firms, has triggered calls for alternative theoretical perspectives to explain these new realities. For example, in 2012, China Investment Corporation paid Ferrovial US $700 million to buy a 10 per cent stake in Heathrow Airport, and it paid US $400 million to Deutsche Bank for a majority stake in the bank's London offices. Lenovo acquired a majority stake in IBM, and Tata Motors took control of the iconic Land Rover and Jaguar groups in the United Kingdom. Below, we briefly discuss two theoretical perspectives that have emerged over the last decade: the linkage, leverage and learning perspective and the springboard perspective.

The linkage, leverage and learning (LLL) perspective posits that EMNEs internationalize by taking the following steps: first, building linkages with firms around the world; second, leveraging such global links to overcome resource/capability barriers; and third, learning to build up their own capabilities cumulatively (Mathews 2006). In other words, and in contrast to the OLI framework, these firms may internationalize in spite of not having initial resources, skills or knowledge. There is increasing empirical support for this theoretical perspective. A recent study of emerging Indian multinationals, for instance, finds that these firms have grown to become credible global challengers by leveraging their learning from strategic acquisitions in advanced economies, acquiring intangible assets and/or following their global clients in search of new market opportunities (Thite et al. 2016). Like the LLL perspective, the springboard perspective argues that EMNEs do not wait to possess complex ownership advantages before internationalizing, but rather they use international expansion as a 'springboard' to acquire strategic resources and capabilities (Luo and Tung 2007). By aggressively acquiring critical assets from established (Western) multinationals, they compensate for their apparent competitive and latecomer disadvantages in global markets, positioning themselves to counter-attack their global rivals' competitive edge in their home economies and to gain competitive advantages in other emerging economies (Luo and Tung 2007).

Having reviewed both established and newer theories on the drivers and motivations for internationalizing firms, we highlight key issues and research opportunities relating to firms engaged in A2A internationalization. A critical question that studies need to address is whether internationalizing African firms behave similarly to (Chinese and Indian) developing economy multinationals that have been discussed more extensively in the EMNE literature, or whether they behave more like established multinationals from advanced economies, internationalizing gradually as they accumulate strategic resources and capabilities, or whether they exhibit unique internationalization behaviours that can help extend extant IB theory.

Ibeh's (2015) exploration of the key motivations that underpin the internationalization of African multinationals using Dunning's (1993) taxonomy finds a strong prevalence of market-seeking motivations. This is hardly surprising. The liberalization of economies and the emergence of a middle class in many countries have created opportunities which firms from other African societies seek to exploit. Moreover, firms in more 'advanced' African economies like South Africa are experiencing slower growth and looking to diversify geographically by entering high-growth, less advanced markets. We discuss this issue in more detail in the next section describing the location determinants of FDI. There is also evidence for resource- and strategic asset-seeking investment arguments. However, Ibeh's study covers both A2A internationalization and investments outside Africa. More empirical research is needed to expand our understanding of the rationale for A2A internationalization, not least because this will provide a basis to ascertain whether or not regional expansion activities have been successful.

Given the increased attention paid to EMNE theories in the IB literature, and because of the several similarities in institutional and firm characteristics between the African and Asian contexts these theories have emerged from, it is important for scholars to engage with them. The scant extant literature on the internationalization of African firms has largely employed traditional IB theories and frameworks, with no studies (to our knowledge) engaging with theories utilizing the LLL and springboard perspectives. Hence, there is an apparent empirical gap with regards to the relevance and appropriateness, as well as the generalizability, of EMNE theories to African firms. Efforts to bridge this gap should begin with examining the similarities and differences between African firms and EMNEs in terms of the following: stage of maturity and growth of the domestic economy, internationalization age of firms, geographic scope of internationalization activities, and the pattern and speed of internationalization. As our review in the introductory section shows, there is considerable diversity in the scale and scope of internationalizing African firms, from big local players, who might be recent or first-time foreign direct investors (like Dangote Group), to established multi-continental or global players (like SABMiller).

Further, researchers need to identify what is really unique about intra-African FDI and firms undertaking internationalization within the Africa region. To this end, empirical research is needed to examine the following questions: Do similar-aged African multinationals internationalize in the same manner as EMNEs or developed economy multinationals? Do African foreign direct investors emphasize different factors than non-African investors in deciding if and how to invest within the region? Do African multi-continental and global players emphasize different factors when investing in Africa and non-African countries? Do intra-African investors wait to possess ownership advantages and reach maturity in their home markets before internationalizing within the region, as traditional IB theories posit? What are ownership advantages in the context of intra-African FDI? Can internationalizing African firms help broaden the concept of ownership advantages beyond the traditional definition involving property rights and/or intangible asset advantages, advantages of common governance and institutional advantages? Do African firms (on the periphery) internationalize with the aim of acquiring strategic capabilities and resources in the more advanced African markets, like Chinese and Indian EMNEs do? How do the springboard and linkage-leverage-learning perspectives apply to internationalizing African firms?

Empirical studies examining these topical issues have the potential to make tangible contributions to the international business literature. We provide some general contextual comments that can help to navigate this uncharted territory. First, A2A internationalization activities are dominated by firms from the two 'giants of Africa', Nigeria and South Africa, and to a lesser extent from Kenya (Rolfe et al. 2015). Outward FDI from South Africa, which is also the most 'advanced' or 'sophisticated' economy in Sub-Saharan Africa, is by far larger than investments from Nigeria and Kenya. Second, firms tend to internationalize to markets that are less advanced than theirs; there are hardly any cases of firms from smaller or less advanced economies investing in the regional giants, even among the 'big three' economies. These contextual realities are a reflection of the relative newness of internationalization in the region, and as discussed earlier in the section on future trends in A2A internationalization, major changes are likely to occur in the scale, scope and pattern of regional investments going forward. The current realities, however, do not appear to lend credence to firms making strategic 'springboard' investments or to firms expanding without possessing resource ownership advantages. Instead, the current realities would seem to support the notion that even among developing economy multinationals, established IB theories still retain the capacity to explain firm internationalization (Narula 2006, 2012; Ramamurti 2012). This is not to suggest that EMNE theories are not relevant for explaining internationalization of African firms. A few African global players, like South African Breweries (SAB), which in 2002 acquired Miller, a major brewer in the USA, amongst other global investments (Imaralu 2013), provide an interesting context to engage EMNE theories. While this is beyond the scope of this volume on A2A internationalization, we encourage IB scholars to conduct research in this area.

Location Determinants of FDI

Location choice decisions made by developing economy multinationals are somewhat neglected in the international business literature (Jain et al. 2013; Rolfe et al. 2015). In the African context, Rolfe et al. (2015) suggest that this could be a result of the historical dominance of FDI in natural resources, where location is essentially predetermined. In recent times, however, there has been a sharp increase in investments in non-resource sectors, and intra-African FDI, especially, covers a wide range of industries: financial services, telecommunications, technology, manufacturing, brewing, construction, transport and retail (Ibeh 2015).

The investment plans of the three firms cited in the quote at the head of this chapter epitomize this trend. Dangote Group, a leading Nigerian conglomerate, is expanding to Cameroon, Cote d'Ivoire, DR Congo, Ethiopia, Gabon, Ghana, Guinea, Liberia, Senegal, Sierra Leone,

South Africa, Tanzania and Zambia (and beyond); ShopRite, the South African retail giant that is already in over 17 markets, is aggressively growing its operations in Nigeria, Mozambique, Angola and Zambia with a US $100 million investment; and Equity Bank, Kenya's successful retail bank, is embarking on a ten-country expansion to Ethiopia, Burundi, the DR Congo, Mozambique, Malawi, Zambia, Zimbabwe, Nigeria, Ghana and Cameroon. What factors drive African firms' decision of which markets to enter in Africa? Do African firms emphasize different factors than non-African firms when deciding where to invest in Africa? Below, we discuss three factors that have a bearing on these questions: market size, colonial ties and regional trade agreements.

Market size as a location decision factor is an interesting issue to research in the context of intra-African FDI. This is partly because Africa is a diverse and unequal continent; of the 48 countries in Sub-Saharan Africa, the three regional elephants account for almost 30 per cent of the population and nearly 60 per cent of gross domestic product (GDP) (World Bank 2015). Nigeria, the sub-regional powerhouse in West Africa, has a GDP of US $568 billion and population of 178 million. With a GDP of US $350 billion and 54 million people, South Africa is the regional leader in the south. Similarly, Kenya's GDP of US $61 billion and population of 45 million make it the largest market in East Africa. This situation makes intra-African location decisions somewhat unique. How important is market size in the location model for the African firms investing in Africa? In one of the few studies looking in depth at location determinants in intra-African FDI, Rolfe et al. (2015) find that market size is not a significant consideration for African firms in deciding where to locate greenfield projects. Interestingly, they find that for non-African firms, location is positively affected by market size. One possible explanation is that the concentration of inward and intra-African FDI into relatively few economies makes them 'overcrowded', and many firms may find that they are unable to compete effectively in such environments. Empirical studies are needed to investigate the importance of market size as a location determinant for African firms.

Africa is a 'divided' continent with heavily militarized borders. Although the lines are blurring between Francophone and Anglophone (and Lusophone) Africa, colonial ties remain, compounded by an

English-French language divide. Rolfe et al. (2015) report a colonial bias in the location of intra-African investments, with Francophone countries receiving considerably less inward FDI from Anglophone countries. This pattern is also evident in some studies on the internationalization of African banks. Ngwu et al. (2015), for instance, find that many Nigerian banks invest first or focus their cross-border investments in Anglophone West African countries. Guaranty Trust Bank perfectly illustrates this pattern. The leading retail bank has subsidiaries in all five Anglophone countries but in only one of ten Francophone countries in West Africa; it also has three subsidiaries in Anglophone East Africa and another in the UK. An exception, perhaps, is Diamond Bank of Nigeria, which has strategically internationalized from its Lagos headquarters to neighbouring Francophone countries, including Benin, Togo and Ivory Coast. Apparently, distance still matters (Ghemawat 2001)—in this case, not geographic distance but most probably administrative distance (for example, absence of colonial ties and absence of shared monetary and political union) and cultural distance (for example, different languages and different social norms). More research is needed to unravel the impact of colonial heritage on A2A internationalization. Further, scholars should conduct in-depth studies of firms that have successfully expanded to several Francophone and Anglophone countries in order to gain insights on how firms can overcome the colonial bias.

Regional Economic Blocs as a Location Determinant

Internationalizing firms often prefer to initiate their international operations in countries that are close to their home market in terms of 'psychic distance' and then gradually expand to markets that are further away (Johanson and Vahlne 1977). In the context of regional expansion, the presence of regional trade agreements and the tendency for most countries in regional blocs to be geographically close to each other means that the psychic distance is usually shorter. In Africa, there are several (sub-)regional trade agreements, and negotiations are ongoing to implement a continent-wide African Continental Free Trade Union in 2017. Three subregional economic blocs stand out: the East African Community (EAC), the Economic Community of West African States (ECOWAS) and the Southern African Development Community (SADC). As highlighted earlier, each of these sub-regions has a dominant country and many other smaller countries, and many firms from the larger economies tend to initiate their internationalization activities within the sub-region. The study by Rolfe et al. (2015) finds that membership in the same regional economic bloc is a significant factor in the internationalization pattern of Nigerian and Kenyan multinationals, but not of South African multinationals. They explain that this could be because the former are late internationalizers that may be adopting a more measured, incremental approach, while South Africa's experienced multinationals have more internationalization knowledge and the experience to move to more distant markets.

More research is needed to increase our understanding of the actual role of regional economic blocs and trade agreements on location decisions of internationalizing firms. In particular, researchers should focus on whether the preference for sub-regional expansion is really due to membership in regional economic communities (and the benefits derived from regional trade agreements) or to the geographic proximity of firms within the sub-region.

Speed of the Internationalization Process

The speed at which firms internationalize has become an increasingly topical issue in the international business literature (Casillas and Moreno-Menéndez 2014). Ibeh's (2015) exploratory study on the rise of African multinationals finds a rapid pace of international expansion in recent years. United Bank for Africa (UBA), for example, has expanded from Nigeria into more than 20 countries since 2007, and MTN, the South African telecommunications giant, has expanded into 15 African countries since 1998. Ibeh argues that this rapid pace of international expansion demonstrates the strong strategic commitment of African firms to internationalization. A pertinent question arises: What explains the speed of A2A internationalization? Beyond trying to get a deeper understanding of the factors accounting for the recent rapid pace of A2A internationalization, researchers should also investigate *how* firms are able to expand so rapidly given the market imperfections and bureaucratic and logistical challenges associated with many African countries. What kinds of resources and capabilities are required to initiate and sustain speedy A2A international operations?

It is not only big local and regional players that are expanding rapidly within the continent. While our review (like much of the burgeoning literature on African multinationals) has focused on (relatively) large multinationals with brand recognition, it is important for researchers to turn attention to smaller (or medium-sized) firms small and medium-sized enterprises (SMEs) in Sub-Saharan Africa. SMEs are important players that account for up to 90 per cent of all businesses in the continent (IFC 2015). In recent years, many early rapidly internationalizing small firms (ERISFs) (Masango and Marinova 2012, 2014) and micro-multinational enterprises (mMNEs) (Ibeh et al. 2004) are challenging the long-held notion that smaller firms, because of their resource constraints, should adopt low-commitment entry modes (specifically, exporting) instead of advanced internationalization modes (Ibeh et al. 2009). Studying ERISFs and mMNEs in the context of A2A internationalization is particularly beneficial as these firms are likely to expand to countries that are in their home region (geographically close) to better handle liabilities of foreignness (Rugman et al. 2011; Dimitratos et al. 2014).

Researchers can build on Masango and Marinova's (2014) study of early rapidly internationalizing small technology firms from South Africa, which maps four distinct categories of firms: 'early rapidly internationalizing small firms'—firms that commence internationalization within six years of their establishment and experience a consistent increase in concurrent cross-border link formation and/or a continuous increase of international sales; 'early internationalizing small firms'—firms that start internationalizing within six years but do not show consistent increase in concurrent cross-border link formation or increasing international sales; 'late internationalizing small firms'—firms that initiate internationalization between six and ten years after establishment and experience a consistent increase in cross-border link formation and/or increasing international sales; and 'domestic market firms'—firms that undertake negligible internationalization on a sporadic, ad hoc basis and generate less than 10 per cent of their sales revenue overseas. They find that firms are able to expand internationally by finding new ways to initiate cross-border operations built on resource fungibility and networking. Building on the foregoing arguments, future studies can address the following research questions: How are mMNEs or ERISFs able to overcome resource constraints, and to what extent are interpersonal and organizational network ties critical to the internationalization process? Do rapidly internationalizing small firms perform better than their counterparts that follow a more gradual process of internationalization? For small firms, are there specific sectors or activities that lend themselves more easily to rapid internationalization than others?

Institutional Voids and Market Imperfections

It is argued that markets require a specific set of institutions that specify the norms and rules of engagement for market players to follow in order for the markets to function efficiently (Mair and Marti 2009; North 1990). As such, the institutional literature suggests that specific institutions, including property rights, the rule of law, and political constraints, are key drivers of economic development (Williamson 2009). While much of the extant scholarly discourse has been focused on institutional construction and the processes through which institutions change over time (Dacin et al. 2002), an important observation is that institutions may experience 'voids' when capital markets, infrastructure, intermediary markets, regulatory systems, contract-enforcing mechanisms and so forth are underdeveloped (Khanna and Rivkin 2001) . Studies have therefore focused on explaining how such institutional voids can be filled. For example, Miller et al.'s (2009) study of Korean high-technology businesses shows that social linkages, as reflected in community relationships and connections, help firms in Korea fill institutional voids to enhance performance. According to Khanna and Palepu (2010), developed market multinationals may seek to adapt their business models to fill institutional voids in developing economies; they may be at a disadvantage, however, because developing market firms with experiential knowledge of environments with high institutional voids 'can exploit their local knowledge by developing models based on their intimate understanding of institutional voids in their home markets' (page 8). Additionally, it has been argued that the experience developing economy firms gain by operating in environments with substantial market imperfections equips them with the managerial and organizational capabilities to successfully compete under similar imperfect market conditions elsewhere (Estrin 2014).

The institutional environment in most African markets is noted for its imperfections: limited access to capital markets, inadequate infrastructure, underdeveloped intermediary markets, and regulatory and contract-enforcing mechanisms that are tainted with widespread corruption add uncertainty and extra transactional costs to firms' operational costs (Luiz and Stewart 2014). The imperfection has also made most African markets difficult to navigate for many multinationals. In building on Estrin's argument for winning in emerging markets, Rolfe et al. (2015) speak to how African firms can leverage their comparative advantage of handling such market imperfections in their domestic African markets to successfully compete in foreign markets with similar conditions. Thus, while developed market multinationals may leverage their strong brands, financial capital and talent to compete in African markets, African firms can leverage their local knowledge of navigating institutional voids to their advantage (London and Hart 2004; Webb et al. 2011).

However, Africa is noted for her diversity in national laws, cultures and geography, suggesting interesting areas for international business research. Significant institutional differences exist in formalized laws, regulations and enforcement approaches across Africa. Differences also exist in informal institutions in regard to norms, values and beliefs. Thus, while first-hand knowledge of the institutional voids may be a source of competitive advantage for African firms expanding to other African markets, the institutional differences across African markets may be argued to reduce African firms' ability to interpret business environment signals in other African markets, thus cancelling out their local market knowledge advantage. In view of the potential for institutional environmental factors to influence economic activities (London and Hart 2004; Webb et al. 2011), therefore, researchers may draw on institutional theories (and other relevant theories) to theorize about and empirically examine how African multinationals leverage their local market knowledge to maximize the effectiveness of their operations (Luo 2003).

To this end, international business research has for years highlighted the notion of how institutional voids can affect implementation of strategic business activities in developing countries (De Soto 2000). In the specific case of Africa, legal institutions are noted to be significantly impaired; as a result firms' relationships with customers, suppliers and employees in African markets tend to be governed by informal structures. Linked to Africa's underdeveloped infrastructure, arguments have been made that mobility and communication can be costly to firms operating in Africa. For example, as a result of institutional voids in Africa, firms tend to use local community leaders (i.e. local opinion leaders, including kings, chiefs, priests, etc.) to disseminate information about market offerings via word-of-mouth advertising (Acquaah 2007). In fact, product endorsement by local kings, chiefs, priests, NGOs and so forth tends to be the norm in Africa. Making donations in churches, mosques and at traditional festival durbars provides firms with opportunities to generate awareness for their products and services while at the same time earning local market legitimacy and reputation. Viswanathan and Rosa (2007) argue that market intelligence gathering activities that are localized are more likely to be effective in generating information about local market needs in less developed societies, many of which are found in African countries. Empirical evidence is therefore crucially needed on how localized intelligence gathering and opportunity exploitation can help African firms penetrate and grow in markets with similar conditions. Theoretical understanding of and empirical evidence about how imperfect market conditions shape firms' market entry and growth strategies remain scanty. Such studies can help extend extant knowledge on the facilitating and inhibiting roles of home and host market conditions in the international expansion of African firms.

A2A Internationalization and Firm Performance

Do firms undertaking internationalization activities perform better than those exclusively focused on domestic markets? This subject has been widely debated in the international business literature, although most of the studies in this area have focused on advanced economy multinationals, with few studies on developing economy multinationals (Contractor et al. 2007). Given the phenomenal speed, scope and scale with which African firms have internationalized within the last decade and the scant extant literature in this area, there is clearly an urgent research need. The A2A internationalization context brings an interesting dimension, as there have been debates about the performance implications of executing a regional versus global strategic orientation (Ruigrok et al. 2013). Research studies are therefore needed to address the following topical issues: Should African firms internationalize or not? How have internationalizing African firms performed compared to those focusing on domestic markets? For internationalizing African firms, what is the performance effect of pursuing sub-regional, continental or global strategies? For A2A internationalizing firms, do they perform better as the degree of regionalization increases? Are there sector-, country-, sub-region-, or region-specific factors that have a moderating effect on internationalization and performance? How do firm-specific factors, such as internationalization age and company size, shape the performance effect of internationalization of African firms?

To begin to answer these questions, it would be beneficial to conduct in-depth studies of successful African multinational firms, as 'success stories' are emerging. MTN, South Africa's telecommunications giant, is a perfect illustration. Established in 1994, the firm started its pan-African expansion in 1998 and now has operations in 21 countries (including five in the Middle East). It is a market leader in many territories and now generates over 70 per cent of its revenues from outside South Africa. Studies in this area can focus on the moderating role of factors such as industry dynamism, top management team composition, and organizational learning on performance. However, not all A2A internationalization activities have produced spectacular results like MTN's. While there have been reports of isolated cases of firm failures across sectors, countries, and sub-regions, there have also been high-profile 'mass failures':

> *Several Nigerian banks entered the Francophone market with high expectations. To their shock, they failed dismally to win over customers. Since then, several Moroccan banks have entered the region and have been far more successful.*

> *Where did the Nigerian banks go wrong in their regional strategy? They forgot to manage perceptions. Regulators were wary of the Nigerian banks and continuously challenged their compliance with local financial management and statutory requirements. Ecobank benefitted from their competitor's mistake and partnered with local firms when they expanded to the region. Their entry has been so successful that they are now known as one of the leading regional banks in Francophone Africa.* Ernst and Young (2013)

In-depth research to unravel the nature, causes and effects of these failed internationalization attempts could yield invaluable lessons, especially for business executives (Ajai 2015; Amankwah-Amoah and Zhang 2015; Amankwah-Amoah and Debrah 2014). A good point of departure will be to analyze whether the failures are primarily due to external, institutional environment factors (for example, macroeconomic and regulatory headwinds, colonial bias) or internal, organizational factors (for example, market entry strategies, choice of local partners). Two recent studies by Ajai (2015) and Amankwah-Amoah and Debrah (2014) of failed internationalizing African firms point clearly to the latter; although many countries across the continent are known to have a challenging institutional environment, their findings show that organizational factors primarily account for firm failures. There is also the argument that African firms (relative to foreign firms) possess a comparative institutional advantage, as they would have developed the competencies necessary to operate in environments with market imperfections and challenging political and regulatory dynamics (Rolfe et al. 2015). Nevertheless, researchers should analyze the roles of external and country- and region-specific institutional factors, especially those that appear to be associated with high failure rates. The case of Nigerian banks' failed internationalization, cited above, provides for an interesting investigation. Led by UBA, Guaranty Trust Bank and Access Bank, Nigerian banks have expanded their footprint across West, Central and East Africa in the last decade, with varying degrees of success in different markets for different banks. As discussed earlier, there is a colonial bias in the location decisions of internationalizing African firms. (How) Does the colonial bias contribute to failed internationalization? What role does the liability of country of origin play in failed internationalization?

Evidence points to managerial and organizational factors contributing to internationalization failures of African firms. Ajai's (2015) exploratory study of firms from South Africa (e.g. Woolworths, Telkom SA, Nando's and Mocality) and Nigeria Industrial and General Insurance (IGI) that experienced at least one failed international venture in Nigeria, Ghana or Kenya identifies the following contributing factors: poor environmental scanning and market analysis, wrong choice of local partners, and poor management of cultural/environmental dynamics. In contrast to the case of Nigerian banks investing in Francophone Africa, there appears to have been a relatively lower distance (culturally, administratively, geographically and economically) in the firms examined by Ajai. All the countries involved were Anglophone and had extensive business and economic relations with each other. For instance, IGI, the Nigerian insurance firm's expansion to neighbouring Ghana, which has a long history of relations with Nigeria, and where many Nigerian firms have invested heavily in the last decade or so. Could some of these failures be explained by the 'psychic distance paradox'? As O'Grady and Lane (1996) argue, investing in psychically close countries does not guarantee success because assumptions of similarity can make executives complacent and prevent them from learning about critical differences. Examining this phenomenon will be beneficial since most cases of A2A internationalization are initiated or concentrated in neighbouring markets.

What role does poor stakeholder and regulator engagement play in failed A2A internationalization? Returning to the quotation about Nigerian banks operating in Francophone countries, one lesson is clear: failure to manage perceptions of customers and regulators is dangerous. This highlights the salient role of non-market strategies, 'a firm's concerted pattern of actions to improve its performance by managing the institutional or societal context of economic competition' (Mellahi et al. 2015: 2). This is especially important in the context of business regionalization. As Suder (2015: 344) argues: 'Non-market power can be key to competitive advantage and can be an important lever for corporate internationalization performance through the strategic utilization of knowledge and influence and the political formalization of business regulation.' For researchers, therefore, it is important to identify the mechanisms through which non-market strategy influences international performance by focusing on two areas: corporate political activity (CPA) and corporate social responsibility (CSR).

Corporate political activity is a topical issue in the African context because political risk is of serious concern and has a significant influence on the inflow of FDI (Osabutey and Okoro 2015; Nyuur and Debrah 2014). In Ajai's (2015) exploratory study cited earlier, however, there was no evidence linking failed international ventures to the inability of firms to adopt effective CPA strategies. More studies are needed to increase our understanding of the factors that moderate the impact of CPA on international performance, especially in the context of highly regulated and 'sensitive' industries (such as banking, telecommunications, infrastructure and natural resources), where governments and regulators tend to play a dominant role.

There is also a need for studies on the use, effectiveness and limitations of CSR as a strategy to engage stakeholders in host economies. Advancing some social good can be especially beneficial to firms operating in Africa, where societies are still struggling with poverty, diseases, income inequality, poor health and poor quality of education. Can international companies operating in such a context enhance their performance by being good corporate citizens? Does commitment to CSR and sustainability initiatives translate into positive financial results in the context of A2A internationalization? What factors moderate the impact of strategic CSR on performance for internationalizing African firms?

Conclusion

The speed, scope and scale at which African firms have been investing in Africa in the last decade have been phenomenal, providing interesting opportunities for researchers to make contributions to the burgeoning literature on emerging market multinationals and to the broader IB literature. This chapter provides a discussion of likely future trends in Africa-to-Africa internationalization and direction on potentially fruitful avenues for academic scholarship. Four future trends in Africa-to-Africa internationalization are predicted: an increase in the scale and scope of geographic expansion of African firms; expansion of African investments/Africa-focused internationalization; emergence of young internationalizing African firms and born regional firms; and emergence of powerful foreign-owned, pan-African multinationals. Given the scant extant literature on Africa-to-Africa internationalization, scholars can make tangible contributions across a range of topical issues: drivers and motivations for internationalization, location determinants of FDI, speed of the internationalization process, and internationalization and firm performance.

Clearly, these interesting developments make it an exciting time for scholars to advance research on Multinational corporations (MNC) behaviour and international business in the African context. Researchers should seek to extend their impact beyond the academic community as it is of importance to other stakeholders. Successful A2A internationalization has the potential to transform economies and societies across Africa, and failures will prove costly (financial losses to firms, job losses, tax revenue losses, etc.). Moreover, with the utilitarian turn in research funding, it is now expected that scholars should provide evidence-based direction and guidance to the decision-makers in the boardroom and the corridors of power. Policy-makers at the national, sub-regional and regional/continental levels need guidance on how to enhance location competitiveness, as well as how to promote and effectively regulate A2A internationalization activities. Business executives can benefit immensely as well. Effectively investigating the topical issues highlighted in this chapter will inform practitioners of the best practices to adopt when confronting the challenges and dilemmas of if, where, when and how to internationalize within Africa, which should ultimately lead to better internationalization decision-making. In sum, we hope this chapter stimulates interesting ideas and research studies that will make a 'triple impact' in the academic, policy and business communities.

Notes

1. "Nigeria: the gorgeous El Dorado seen by Aliko Dangote", March 13, 2014. Available online at: http://www.africatopsuccess.com/en/2014/03/13/nigeria-the-gorgeous-el-dorado-seen-by-aliko-dangote/.

2. "Shoprite shifts investment focus to Africa", August 19, 2014. Available online at: http://www.moneyweb.co.za/uncategorized/shoprite-shifts-investment-focus-to-africa/.
3. "Equity Bank readies Sh200bn for ten country expansion", April 1, 2015. Available online at: http://www.businessdailyafrica.com/Equity-Bank-plans-Sh200-billion-ten-country-expansion-/-/539552/2672024/-/tudjv1z/-/index.html.

References

Acquaah, M. (2007). Managerial social capital, strategic orientation, and organizational performance in an emerging economy. *Strategic Management Journal, 28*, 1235–1255.

Adeleye, I., White, L., Ibeh, K., & Kinoti, A. (2015). The changing dynamics of international business in Africa: Emerging trends and key issues. In I. Adeleye, K. Ibeh, A. Kinoti, & L. White (Eds.), *The changing dynamics of international business in Africa* (pp. 1–16). Basingstoke: Palgrave Macmillan.

Adeniyi, O. (2015). Dangote, Adenuga and the Nigerian Condition. *ThisDay.* Retrieved June 11, from http://www.thisdaylive.com/articles/saraki-dogara-and-apcs-naivety-/211669

Ajai, O. (2015). Failure of Africa-to-Africa internationalization: Key factors and lessons. In I. Adeleye, K. Ibeh, A. Kinoti, & L. White (Eds.), *The changing dynamics of international business in Africa* (pp. 148–168). New York: Palgrave Macmillan.

Amankwah-Amoah, J., & Debrah, Y. (2014). Air Afrique: The demise of a continental icon. *Business History, 56*(4), 517–546.

Amankwah-Amoah, J., & Zhang, H. (2015). 'Tales from the grave': What can we learn from failed international companies? *Foresight, 17*(5), 1–15.

Beck, T., Fuchs, M., Singer, D., & Witte, M. (2014). Making cross-border banking work for Africa. Deutsche Gesellschaft für Internationale Zusammenarbeit (GIZ), Bonn and Eschborn. Chicago.

Boojihawon, D. K., & Acholonu, K. (2013). Internationalization process of African banks: An exploratory study. *African Journal of Economic and Management Studies, 4*(2), 244–266.

Boston Consulting Group. (2010). The African Challengers: Global Competitors Emerge from the Overlooked Continent. Retrieved from https://www.bcg.com/documents/file44610.pdf

Boso, N., Story, V. M., Cadogan, J. W., Micevski, M., & Kadic-Maglajlic, S. (2013). Firm innovativeness and export performance: Environmental, networking, and structural contingencies. *Journal of International Marketing, 21*(4), 62–87.

BusinessDaily. (2015). Equity Bank readies Sh200bn for ten country expansion. Retrieved April 1, from http://www.businessdailyafrica.com/Equity-Bank-plans-Sh200-billion-ten-country-expansion-/-/539552/2672024/-/tud-jv1z/-/index.html

Casillas, J. C., & Moreno-Menéndez, A. M. (2014). Speed of the internationalization process: The role of diversity and depth in experiential learning. *Journal of International Business Studies, 45*(1), 85–101.

Contractor, F. J., Kumar, V., & Kundu, S. K. (2007). Nature of the relationship between international expansion and performance: The case of emerging market firms. *Journal of World Business, 42*(4), 401–417.

Dacin, M. T., Goodstein, J., & Scott, W. R. (2002). Institutional theory and institutional change: Introduction to the special research forum. *Academy of Management Journal, 45*(1), 45–56.

De Soto, H. (2000). *The mystery of capital: Why capitalism triumphs in the West and fails everywhere else*. New York: Basic Books.

Dimitratos, P., Amorós, J. E., Etchebarne, M. S., & Felzensztein, C. (2014). Micro-multinational or not? International entrepreneurship, networking and learning effects. *Journal of Business Research, 67*(5), 908–915.

Dunning, J. H. (1977). Trade, location of economic activity and the MNE: A search for an eclectic approach. In B. Ohlin, P. Hesselborn, & P. M. Wijkman (Eds.), *The international allocation of economic activity*. London: Macmillan.

Dunning, J. H. (1993). *Multinational enterprises and the global economy*. Workingham, Berkshire: Addison Wesley.

Dunning, J. H. (2006). Comment on dragon multinationals: New players in 21st century globalization. *Asia Pacific Journal of Management, 23*(2), 139–141.

Ernst and Young. (2013). What it takes to succeed in Francophone Africa. Retrieved from http://www.ey.com/Publication/vwLUAssets/What_it_takes_to_succeed_in_Francophone_Africa/$FILE/130722%20Francophone%20SGF%20thought%20pieceindd.pdf

Estrin, S. (2014). Internationalization of firms from emerging markets: Location choice and the impact of institutions and state ownership. *International Business and Institutions After the Financial Crisis, 9*.

Ghemawat, P. (2001). Distance still matters. *Harvard Business Review, 79*(8), 1–11.

Grosse, R. (2015). Standard Bank: An African tiger. In I. Adeleye, K. Ibeh, A. Kinoti, & L. White (Eds.), *The changing dynamics of international business in Africa* (pp. 220–241). New York: Palgrave Macmillan.

Ibeh, K. I. N. (2015). Rising Africa and its nascent multinational corporations. In I. Adeleye, K. Ibeh, A. Kinoti, & L. White (Eds.), *The changing dynamics of international business in Africa* (pp. 123–147). New York: Palgrave Macmillan.
Ibeh, K. I. N., Borchert, O., & Wheeler, C. (2009). Micro-multinationals: Transcending resource challenges in international business. In K. I. N. Ibeh & S. Davies (Eds.), *Contemporary challenges to international business* (pp. 85–105). Basingstoke, UK: Palgrave Macmillan.
Ibeh, K. I. N., Johnson, J. E., Dimitratos, P., & Slow, J. (2004). Micro-multinationals: Some preliminary evidence on an emergent star of the international entrepreneurship field. *Journal of International Entrepreneurship, 2*(4), 289–303.
Ibeh, K. I. N., Wilson, J., & Chizema, A. (2012). The Internationalization of African firms, 1995–2011: Review and Implications. *Thunderbird International Business Review, 54*(4), 411–428.
IFC. (2015). Sub-Saharan Africa: SME initiatives. Retrieved from http://www.ifc.org/wps/wcm/connect/region__ext_content/regions/sub-saharan+africa/advisory+services/sustainablebusiness/sme_initiatives/sme_initiatives
Imaralu, D. 2013. 10 African companies going global in 2013. *Ventures Africa*. Retrieved from http://venturesafrica.com/10-african-companies-going-global-in-2013
Jain, N., Lahiri, S., & Hausknecht, D. (2013). Emerging market multinationals' location choice: The role of firm resources and internationalization motivations. *European Business Review, 25*(3), 263–280.
Johanson, J., & Vahlne, J.-E. (1977). The internationalization process of the firm: A model of knowledge development and increasing foreign market commitments. *Journal of International Business Studies, 8*(1), 23–32.
Khanna, T., & Palepu, K. (2000). The future of business groups in emerging markets: Long-run evidence from Chile. *Academy of Management Journal, 43*(3), 268–285.
Khanna, T., & Palepu, K. G. (2010). *(With Richard Bullock). Winning in emerging markets: A road map for strategy and execution*. Boston: Harvard Business Press.
Khanna, T., & Rivkin, J. (2001). Estimating the performance effects of business groups in emerging markets. *Strategic Management Journal, 22*(1), 45–74.
Klein, S., & Wocke, A. (2007). Emerging global contenders: The South African experience. *Journal of International Management, 13*(3), 319–337.
Krüger, R., & Strauss, I. (2015). Africa rising out of itself: The growth of intra-African FDI. *Columbia FDI Perspectives*, 139, January 19. Columbia University. Columbia Center on Sustainable International Investment.

London, T., & Hart, S. (2004). Reinventing strategies for emerging markets: Beyond the transnational model. *Journal of International Business Studies, 35*(5), 350–370.

Luiz, J., Townsend, S., & Beswick, C. (2015). Game in Africa: Seizing the opportunity. In I. Adeleye, K. Ibeh, A. Kinoti, & L. White (Eds.), *The changing dynamics of international business in Africa* (pp. 242–261). New York: Palgrave Macmillan.

Luiz, J. M., & Stewart, C. (2014). Corruption, South African multinational enterprises and institutions in Africa. *Journal of Business Ethics, 124*(3), 383–398.

Luo, Y. (2003). Industrial dynamics and managerial networking in an emerging market: The case of China. *Strategic Management Journal, 24*, 1315–1327.

Luo, Y., & Tung, R. L. (2007). International expansion of emerging market enterprises: A springboard perspective. *Journal of International Business Studies, 38*(4), 481–498.

Mair, J., & Marti, I. (2009). Entrepreneurship in and around institutional voids: A case study from Bangladesh. *Journal of Business Venturing, 24*(5), 419–435.

Masango, S. G., & Marinova, S. T. (2012). Development of international entrepreneurial opportunities by South African early and rapidly internationalizing small firms. In M. Marinov & S. Marinova (Eds.), *Impacts of emerging economies and firms on international business* (pp. 302–316). New York: Palgrave Macmillan.

Masango, S. G., & Marinova, S. T. (2014). Early rapidly internationalizing small firms from South Africa. In M. Marinov & S. Marinova (Eds.), *Success and challenges of emerging economy multinationals* (pp. 158–183). New York: Palgrave Macmillan.

Mathews, J. A. (2006). Dragon multinationals: New players in 21st century globalization. *Asia Pacific Journal of Management, 23*(1), 5–27.

McNamee, T., Pearson, M., & Boer, W. (2015). *Africans investing in Africa: Understanding business and trade, sector by sector*. New York: Palgrave Macmillan.

Mellahi, K., Frynas, J. G., Sun, P., & Siegel, D. (2015). A Review of the Nonmarket Strategy Literature Toward a Multi-Theoretical Integration. *Journal of Management*, 0149206315617241.

Miller, D., Lee, J., Chang, S., & Le Breton-Miller, I. (2009). Filling the institutional void: The social behavior and performance of family vs non-family technology firms in emerging markets. *Journal of International Business Studies, 40*(5), 802–817.

Narula, R. (2006). Globalization, new ecologies, new zoologies, and the purported death of the eclectic paradigm. *Asia Pacific Journal of Management, 23*(2), 143–151.

Narula, R. (2012). Do we need different frameworks to explain infant MNEs from developing countries? *Global Strategy Journal, 2*(3), 188–204.

Ngwu, F., Adeleye, I., & Ogbechie, C. (2015). Africa-to-African internationalization: Rhetoric, reality and risks of intra-African regional expansion. In S. Nwankwo & K. Ibeh (Eds.), *The Routledge companion to business in Africa* (pp. 9–31). New York: Routledge.

North, D. C. (1990). *Institutions, institutional change and economic performance.* New York: Cambridge University Press.

Nwaoguji, C. (2015). Why we invested $400m in Zambia cement plant—Dangote. *The Sun.* Retrieved August 11, from http://sunnewsonline.com/new/why-we-invested-400m-in-zambia-cement-plant-dangote

Nyuur, R. B., & Debrah, Y. A. (2014). Predicting foreign firms' expansion and divestment intentions in Host countries: insights from Ghana. *Thunderbird International Business Review, 56*(5), 407–419.

O'Grady, S., & Lane, H. (1996). The psychic distance paradox. *Journal of International Business Studies, 27*(2), 309–333.

Osabutey, E. L. C., & Okoro, C. (2015). Political risk and foreign direct investment in Africa: The case of the Nigerian telecommunications industry. *Thunderbird International Business Review, 57*(6), 417–429.

Parente, R. C., Cyrino, A. B., Spohr, N., & de Vasconcelos, F. C. (2013). Lessons learned from Brazilian multinationals' internationalization strategies. *Business Horizons, 56*(4), 453–463.

Planting, S. (2014). Shoprite shifts investment focus to Africa. Retrieved August 19, from http://www.moneyweb.co.za/uncategorized/shoprite-shifts-investment-focus-to-africa

Ramamurti, R. (2012). What is really different about emerging market multinationals? *Global Strategy Journal, 2*(1), 41–47.

Rolfe, R., Perri, A., & Woodward, D. (2015). Patterns and determinants of intra-African foreign direct investment. In I. Adeleye, K. Ibeh, A. Kinoti, & L. White (Eds.), *The changing dynamics of international business in Africa* (pp. 101–122). New York: Palgrave Macmillan.

Rugman, A., Lee, I. H., & Terjesen, S. (2011). Are born global firms really born regional?. *Frontiers of Entrepreneurship Research, 31*(16), 11. Retrieved from http://digitalknowledge.babson.edu/fer/vol31/iss16/11

Ruigrok, W., Georgakakis, D., & Greve, P. (2013). Regionalization strategy and performance: The moderating role of industry dynamism and top management team diversity. *Multinational Business Review, 21*(1), 6–24.

Saville, A., & White, L. (2015). Ensuring that Africa keeps rising: The economic integration imperative. *South African Journal of International Affairs, 22*(1), 1–21.

Suder, G. (2015). Regional trade agreements: Non-market strategy in the context of business regionalization. In T. C. Lawton & T. S. Rajwani (Eds.), *The Routledge companion to non-market strategy* (pp. 332–347). New York: Routledge.

The African Report. (2014). Retrieved from http://www.theafricareport.com/Africa-in-2014.html

Thite, M., Wilkinson, A., Budhwar, P., & Mathews, J. (2016). Internationalization of emerging Indian multinationals: Linkage, leverage and learning (LLL) perspective. *International Business Review, 25*(1), 435–443.

Viswanathan, M., & Rosa, J. A. (2007). Product and market development for subsistence marketplaces: Consumption and entrepreneurship beyond literacy and resource barriers. *Advances in International Management, 20*, 1–17.

Webb, J. W., Ireland, R. D., Hitt, M. A., Kistruck, G. M., & Tihanyi, L. (2011). Where is the opportunity without the customer? An integration of marketing activities, the entrepreneurship process, and institutional theory. *Journal of the Academy of Marketing Science, 39*(4), 537–554.

Williamson, C. R. (2009). Informal institutions rule: Institutional arrangements and economic performance. *Public Choice, 139*(3–4), 371–387.

World Bank. (2015). Data: Sub-Saharan Africa. Retrieved from http://data.worldbank.org/region/SSA

Yiu, D., Lau, C., & Bruton, G. (2007). International venturing by emerging economy firms: the effects of firm capabilities, home country networks, and corporate entrepreneurship. *Journal of International Business Studies*, 38(4), 519–540. http://dx.doi.org/10.1057/palgrave.jibs.8400278

Part II

Research Articles on Africa-to-Africa Internationalization

3

Examining the Factors Influencing the International Expansion of Nigerian Banks

Ebimo Amungo

Introduction

International market entry by Nigerian banks started when some banks established representative offices and branches in New York and London in the 1980s to facilitate trade for some of their clients. In 2000 the Central Bank of Nigeria (CBN) issued universal banking licenses that allowed banks to establish foreign sub-subsidiaries. In 2005 a CBN policy required Nigerian banks to increase their tier 1 capital from N2billion to N25billion. After the consolidation, the Nigerian banking market became the second largest in Sub-Saharan Africa (SSA), after South Africa (Kasekende et al. 2009). Some of Nigeria's largest banks then developed strategies for growth that included international expansion. This happened at a time when a number of established European banks were retreating from Africa (Florian 2012).

E. Amungo (✉)
Nigerian Turkish Nile University, Abuja, Nigeria
e-mail: eamungo@gmail.com

I. Adeleye et al. (eds.), *Africa-to-Africa Internationalization*, AIB Sub-Saharan Africa (SSA) Series, DOI 10.1007/978-3-319-30692-6_3

This phenomenal expansion of Nigerian banks and banks from other African countries into SSA (notably South Africa, Togo, Kenya, etc.) has started to elicit the interest of scholars of international business (Boojihawon and Acholonu 2013). Still, few studies have taken a country-specific view of the internationalization of African banks (Luiz and Charalambous 2009). This study notes the phenomenon as it relates to the foreign market entry decisions of Nigerian banks. The originality of the study is its addition of country-specific knowledge on the internationalization strategies of banks from a low-income SSA country.

The study sought to unveil the factors that are most pertinent in shaping the internationalization decisions of Nigerian banks. The study used a mixed quantitative and qualitative research approach. Five Nigerian banks, namely, United Bank for Africa (UBA), Diamond Bank, Keystone Bank, Guaranty Trust Bank (GTB) and Access Bank, were examined in a multiple case study.

After reviewing the literature, propositions were declared prior to the start of field work. For each bank, primary data was obtained from top management staff involved in strategy formulation and implementation. Likert scale questionnaires and interviews were used. Secondary data was obtained from a variety of sources. Data was analyzed using the normal fitting algorithm approach, a statistical tool for converting ordinal scale data into interval data (Stacey 2005). The results and findings were compared to the propositions declared, and the propositions were modified when necessary.

Literature Review

Internationalization by firms has been defined is the process of increasing involvement in international markets. Czinkota (2004) noted that there are a number of proactive and reactive motivations for firms to internationalize. Proactive motives come about when a firm possesses profit or technological advantages, unique products, exclusive information, managerial urge, tax benefits or economies of scale. Reactive motivations are forced on the firm by competitive pressures in the domestic market, such as overproduction, declining domestic sales, excess capacity, saturated domestic markets and lack of proximity to customers or the need to follow clients.

Banks embark on international market entry for most of the reasons that multinational enterprises in general internationalize, but some scholars have observed that the nature and characteristics of banking engender slight variations in their internationalization. Studies have noted that banks follow their clients that have made international market entries (Goldberg and Johnson 1990). Information on clients' banking needs is used to explain the "follow-the-client hypothesis", including the fact that firms prefer to do business with a small number of banks so as not to reveal sensitive information to many financial firms.

The opportunity for profit in host countries, such as a higher expected rate of economic growth and profitability of the host country banking market, is also a main determinant of outward banking foreign direct investment (FDI) (Buch and DeLong 2004). Furthermore, tax, interest and exchange rate differentials between a bank's home and host countries may create opportunities for arbitrage and transfers which banks seek to exploit.

Banks sometimes possess qualities and assets that enable them to operate more efficiently in a foreign market. These advantages include size, distribution channels and managerial competence. A large size enables banks to translate their scale efficiencies to foreign markets at a relatively low cost and compete with local institutions. Tschoegl (2003) found that most of the largest subsidiaries of foreign banks in the United States of America (USA) were also among the largest banks in their domestic markets.

The structure and competitiveness of home banking markets can influence banks' performance and efficiency. A competitive banking market means that some banks are squeezed out of the market and thus might embark on foreign market entry to seek better margins and profits elsewhere. Banks may also react to the actions of their competitors by following them to markets or avoiding some markets that their competitors have already entered. This is the oligopolistic behaviour theory of foreign direct investment (Knickerbocker 1973; William 1997).

When there are restrictions in the home country limiting a bank's home operations, growth or expansion, it might want to "escape" by expanding internationally. In the same vein, a host country's openness to the establishment of new foreign branches and subsidiaries, as well as tax incentives, may also be important (Miller and Prakhe 1998).

Aggarwal and Durnford (1989) noted that a bank can diversify its income base by operating in a foreign country and obtaining gains in terms of its risk/return profile. A common cultural background may also facilitate bank international expansion into a particular geographic market. Guillén and Tschoegl (1999) noted a significant effect of cultural proximity in the expansion of Spanish banks into Latin America.

Banks and Theories of Internationalization

In seeking a better understanding of the determinants of the internationalization of firms, scholars have formulated a number of theories to explain the process. These theories include the process theory of internationalization, eclectic theory, the resource-based view (RBV) and transaction cost analysis (TCA), among others.

The process theory of internationalization states that increased knowledge of foreign markets allows firms to increase their commitment of resources to the market (Johanson and Vahlne 1977). This may be at the heart of the internationalization of banks that seem to enter foreign markets with low commitment and gradually increase their investment with increased knowledge of the market. Process theory also notes the importance of psychic distance as a determinant of banks' foreign market choices, and studies have shown that banks tend to internationalize in foreign markets with low psychic distance (Guillén and Tschoegl 1999).

The eclectic theory emphasized ownership (O-) advantages of the firms, location (L-) advantages of the host country, and internalization (I-) advantages that makes firms decide on what mode of entry to adopt in a host country. The eclectic theory states that firms must possess some O-advantages that enable them to profit from extending their operations into other national markets. For banks, these O-advantages include specialised banking services, reputation for efficiency, managerial skills, technological edge, size and international experience (Cho 1986).

Similarly, host countries possess L-advantages that make them attractive to multinational banks (MNBs). These include regulations that make banking easier, less risky and less uncertain. They also include market size, profit opportunities and level of governance in the host country (Outreville 2007). According to Cho (1986), I-advantages include availability and cost of fund transfers within the MNB, efficient customer contracting, and transfer price manipulation, which potentially reduces variability.

The resource-based view (RBV) supports the notion that firms are able to leverage unique, valuable and rare resources for competitive advantage (Barney 1991). These resources and capabilities include physical, human and organizational assets that can be used to implement value-creating resources for competitive advantage. For banks, managerial capabilities, brand name, reputation, size and organizational culture are all assets that can confer competitive advantages.

A transaction cost analysis (TCA) approach to the internationalization of banks is focused on factors that hamper banks' ability to mitigate the cost of information about borrowers and enforce contracts (Cull and Peria 2010). These factors include environmental uncertainty brought about by macroeconomic instability and political risk as well as by regulatory, geographic, cultural and institutional distance. Factors that reduce environmental uncertainties, like integration through culture and language spoken in the home and host countries, are found to be significant in the decision to invest abroad. In addition, host country macroeconomic stability, political risks and governance levels are other factors that affect banks' foreign market entry decisions (Outreville 2007).

Theoretical Framework and Propositions

The theoretical framework and propositions are important aspects of positivist case study research. They are used in identifying the unit of analysis, boundary and scope of the research. Piekkari et al. (2009) noted that the positivist tradition for case studies favours a design logic in which field work is preceded by the careful development of a blueprint.

The theory identifies the various concepts in the literature, and propositions are declared statements about causation. The concepts, when developed for measurement, become variables with the causal (independent) and outcome (dependent) variables identified. Yin (2009) advocates that propositions should be declared from the theory and investigated and (sometimes) falsified through empirical findings.

This research used a synthesis of the eclectic theory, RBT and TCA, as well as empirical findings relating to them, are used as the framework for the research. In this light, the dependent variables, namely motivating factors for international market entry by Nigerian banks, were the main focus of the research, which aimed to identify variables influencing the banks' decision to enter foreign markets.

Factors that Influence Bank International Market Entry

Bank-Specific Factors

Banks engage in multinational banking due to certain bank-specific factors, including size and international experience, desire to seek new markets and growth opportunities, desire to follow clients into new foreign markets, as well as the characteristics of managers and decision makers who may try to steer the bank towards a globalization strategy. Furthermore, home country business conditions, such as regulatory laws, competition in the domestic market and the strategic actions of other industry players, can play a role in motivating banks to expand internationally.

When banks follow their home country clients into foreign markets, they need to develop products and managerial competence that make them cost effective and efficient in the new location. These are O-advantages that banks seek to exploit in foreign markets. Banks also seek new markets with profit opportunities. For example, high expected economic growth in the host country that offers profitable business opportunities (Magri et al. 2005) is a host country L-advantage.

Also, managers may intentionally seek entry into foreign markets both to react to the actions of competitors and to exploit excess human and financial resource slack. This so-called *managerial intentionality* has been noted by Hutzschenreuter et al. (2007).

Based on these observations, this proposition is suggested:

Proposition 1 A bank's desire to expand internationally will be influenced by a need to follow its clients into foreign markets, seek growth and profit opportunities, exploit its ownership advantage (O-advantage), and fulfil the aspirations of its managers.

Home Country Conditions

Regulations governing banking sometimes "push" banks to internationalize. Some banks must seek approval from home country regulators before opening operations in foreign markets (Cerrutti et al. 2007). Restrictive regulatory laws may also influence banks' need to expand internationally. It has been noted that government policies like deregulation lead to more competitive banking markets. In the face of increased domestic competitive pressure, banks may internationalize to seek better margins in new markets. Guillén and Tschoegl (1999) found this to be the case with Spanish banks that sought new markets in Latin America following increased domestic competitive pressure after financial integration in the European Union (Fig. 3.1).

Based on these observations, this proposition is suggested:

Proposition 2 A bank's motivation to expand internationally will be influenced by home country regulations and competitive pressure in the domestic banking market.

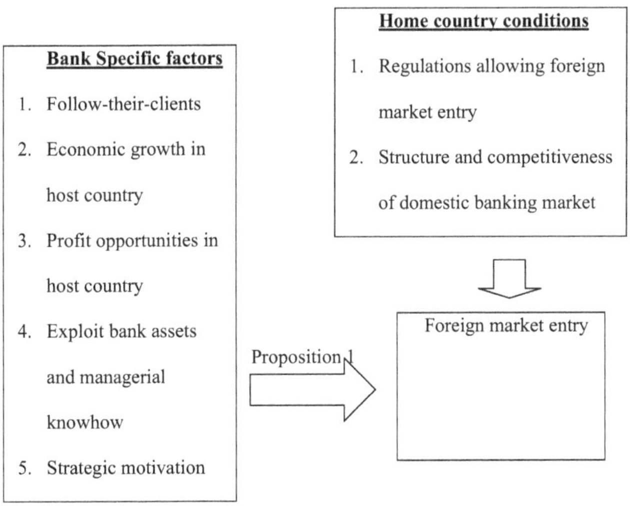

Fig. 3.1 Framework of the research with propositions

Data Collection and Analysis

Sampling Frame

At the end of 2012 there were 21 commercial banks in Nigeria, of which nine were licensed to have international operations. From this population, five banks that embarked on foreign market entries were chosen by purposive sampling as the cases for this study. These five banks made up 40 of the 53 total (75 %) foreign entries made by Nigerian banks between 2005 and 2012.

The five banks chosen were United Bank for Africa (eighteen international subsidiaries), Access Bank (nine international subsidiaries), Guaranty Trust Bank (seven international subsidiaries), Diamond Bank (four international subsidiaries) and Keystone Bank (four international subsidiaries). The selection criteria were that all the banks have operations in international markets for the period of the study (2005–2012) and that all have operations in four or more countries.

Sampling of respondents and interviewees emphasized top management at the banks' headquarters and managing directors of international subsidiaries. Likert scale questionnaires were sent to four top management and board members of each bank. The questionnaire was designed to appraise how important certain stated factors were to a bank's management decision to embark on foreign market entry. Additionally, two managers out of the four from each bank who responded to the questionnaire were interviewed to gain further insight into their bank's strategies. In order to triangulate primary evidence, secondary data was also employed in a mixed methodology approach. The secondary data was sourced from bank annual reports and websites and databases of agencies like the World Bank and the International Monetary Fund (IMF).

Analysis of Likert Scale Data

Primary data was analyzed using the normal distribution fitting analysis (NDFA) approach. Stacey (2005) has shown this approach to be more reliable and valid in converting ordinal level data into interval level data, thus creating a numeric scale. According to Stacey (2005), constructs such as attitudes, perceptions and preferences are generally impossible to evaluate through direct observation; therefore, researchers resort to indirect data sources, typically using some sort of self-report methodology. The data gathered in the present study was qualitative and thus needed to be subjected to statistical transformation into quantitative data if parametric statistical methods were to be used. With NDFA this transformation can be done with greater reliability and validity than with most other stated methods, including the correspondence analysis method.

Essentially, the fundamental assumption of the methodology is that there is a distribution of perceptions about the range of issues/factors/items/variables presented in the survey. Because the response format is ordinal, it has no absolute, measurable, calibrated numeric values; therefore, the numeric measurement scale may be defined such that the distribution of responses follows a normal distribution (Stacey 2005). Along this numeric measurement scale, there are threshold values that separate participants' responses into ordinal categories. In the case of this research, the categories were "Not important", "Less important", "Important", "Very important" and "Extremely important". Four thresholds separated the five response categories.

Using normal statistical distribution parameters, such as population means and variance, the distribution of responses that is expected for each survey item can be calculated using the NORM.DIST function in Microsoft Excel. However, from the field data gathered from the questionnaire, we had the actual (i.e. observed) number of responses.

The methodology assumes arbitrary values for the means and variance of each of the survey items as well as the threshold values. While still using Microsoft Excel, the next step is to calculate a Chi-square goodness-of-fit statistic between the observed frequencies and the numeric model. If the Chi-square statistic is insignificant, there is no significant difference between the observed data and the numeric model and the means and variance in the model are reliable estimates of the means and variance of the survey responses.

Results

The data was collected and analyzed with the aim of answering the main question of this research. Evidence from the primary and secondary data was used to seek support for or to guide modifications to the propositions. Using these results, Proposition 1 was addressed.

Primary data was gathered from questionnaire responses, and the average responses to each question were collated, tabulated and analyzed using the NDFA approach (Tables A1 and A2, see appendix). In the sections that follow, this primary data is supplemented by secondary evidence from a variety of cited sources.

Internationalization to Follow Clients into Foreign Markets

Managers stated that client-following was a "very important" motivation for international expansion by Nigerian banks. Secondary data shows significant trade flows between Nigeria and other African countries. A report by the Brookings Institution points out that Africa's biggest economies are the biggest inter-regional traders. The report further states that Nigeria was Africa's second-biggest intra-regional exporter (Brookings Institution 2012). Additionally, comparative data also shows a high concentration of Nigerian banks in the countries that enjoy the largest exports from Nigeria, namely, Ghana, Côte D' Ivoire and Senegal. These are also countries that enjoy significant FDI from Nigerian firms (Table 3.1).

Thus, secondary data showing trade flows generally seems to support the primary response that client-following was a very important factor in a bank's foreign market entry decision.

Internationalization to Seek Opportunities in Growth Economies

Decision makers in the banks viewed the gross domestic product (GDP) growth rates of host countries as "very important" determinants of foreign

Table 3.1 Exports from Nigeria and the number of Nigerian bank subsidiaries in select SSA countries

Country	Number of Nigerian banks in the country	Exports from Nigeria 2008	2009	2010
Ghana	5	1847.47	301.93	437.44
Côte d' Ivoire	6	1818.50	1496.56	1256.43
Sierra Leone	7	7.41	4.56	3.44
Senegal	3	927.61	283.66	190.82
Burkina Faso	1	1085	8.30	51.40

Source: Africa Union Commission Yearbook on status of intra-African trade (2012)

market entry. This item was the highest ranked item according to the data analysis.

SSA countries have been the primary destination of Nigerian banks, and data from the IMF indicates that most SSA countries have been experiencing high growth rates in the past decade. Greater political stability has fuelled the economic growth in many SSA countries (World Bank 2010; IMF 2010).

In support of the primary data, secondary evidence shows that the countries with the highest population of Nigerian banks, namely Ghana (four banks), Sierra Leone (six banks) and Côte D' Ivoire (six banks), have experienced some of the highest GDP growth rates in SSA, and indeed in the world (see Table 3.2).

Internationalization to Seek Profit Opportunities in Host Countries

Responses by managers indicated that profit opportunities in host countries were a significant determinant of international expansion. Profit opportunities due to differentials in exchange rates and tax rates were considered "less important" than profit opportunities due to differentials in interest rates; profitability of the host countries' banking markets was found to be "important".

Table 3.2 GDP growth rates and macroeconomic indices of select SSA countries as compared to some Organisation for Economic Co-operation and Development (OECD) countries

Country	GDP growth rate(2010)	Interest rate (prime lending rates of commercial banks) 2011	Corporate tax rate (2011)
Cameroon	2.6	14.0	49.1
Congo DR	7.2	43.75	337.7
Côte d'Ivoire	3.0	4.3	44.3
Gabon	5.7	15.0	43.5
Gambia	5.0	28.0	283.5
Ghana	6.6	18.0	33.6
Kenya	5.3	15.05	42.6
Liberia	5.5	13.0	43.7
Nigeria	7.9	16.0	32.7
Sierra Leone	4.9	21.0	32.0
South Africa	2.8	9.0	31.0
UK	2.1	4.06	37.3
USA	3.0	3.25	46.7

Source: World Bank Development Indicators (2012), CIA factfile

Secondary data seems to support this finding. Regarding interest rate differentials between home and host countries, the two interest rate measures used in extant research are the prime lending rate of commercial banks to borrowers and the risk-free interest rate, which measures the rate at which governments sell so-called risk-free treasury bills. Analysis of secondary evidence seems to suggest that interest rate differentials between home and host countries were unlikely to be an important consideration for international expansion. Managers did not consider exchange rate differentials between their home and host countries to be important in their decision to enter foreign markets. Respondents noted that host country tax rate differentials were "less important" in their foreign market entry decisions.

Primary evidence shows that the profitability of SSA banking markets was an "important" factor for entry by Nigerian banks. The profitability of a banking market may be measured by returns on assets (ROAs) and returns on equity (ROEs), and secondary data shows that SSA banks have high values for both measures. In an empirical study of the profitability of banks in SSA, Flamini et al. (2009) found that commercial banks are very profitable in SSA, and they posited that apart from credit risk, higher ROAs are associated with larger bank size, activity diversification and private ownership of banks.

Internalization to Exploit Banks' Assets, Processes and Management Skills

Primary evidence shows that expansion to exploit O-advantages was an "important" factor in foreign market entry decisions. These O-advantages include a bank's reputation, size and capital, management processes and know-how, risk management and credit appraisal skills, and technology. Additional secondary evidence seems to support these primary responses.

Size

Respondents noted that the size and capital of their banks was a "very important" consideration for managers in their foreign market entry decision. Following its consolidation in 2005, the Nigerian banking market became the second biggest in SSA (Kasekende et al. 2009). Data from *The Banker* magazine shows that by 2010 Nigerian banks were among the largest banks in Africa by tier 1 capital and assets, at the time several were ranked among the top 1000 banks in the world (Table 3.3). Additional evidence shows that international market entry is typically pursued as a strategy mainly by the banks with the greatest capital and assets.

Reputation

Managers stated that the reputation of their banks was an "important" O-advantage to exploit in host markets. Studies have used the ranking of a bank in *The Banker* magazine as a proxy for its reputation (Qian and Delios 2008). Secondary data shows that by 2007 seven Nigerian banks were ranked among the top 1000 banks in the world according to the size of their tier 1 capital and assets. Additionally, ten Nigerian banks were ranked among the top twenty banks in Africa by 2010 (see Table 3.3).

Table 3.3 Size, capital, profitability, ranking and number of foreign market entries of Nigerian banks

Bank	Tier 1 capital ($M)	Assets ($M)	ROA (%)	ROE (%)	Ranking in Africa (2011)	No. of foreign operations (2012)
GTB	1362	7646	4.2	23.6	15	6
UBA	1084	10,737	0.2	1.9	20	18
Access Bank	1149	5342	2.0	9.3	18	10
Diamond Bank	750	3948	0.8	4.5	30	4
First Bank	2221	15,301	1.9	12.9	9	5
Zenith Bank	2405	12,578	2.6	13.8	8	5
Skye Bank	695	4474	1.7	10.9	31	3

Source: The Banker's Magazine, The African Banker Magazine, banks annual reports

Management Skills, Processes and Know-How

Primary evidence from the respondents denotes that managerial know-how and processes are valuable and "important" assets that can be exploited in foreign markets. Managers interviewed for additional insights pointed out that some Nigerian banks have developed unique management skills and processes that provide them with a competitive advantage in other SSA countries. Managers listed cost and profit efficiencies and expertise in doing business in a challenging environment as unique management knowledge.

Secondary evidence supports this finding. The profitability of a bank or banking market has been used as a proxy for management competence and performance (Focarelli and Pozzolo 2001). With an ROA averaging 3.01 in 2005 and 2.07 in 2006, the Nigerian banking market was one of the most profitable in SSA. Kasekende et al. (2009) stated that following the reform program of 2005 in Nigerian banking, most of the performance indicators of Nigerian banks satisfied high quality benchmarks, such as ROA, ROE, capital strength, asset size and soundness. Furthermore, Kiyota (2011) found that Nigerian banks, along with other SSA-owned international banks, developed profit and cost efficiencies that enabled them to expand and compete against domestic banks in SSA.

Added to this, bank managements have developed unique capabilities in the cause of providing banking services in Nigeria. Managers interviewed believed that the most important aspect of this know-how was their expertise in doing business in a challenging business environment.

Secondary evidence reveals similarities in the physical and institutional environments between Nigeria and many SSA countries, but circumstances have sometimes presented more difficulty for banks in Nigeria. These physical similarities include low levels of electricity generation and consumption per capita and poor telecommunications infrastructure. Similarities in the level of institutional development include the same levels of development of borrower information and of the judiciary. Nigeria and many SSA countries also share similarities in levels of corruption and rule-based governance, like creditor protection and property rights (Table 3.4).

Table 3.4 Indicators of development in select SSA, South American, Asian and OECD countries

Country	Telephone subscriptions per 100 (2009)		Electricity per capita (2009)	Dept. of credit information (1–10)	Ease of Doing Business ranking (2012)	Property rights and rule-based governance (2011)
	Fixed line	Mobile				
Cameroon	3	44	271	2		2.5
Congo DR	0	18	104	0	178	2.0
Côte d'Ivoire	1	76	203	1	167	2.0
Gabon	2	107	922	2	156	
Gambia	3	86	–	0	149	3.0
Ghana	1	71	265	3	63	3.5
Kenya	1	62	147	4	109	2.5
Liberia	0	39		1	151	2.5
Nigeria	1	55	121	0	137	2.5
Sierra Leone	0	34	–	0	141	2.5
South Africa	8	101	532	6	35	
UK	4	130	5692	6	6	
USA	49	90	12,914	6	4	

Source: WD Source: WDI, World Bank Doing Business Index (2012)

The challenges faced by businesses due to the low levels of institutional development in Nigeria are revealed by the country's low rank of 137 in the 2012 World Bank Ease of Doing Business Index. This index outlines the level of development of institutions and the availability of regulations that facilitate the setting up and enforcement of property rights for businesses in various country's.

This evidence suggests that Nigerian banks have developed capabilities, know-how and processes for conducting business profitably in an environment with low infrastructural and institutional development. It is these capabilities that give them a competitive advantage in other SSA countries (Claessens and van Horen 2008).

Risk Management and Credit Appraisal Know-How

A bank's credit risk appraisal knowledge was viewed as an "important" asset. The managers interviewed saw the ability of their officers to appraise risk when lending money to borrowers, especially in markets with little or no credit information on borrowers, as an intangible asset that gave them a competitive advantage when transferring to foreign markets.

Credit risk is high in most SSA countries, including Nigeria, because of limited information on borrowers and low creditors' rights (see Table 3.4). Despite these risks, data shows that credit to the private sector as a percentage of GDP by banks in Nigeria is among the highest in SSA. Thus, secondary data, in line with the primary responses, suggests that Nigerian banks have developed other means of risk appraisal and information generation about borrowers. Most notable among these measures to mitigate risk is relationship banking. Kasekende et al. (2009) noted the increased investment of Nigerian banks in personal (relationship) banking following the consolidation program of 2005.

Secondary data shows the investment of Nigerian banks in branch networks to mobilize information on clients and deposits (Table 3.5).

Table 3.5 Number of branches of case study banks in selected SSA countries at the end of 2012

Bank	Ghana	Sierra Leone	Gambia	Burkina Faso	Benin	Côte d'Ivoire
Access	32	4	5	–	–	2
UBA	24	5	–	20	11	5
GTB	22	9	15	–	–	1
Diamond	–	–	–	–	18	1
Keystone	–	–	6	–	–	–

Source: Banks' annual reports

Knowledge of Business Cultures in Host Markets

Managers asserted that knowledge of the business cultures and institutions of host countries was a "less important" factor for the banks in their decisions to enter foreign markets. Secondary evidence corroborates the assertion of the respondents, as most Nigerian banks entered foreign markets in SSA with a high equity entry mode (subsidiaries) despite not having operated in these markets before and without any prior experience of foreign market entry.

Technological Assets

Primary evidence from interviewees shows that exploitation of the technological assets of a bank was a "very important" motive for internationalization. Secondary evidence also shows increased investment in distribution channels like ATM machines made by Nigerian banks in both their home and international operations.

International Expansion for Strategic Reasons

Bank internationalization can be a deliberate strategic decision. Primary data reveals the relative importance of different components of strategic motivation as factors that influenced international market entry. These may include risk diversification, oligopolistic reaction and management's intentional decision to expand. Interviewees noted that risk diversification was an "important" motivating factor for international expansion. Managers also asserted that oligopolistic reaction was an "important" factor in their decision to enter foreign markets. Qian and Delios (2008) used the pace of international market entry by banks from the same country into a particular host country as a proxy for oligopolistic reaction.

Secondary evidence seems to suggest a "bandwagon effect" in the expansion of Nigerian banks into foreign markets. An example is the pace of entry into Ghana by Nigerian banks. Entry into Ghana by UBA in 2004 was followed swiftly by entry by other Nigerian banks. By 2008 there were six Nigerian banks in Ghana. This suggests that entry into Ghana by UBA may have triggered a bandwagon effect that led other banks to enter also (Table 3.6). Thus, primary and secondary evidence show that Nigerian banks reacted to the actions of their competitors in expanding internationally.

Respondents noted that the role of managerial intentionality was cited as a "very important" reason for the decision to internationalize. Indeed, this item was ranked third by respondents. Secondary evidence on managerial intentionality can also be inferred from the official vision statements of the banks. Access Bank desires "to be the most respected bank in Africa". GTB wants "to be one of the top three banks in Africa by 2016". UBA yearns "to be Africa's global bank", while Diamond Bank aims to be "a strong financial services institution with effective presence in Nigeria, Africa and indeed all key financial centres of the world".

Thus, both the primary and secondary evidence agree that managerial intentionality is a significant strategic reason for banks' international expansion (Table 3.7).

Table 3.6 Foreign market entries made by some Nigerian banks between 2000 and 2012

	Number of foreign market entries					
Bank	2000	2004	2006	2008	2010	2012
GTB	–	2	3	4	5	6
UBA	–	1	2	7	16	18
Access	–	–	1	7	10	10
Diamond	–	1	1	1	1	4
Zenith	–	–	2	3	4	5
Keystone Bank	–	–	1	2	4	4
Skye	–	–	–	2	3	3

Source: Banks' annual reports

Table 3.7 Primary and secondary evidence for Proposition 1 (P1)

P1: Interview question topics	Primary evidence	Secondary evidence	Conclusions on P1
Client-following	Very Important	Consistent	Consistent
GDP growth rate of host	Very Important	Consistent	Consistent
Interest rate differentials	Important	Consistent	Consistent
Exchange rate differentials	Less important	Contradictory	Inconsistent
Tax rate differentials	Less important	Contradictory	Inconsistent
Profitability of host banking market	Important	Consistent	Consistent
To exploit bank's size	Very important	Consistent	Consistent
To exploit bank's reputation	Important	Consistent	Consistent
To exploit bank's management skill	Important	Consistent	Consistent
To exploit credit appraisal know-how	Important	Consistent	Consistent
To exploit bank's knowledge of host country business culture	Less Important	Contradictory	Inconsistent
To exploit bank's technology assets	Very important	Consistent	Consistent
Strategic motivation to diversify risk	Important	Consistent	Consistent
Strategic reaction to competitor action	Important	Consistent	Consistent
Management's desire to expand brand	Very important	Consistent	Consistent

Conclusions on Proposition 1

From the evidence, therefore, Proposition 1 is largely supported. We now address the evidence relating to Proposition 2, which states that "a bank's motivation to expand internationally will be influenced by home country regulations and competitive pressure in the domestic banking market".

Home Country Conditions

Regulations

Primary evidence shows that regulations by the CBN that permitted foreign market entry by Nigerian banks were an "important" factor in the decision by individual banks to enter foreign markets. Secondary evidence shows that there were extant regulations from the CBN permitting international market entry by the banks

Structure and Competitiveness of the Domestic Banking Market

Respondents stated that the structure and competitiveness of the Nigerian banking market was a "less important" factor influencing their decision to expand internationally. Managers who were interviewed denied the notion that their foreign market entry was due to competitive pressure in the Nigerian banking market.

Secondary evidence on the structure and competitiveness of the Nigerian banking market can be inferred from the findings of several empirical studies that found the structure to be oligopolistic (Bikker and Spierdijk 2008; Zhao and Murinde 2011; Okulue et al. 2012)

An oligopolistic structure suggests that the Nigerian banking market is neither monopolistic nor perfectly competitive. Thus, the industry was not so concentrated as to confer market power on only a few banks and force others to seek new markets, nor was it very competitive.

Thus, secondary evidence suggests that the structure of the Nigerian banking market might not have been a determining factor in the foreign market entry by Nigerian banks (Table 3.8).

Table 3.8 Primary and secondary findings for Proposition 2 (P2)

P2: Interview question topics	Primary evidence	Secondary evidence	Conclusions on P2
Home country regulations	Important	Consistent	Consistent
Structure and competitiveness of home country banking market	Less Important	Contradictory	Inconsistent

Conclusions on Proposition 2

Thus, Proposition 2 is only partially supported by the evidence gathered.

Findings and Revisions to Propositions

Some measure of inconsistency was found between the propositions declared at the beginning of the research and the findings from the primary and secondary evidence gathered. In line with the positivist case study approach, these propositions may be revised or modified.

Proposition 1

Primary and secondary evidence indicate that foreign market entry by Nigerian banks was driven mainly by managerial intentionality, client-following, exploitation of the assets that the banks possessed and profit opportunities in most SSA banking markets. Internationalization was a deliberate strategic objective of Nigerian banks to become dominant players in the financial services sector in Africa. Africa has become the strategic scope of many Nigerian banks, and the banks' mission and vision statements focus on the African banking market. Additionally, these banks possess tangible and intangible assets that they sought to exploit in SSA markets and which helped them to overcome the liability of foreignness. These assets include the banks' size and capital, reputation and brand name, management skills, credit appraisal know-how and technological assets.

Regarding profit opportunities in the host countries, some factors that previous studies had identified as being important in determining foreign market entry by MNBs were found to be less important to the foreign market entry decisions of Nigerian banks. Arbitrage from differentials in interest, exchange and tax rates between home and host countries were found to be less important, while the profitability of the host country banking market was found to be important.

Evidence on the strategic motivation for foreign market entry shows that banks found the diversification of risk and the need to respond to competitors' actions to be "important" factors for foreign market entry. Managerial intentionality, on the other hand, was found to be "very important". Managerial intentionality was manifested by the desire of Nigerian banks to be dominant financial services providers across Africa. Proposition 1 was found to be largely supported, but the proposition has been reordered to reflect the most important factors that prompted foreign market entry by the banks.

Thus, Proposition 1 has therefore been revised (changes in italics) to

"A bank's motivation to expand internationally will be influenced by a need to *follow its clients into foreign markets*, *seek profit opportunities in the hosts' banking markets*, and *fulfil the strategic aspirations of its managers*."

Proposition 2

Evidence shows that home country regulations were important to the banks investigated in determining foreign market entry. On the other hand, competitive pressure in the home country banking market was found to be less important. Thus, Proposition 2 was only partially supported.

Proposition 2 has therefore been revised to

"A bank's motivation to expand internationally will be influenced by home country regulations and competitive pressure in the domestic banking market, *unless the banks are from home countries with low levels of financial development.*"

Implications of the Research Findings

This research has revealed strong relationships between bank motivations for internationalization and factors that are under the control of governments. The CBN-initiated consolidation of the Nigerian banking market in 2005 was successful and led to an increase in the capital and assets of banks. A significant effect of this increased capital was a quest by the managers of several Nigerian banks to have their banks become dominant financial service providers in Africa. This change in the strategic scope of these banks led to a scramble to enter SSA markets. At the same time, host country governments were active in attracting banking FDI. Additionally, it was found that banks that possess significant amounts of tangible and intangible assets can operate profitably in host markets. This effect is amplified if those markets possess significant opportunities for profit.

Contributions

This research has essentially developed an explorative explanation of the phenomenon of internationalization of Nigerian banks. The research emphasized the various national, cultural and institutional contexts of SSA countries that may have influenced the findings. For these reasons, this research was highly contextual and the findings are largely idiosyncratic, but it should be noted that the research has sought high levels of validity and reliability through the positivist case study approach.

Limitations and Suggestions for Further Studies

This research was mainly explorative. It relied on a small sample of banks and respondents in Nigeria and some SSA countries chosen through non-parametric sampling methods. Despite methodological measures taken to increase validity and reliability, the realist leanings of the study emphasized the local context of individual respondents as well as the local context in which the research was conducted. This, however, implies multiple realities and the inapplicability of highly generalized, deductive theories.

There are now a number of companies in Africa that can be called "African multinationals". These include South African telecommunications firm MTN and retailer ShopRite and Nigerian cement manufacturer Dangote Industries, among others. These firms have made significant market entries into many countries in SSA and the Middle East. Factors influencing their decisions to enter foreign markets and the chosen mode of entry of these African multinational companies should be further studied.

Appendix

Table A1 Tabulation of observed and expected responses and distribution parameters and analysis using normal distribution fitting analysis (NDFA) algorithm

	1	2	31	32	33	34	41	42
Observed frequencies	To extend banking services to your clients who have expanded abroad	GDP growth rate of host country	3.1. Interest rate differential between Nigeria and host country	3.2. Exchange rate differential between Nigeria and host country currency	3.3. Tax rate differential between Nigeria and host country	3.4. Profitability of host country banking market (high returns on asset [ROA] & returns on equity [ROE])	4.1 To exploit the bank's size and capital	4.2 To exploit the bank's reputation
Not important	0	0	0	0	1	0	0	1
Less important	1	1	8	13	14	2	0	0
Important	5	5	4	4	4	8	6	6
Very important	7	6	6	3	1	7	12	11
Extremely important	7	8	2	0	0	3	2	2
$n =$	20	20	20	20	20	20	20	20
Distribution parameters								
$\mu =$	0.7074	0.7889	−0.2976	−0.8399	−1.0837	0.2114	0.4073	0.1099
$\sigma^2 =$	0.9406	1.1240	1.1415	0.5714	0.4328	0.6427	0.2934	1.0719
Expected frequencies								
Not important	0.0	0.1	0.9	1.0	1.2	0.0	0.0	0.3
Less important	1.4	1.5	6.1	10.4	13.1	2.5	0.4	4.0
Important	3.9	3.6	5.9	6.5	4.9	6.4	5.4	5.7
Very important	8.0	7.4	5.3	2.0	0.7	8.5	12.4	6.8
Extremely important	6.6	7.5	1.8	0.1	0.0	2.5	1.8	3.2
χ^2 contributions								
Not important	0.0384	0.0650	0.9223	0.9645	0.0452	0.0399	0.0000	1.3539
Less important	0.1207	0.1787	0.5896	0.6245	0.0606	0.0952	0.3989	3.9780
Important	0.3139	0.5417	0.6184	0.9474	0.1814	0.3900	0.0742	0.0212
Very important	0.1350	0.2484	0.1056	0.4734	0.1286	0.2807	0.0146	2.5882
Extremely important	0.0227	0.0392	0.0205	0.0908	0.0076	0.0972	0.0206	0.4705
40.5926	0.6307	1.0730	2.2564	3.1006	0.4234	0.9030	0.5083	8.4118
Solver parameters	τ1	τ2	τ3	τw4				
Thresholds	−2.0965	−0.7056	0.1051	1.1324				
Means	0.7768	0.8662	−0.3268	−0.9223	−1.1900	0.2322	0.4473	0.1207
Variances	1.1342	1.3553	1.3763	0.6890	0.5218	0.7749	0.35537	1.2924
To prevent division by zero: 0								
t-value	3.2618	3.3276	−1.2457	−4.9692	−7.3672	1.1795	3.3633	0.4746
p-value	0.0043	0.0037	0.2288	0.0001	0.0000	0.2536	0.0035	0.6408

The results reported in Table A1 are now summarized in Table A2

43	44	45	46	51	52	53	61	62	
4.3. To exploit the bank's management skills, processes and know-how	4.4. To exploit the bank's management and credit appraisal know-how	4.5. To exploit the bank's knowledge of institutional and business culture of various international markets	4.6 To exploit the bank's technological assets	5.1. To diversify risk	5.2. To respond to other industry players' expansion (oligo-polistic reaction)	5.3. Manage-ment's desire to expand brand internatio-nally (managerial intentionality)	6.1 Regula-tions of CBN regarding international expansion (as of 2005)	6.2. Structure and compe-titiveness of Nigerian banking market	
1	0	0	0	0	1	0	0		
0	1	4	0	7	5	1	5	8	
8	8	11	9	4	8	2	6	8	
9	9	5	11	9	4	14	3	2	
2	2	0	0	0	2	3	6	2	
20	20	20	20	20	20	20	20	20	
−0.0041	0.2421	−0.2564	0.1354	−0.1879	−0.2850	0.5331	0.2137	−0.3946	
1.0083	0.4180	0.2762	0.0574	0.7339	1.0636	0.3988	1.8050	0.9619	
0.4	0.0	0.0	0.3	0.8	0.0	0.9	0.8		
4.5	1.4	3.9	0.0	5.2	6.0	0.5	4.1	6.7	
6.0	6.9	11.2	9.0	7.2	6.1	4.5	4.4	6.4	
6.6	10.0	4.8	11.0	6.1	5.4	11.6	5.7	4.9	
2.6	1.7	0.1	0.0	1.2	1.7	3.4	4.9	1.2	
1.0614	0.0030	0.0046	0.0000	0.2588	0.0558	0.0003	0.8550	0.8268	
4.4760	0.1261	0.0016	0.0027	0.6254	0.1803	0.5068	0.2061	0.2589	
0.6529	0.1773	0.0022	0.0000	1.4361	0.5821	1.3733	0.5669	0.4088	
0.9102	0.0988	0.0058	0.0000	1.3893	0.3447	0.4989	1.2815	1.7242	
0.1293	0.0588	0.0822	0.0015	1.2329	0.0555	0.0531	0.2269	0.5426	
7.2298	0.4640	0.0964	0.0042	4.9425	1.2185	2.4324	3.1364	3.7612	Chi-text *p*-value 0.9925
−0.0045	0.2659	−0.2816	0.1486	−0.2063	−0.3130	0.5854	0.2347	−0.4333	
1.2158	0.5040	0.3330	0.0692	0.8849	1.2824	0.4808	2.1763	1.1598	
−0.0183	1.6748	−2.1822	2.5278	−0.9808	−1.2359	3.7755	0.7115	−1.7993	
0.9856	0.1113	0.0426	0.0211	0.3397	0.2324	0.0014	0.4859	0.0888	

Table A2 Summary of values and their interpretation following analysis of responses to questionnaire

Item/factor	n	μ	σ^2	Rank	t-value	p-value	Significance	Degree of importance of factor
1. To extend banking services to your clients who have expanded abroad	20	0.71	0.94	2	0.26	043	Significantly greater than average, at $\alpha = 0.01$	Very Important
2. GDP growth rate of host country	20	0.79	1.12	1	3.33	0.0037	Significantly greater than average, at $\alpha = 0.01$	Very Important
3.i. Interest rate differential between Nigeria and host country	20	−0.30	1.14	14	−1.25	0.2288	Not significantly different from average	Important
3.ii. Exchange rate differential between Nigerian and host country currency	20	−0.84	0.57	16	−4.97	0.0001	Significantly less than average, at $\alpha = 0.01$	Less Important
3. iii. Tax rate differential between Nigeria and host country	20	−1.08	0.43	17	7.37	0.0000	Significantly less than average, at $\alpha = 0.01$	Less Important
3. iv. Profitability of host country banking market (high ROA and ROE)	20	0.21	0.64	7	1.18	0.2536	Not significantly different from average	Important
4. i. To exploit the bank's size and capital	20	0.41	0.29	4	3.36	0.0035	Significantly greater than average, at $\alpha = 0.01$	Very Important
4. ii. To exploit the bank's reputation	20	0.11	1.07	9	0.47	0.6408	Not significantly different from average	Important
4. iii. To exploit the bank's management skills, processes and know-how	20	0.00	1.01	10	−0.02	0.9856	Not significantly different from average	Important

4. iv.	To exploit the bank's risk management and credit appraisal know-how	20	0.24	0.42	5	0.67	1113	Not significantly different from average	Important
4. v.	To exploit the bank's knowledge of institutional and business culture of various international markets	20	−0.26	0.28	12	−2.18	0.0426	Significantly less than average, at $\alpha = 0.05$	Less Important
4. vi.	To exploit the bank's technological assets	20	0.14	0.06	8	2.53	0211	Significantly greater than average, at $\alpha = 0.05$	Very Important
5. i.	To diversify risk	20	−0.19	0.73	11	−0.98	0.3397	Not significantly different from average	Important
5. ii.	To respond to other industry players' expansion (oligopolistic reaction)	20	−0.29	1.06	13	−1.24	0.2324	Not significantly different from average	Important
5. iii.	Management's desire to expand brand internationally (managerial intentionality)	20	0.53	0.40	3	3.78	0.0014	Significantly greater than average, at $\alpha = 0.01$	Very Important
6. i.	Regulations of CBN regarding international expansion (as of 2005)	20	0.21	1.80	6	0.71	0.4859	Not significantly different from average	Important
6. ii.	Structure and competitiveness of Nigerian banking market	20	−0.39	0.96	15	−1.80	0.0888	Significantly less than average, at $\alpha = 0.01$	Less Important

Legend: n, sample size; μ, mean; σ^2 standard deviation

References

Aggarwal, R., & Durnford, J. (1989). Market assessment of international banking activity: A study of US bank holding companies. *Quarterly Review of Economics and Business, 29*(1), 58–67.

Barney, J. B. (1991). Firm resources and sustained competitive advantage. *Journal of Management, 17*(1), 99–120.

Boojihawon, D. K., & Acholonu, K. K. (2013). Internationalisation process of African banks: an exploratory study. African Journal of Economic and Management Studies, 4(2), 244–266.

Buch, C. M., & DeLong, G. (2004). Cross-border bank mergers: What lures the rare animal?. Journal of Banking & Finance, 28(9), 2077–2102.

Cerrutti, E., Dell'Ariccia, G., & Peria, M. S. M. (2007). How banks go abroad: Branches or subsidiaries. *Journal of Banking and Finance, 31*(6), 1669–1692.

Cho, K. R. (1986). Determinants of international banks. *Management International Review, 26*(1), 10–23.

Claessens, S., & van Horen, N. (2008). *Location decision of foreign banks and competitive advantage* (World Bank Policy Research Working Papers No. 4113). Washington, DC: World Bank.

Cull, R., & Peria, M. S. M. (2010). *Foreign bank participation in developing countries* (Policy Research Working Paper 5398). Washington, DC: The World Bank Development Research Group.

Czinkota, M. R. (2004). *The export marketing imperative*. London, UK: Thomson Learning.

Flamini, V., McDonald, C., & Schumacher, L. (2009). *The determinants of commercial bank profitability in Sub-Saharan Africa* (Working Paper WP/09/15). Washington, DC: IMF.

Florian, L. (2012). Financial sector competition in West African Economic and Monetary Union, *Etudes et Documents 2012.14, Document Du Travial De La Série*. Clermont-Ferrand, France: CERDI, Université d'Auvergne et CNRS.

Focarelli, D., & Pozzolo, A. F. (2001). The patterns of cross-border bank mergers and shareholding in OECD countries. *Journal of Banking and Finance, 25*(12), 2305–2337.

Goldberg, L. G., & Johnson, D. (1990). Determinants of U.S. Banking Activity Abroad. *Journal of International Money and Finance, 9*(2), 123–137.

Guillén, M. F., & Tschoegl, A. E. (1999). *At last the internationalization of retail banking? The case of the Spanish banks in Latin America* (Working Paper No. 99–41). Philadelphia. PA: The Wharton School, University of Pennsylvania.

Hutzschenreuter, T., Pederson, T., & Volberda, H. W. (2007). The role of path dependency and managerial intentionality: A perspective of the international business research. *Journal of International Business Studies, 38*(7), 1055–1068.

Johanson, J., & Vahlne, J. E. (1977). The Internationalization process of the firm. *Journal of international Business Studies, 8*(1), 23–32.

Kasekende, L., Mlambo, K., Murinde, V., & Zhao, T. (2009). Restructuring for competitiveness: The financial services sector of Africa's four largest economies. *The Africa Competitiveness Report 2009*. Abidjan, Côte d'Ivoire: African Development Bank.

Kiyota, H. (2011). *Efficiencies of commercial banks in Sub-Saharan Africa: A comparative analysis of domestic and foreign banks* (Working Paper Series No. 2011/58). New York, NY: United Nations University.

Luiz, J. M., & Charalambous, H. (2009). Factors influencing foreign direct investment of South African financial services firms in Sub-Saharan Africa. *International Business Review, 18*(3), 305–317.

Magri, S., Mori, A., & Rossi, P. (2005). The entry and the activity level of foreign banks in Italy: An analysis of the determinants. *Journal of Banking and Finance, 29*(5), 1295–1310.

Miller, S. R., & Prakhe, A. (1998). Patterns in the expansion of US bank's foreign operations. *Journal of International Business Studies, 29*(2), 359–389.

Okulue., U. D., Uchenna, A. W., Obinna, U. G., & Nonye, U. G. (2012). The structure of the Nigerian banking sector and its impact on bank performance. *Journal of Economics and Sustainable Development, 3*(7), 30–40.

Outreville, J. F. (2007). Foreign affiliates of the world largest financial groups: Location and governance. *Research in International Business Finance, 21*(1), 19–31.

Piekkari, R., Welch, C., & Paavilainen, E. (2009). Case study as a disciplinary convention: Evidence from international business journals. *Organizational Research Methods, 12*(3), 567–589.

Qian, L., & Delios, A. (2008). Internalization and experience: Japanese banks international expansion, 1980–1998. *Journal of International Business Studies, 39*(2), 231–248.

Stacey, A. G. (2005). Reliability and validity of item means and standard deviation of ordinal level response data. *Management Dynamics, 13*(3), 2–25.

Tschoegl, A.E. (2003). *Who owns the major US subsidiaries of foreign banks? A note* (Working Paper Series No. 03-11). Philadelphia, PA: The Wharton School, University of Pennsylvania.

World Bank (2012). *World development indicators*. Washington, DC: World Bank.

Yin, R. K. (2009). *Case study research. Design and methods* (4th ed.). Thousand Oaks, CA: Sage Publications.

Zhao, T., & Murinde, V. (2011). Bank deregulation and performance in Nigeria. *African Development Review, 23*(1), 30–43.

4

Corporate Political Activity and Intra-African Foreign Direct Investments: Evidence from Uganda's Electricity Industry

Charles Godfrey Mbalyohere

Introduction

This study was inspired by a growing need for Africa to tap into the global foreign direct investment (FDI) patterns that indicate an ever-larger share for new emerging markets in general (UNCTAD 2011, 2014). A major concern, however, is the observation that while the absolute share for emerging markets has been growing, Africa's relative share has not grown proportionately (Bartels et al. 2009). One suggestion to counteract this is to improve the quantity and quality of intra-African FDI (Adeleye et al. 2015). In order for this to happen effectively, however, there is a need to re-examine the relationships between governments across the continent and the firms driving intra-African FDI. This suggests that studies about government-business relations that have thus far focused on the maturing emerging markets need to encompass the broader corpus of emerging markets, not least

C.G. Mbalyohere (✉)
Rose Cottage, Milton Keynes, UK
e-mail: charles.mbalyohere@open.ac.uk

I. Adeleye et al. (eds.), *Africa-to-Africa Internationalization*, AIB Sub-Saharan Africa (SSA) Series, DOI 10.1007/978-3-319-30692-6_4

in Sub-Saharan Africa (Luo 2004; Sun et al. 2010; Lawton et al. 2014). The chapter hence describes an exploratory investigation in this regard, using Uganda's electricity industry as a research context, to capture recent patterns from a corporate political activity (CPA) perspective on investment.

Following Hillman and Hitt's (1999) seminal work, which also draws on earlier work by Baysinger (1984), CPA is defined as *corporate attempts to influence government policy in ways that are favourable to the firm.*[1] While in the past key firms have been state-owned enterprises configured to simply implement government policy, the growing accommodation of pro-market reforms all over Africa and the market entry of foreign multinational enterprises (MNEs) has necessitated the reconfiguration of relationships between firms and governments using CPA strategies. This has further been prompted by the ever-growing number of local firms competing with MNEs, seeking to use their understanding of the local situation for competitive advantage. Beyond the effects of this phenomenon in the respective countries, an important new aspect is the growing realisation of the possibilities for stronger regionalisation as part of pan-African strategies designed to exploit the scale and scope of the continent's potential. This has particularly been driven by MNEs from South Africa, Kenya and Nigeria and has resulted in a strong demonstration of the value of intra-African trade and investment. Given the emerging and hence fragile nature of supra-national regulatory and policy-making institutions to support these regional engagements, direct lobbying of and engagement with both the host and home governments by affected MNEs has become an important factor in enabling and driving the process. The classical firm bottom line in the new markets has, to a large extent, depended on how successfully this CPA process has occurred; a successful CPA process has many times helped to clarify investment regulations and improved ease of access to land and other fixed assets, enhanced flexibility in enforcing tax codes and aided in determination of firm ownership rules, among other things.

In extant literature on CPA as an emerging research domain with implications for the strategic management of MNEs, the focus has been on advanced market contexts and, increasingly, also on maturing emerging markets (Hillman et al. 2004; Lawton et al. 2013; Sun et al. 2010). There is hence a gap in studies that explicitly address the wider body of emerging markets, for example those in Africa. These markets have yet to develop solid market institutions; therefore, as part of an emerging interpretation of capitalism, non-market strategic perspectives, exemplified by CPA, attain a very important bridging role. This chapter hence contributes to filling this gap and reinforcing the literatures that underline the importance of CPA in the strategic management of MNEs in Africa, especially as part of intra-African FDI trends.

Theoretical Background

A substantive corpus of research (e.g. Hill et al. 1990; Hoskisson et al. 2000; Peng et al. 2008) has addressed the institutional implications of FDI in maturing emerging countries like China and India. However, the empirical evidence about the wider body of emerging markets remains thin (e.g. Frynas et al. 2006; Webb et al. 2010; Adeleye et al. 2015). But in light of the ever-increasing share of global FDI received by these new markets and their predicted importance in the 'new frontiers' of global economic growth (Raman 2009; UNCTAD 2011, 2014; Adeleye et al. 2015), there is a need for more research to illuminate the situation.

Given preliminary research about an associated emergence of new internationalising firms from these markets and how they benefit from their home bases (e.g. Daniel et al. 2003; Cuervo-Cazurra 2006, 2008; Luiz and Ruplal 2013), questions arise about the nature of this emergence, and its shaping by CPA. The details of how this new breed of firm is emerging and the strategic issues involved remain obscure. If there is a gap in understanding the economics-oriented dynamics of entry into and adaptation to these new emerging markets, the gap is worse from a non-market strategic perspective, given its relatively recent prominence even in advanced markets (e.g. Bonardi 2011; Doh et al. 2012; Lawton et al. 2014). A particularly important non-market strategic capability is developing relationships with key political actors such that they support favourable policy and institutional decisions (e.g. Hillman et al. 2004; Baines and Viney 2010; Bonardi 2011). By being historically embedded in these emerging markets, emerging market multinational enterprises (EMNEs) accumulate extensive experience concerning the behaviour of these actors in the political and institutional environment surrounding them. Effectively, EMNEs nurture the political capabilities needed to operate successfully in these fragile institutional contexts.

In this contribution, 'political capabilities' are defined as the strategic decision-making options that a firm accrues by combining resources, including human, relational, reputational and financial resources, in order to achieve corporate political objectives (e.g. Hillman et al. 2004; Bonardi and Keim 2005; Frynas et al. 2006). CPA, which accordingly accommodates these political capabilities, has already been defined in the introduction. The evolution from resources to capabilities is understood to reflect the suggestions of the resource-based view of strategy that envisions further evolution to strategic core competences and ultimately to strategic competitive advantage (e.g. Prahalad and Hamel 1990; Barney 1991; Helfat and Peteraf 2003). While there is extensive understanding of the transformation of market-based economic resources, there is thus far only a skeletal understanding of the transformation of non-market-based resources.

This current study extends our understanding of the emerging CPA domain by exposing it to new and rapidly changing investment contexts in Sub-Saharan Africa. While some previous studies have dwelt on market-based strategies in the region, the role of non-market strategies, as manifested in CPA, for example, has not been comprehensively addressed. Yet the region offers a particularly rich context in which to study CPA, not least as an important element of pro-market reforms and the shaping of an African understanding of market capitalism (Jackson and Deeg 2008). Efforts to develop stronger regional market blocs and the synergies between them further strengthen the uniqueness of the continent for this type of study. Corresponding MNEs are accordingly developing a rich portfolio of heterogeneous CPA strategies and underlying political capabilities, by means of which investment patterns and trends in these new emerging markets are being substantially redefined. The chapter hence seeks to address the knowledge gap on CPA activity in an increasingly important region for the global economy.

Methodology

The research used an exploratory, qualitative, multi-case-based approach to gather data. Such an approach has been recommended for areas of research that are novel and require preliminary insights (Eisenhardt 1989; Dyer and Wilkins 1991; Yin 2003). The wider philosophical rationale is that the broad interpretivist approach, specifically the social constructionist paradigm that was applied here, enables the researcher to investigate and make sense of reality using a reflexive, iterative and rich approach (Crotty 1998; Hammersley and Atkinson 2007, pp. 14–18; Easterby-Smith et al. 2008, pp. 58–60). Further, such an approach enables the researcher to access deeper levels of complexity of a situation, whilst allowing greater contextual focus (Miles and Huberman 1994, p. 10).

Three firms—one of them in a joint venture with an advanced market firm—were included in the study. They are all located in the electricity generation sector. One firm (Frinam) originates from South Africa, and another (Pisu) originates from Kenya. The last one (Avin) is based in the host country (Uganda). Pisu is in a joint venture with Energy Global of the USA. All of the names are pseudonyms, in keeping with the ethical research underpinnings that guided the study. Profile details for each case are provided in Table 4.1 below.

Table 4.1 Summary profiles of the cases in the study

	Research case		
Parameters	Pisu/Energy Global (a joint venture)	Frinam	Avin
Year of market entry	2005	2003 (pre-entry 1999)	2003
Home country	Kenya/USA	South Africa	Uganda
Mode of market entry	Joint venture	Greenfield (in partnership with government)	Market diversification as a local firm
Type of project	PPP	Hybrid PPP	IPP
No. of core employees in power unit	About 120 (about 500 at peak of construction, not counting over 5000 unskilled labourers)	About 100	About 50
Electricity generation capacity (MW)	250	380 (old dam plus extension)	50
Other electricity projects in Africa	Ruzizi dam project (DRC, Rwanda, Burundi and Tanzania)	Several projects of various forms in Southern and Western Africa	Sugar projects in S. Sudan and Rwanda that have potential for cogeneration

Source: Electricity Regulatory Authority (ERA) and Ministry of Energy and Mineral Development, Uganda
Legend: PPP = public private partnership; IPP = independent power producer; MW = megawatts; DRC = Democratic Republic of the Congo

The cases were selected because collectively they cover approximately 85 % of Uganda's current hydropower generation and represent a rich mix of intra-African FDI. Data collected included responses to semi-structured interviews, field notes, company archives, institutional archives and media reports. The data was analysed using thematic analysis supported by Nvivo 10 software. Interview partners (see Table 4.2 below) were selected for their seniority and experience. As the table illustrates, the partners represented a high level of diversity of institutional and corporate political background. The interviews lasted one hour on average and in a few cases were done twice in the course of fieldwork in order to get a deeper understanding of a situation. Interviews were recorded with permission and transcribed for analysis. A total of 40 interviews and over 100 archival documents were used for this study (see appendix).

Table 4.2 Overview of the interview partners and their specialities

Description of interview partners	Area of speciality	Number of interview partners
Current and past mid- to senior-level managers in case organisations	Corporate political activity (CPA) and its evolving characteristics; impact on emerging rules and norms	17
Uganda Ministry of Energy officials	Energy policy, specifically electricity	5
Senior government advisors in the energy industry (academics, local and international consultants)	External views on CPA and institutional implications since 1999	5
Members of parliament and their senior assistants (parliamentary committee on energy regulation)	Legislative perspectives, political stakeholdership	3
Association of energy industry stakeholders	Broader industry stakeholdership—social, economic and political perspectives	5
Key actors in the institutional field (electricity producers, transmitters and distributors; institutional entrepreneurs)	Legitimacy, non-market strategy (its implications for various institutionalisation processes), corporate political activities, local vs MNE perspective	5

Uganda's Electricity Sector: A Synopsis

While Uganda has been one of the few modestly durable success stories of economic and political reform and revival in Africa in recent decades, its continued economic prosperity requires sustained macroeconomic stability backed up by increasing economic productivity. A key limiting factor is the high rate of growth in demand for a stable power supply that is accompanying the rapid growth and expansion of the economy (Mawejje et al. 2012; Tumwesigye et al. 2012).

Uganda's electricity sector is regulated under the Electricity Act of 1999, which replaced the Electricity Act of 1964 (Engurait 2005; Keating 2009). At the time of implementation, this was the most extensive power sector reform ever undertaken on the African continent. Under the new act, the Uganda Electricity Board (UEB) was unbundled into three separate, government-owned entities: (1) Uganda Electricity **Generation** Company Limited (UEGCL), (2) Uganda Electricity **Transmission** Company Limited (UETCL) and (3) Uganda Electricity **Distribution** Company Limited (UEDCL). Concessions were also given to private companies to perform generation and distribution as part of private public partnerships with the newly created government-owned entities. There was also the option to enter the market as an independent power producer (IPP). Further, a new regulator, the Electricity Regulation Authority (ERA), was formed as an independent regulator under the policy guidance of the Ministry of Energy and Mineral Development (MEMD). Finally but not least, a Rural Electrification Agency (REA) was formed to focus on pushing for the increased electrification of rural areas. The government maintained a monopoly on power transmission through UETCL.

The sector can be considered strategic by virtue of its multiple impacts on many other sectors in the economy, its significant contribution to the national revenue profile and its potential to help alleviate poverty, especially in rural areas where the majority of the population still resides (Tumwesigye et al. 2012; Haanyika 2006; Engurait 2005). Access to electricity in rural areas is estimated at an alarming 6 %, while the national rate is only 15 %, which is far below Sub-Saharan Africa's average of 30 % (Businge 2014; World Bank 2014).

Currently, the country has an installed hydroelectric capacity of around 700 megawatts (MW), which is predominantly a product of dam installations at the source of and along River Nile. This includes the Bujagali Hydroelectric Power Station, with an installed capacity of 250 MW, which was commissioned in October 2012 to mark Independence Day. The country has the potential to produce up to 2000 MW of hydroelectric power with further installations along the Nile, a prospect that might help alleviate the massive demand and spur investment (Tumwesigye et al. 2012).

Findings

The research findings are structured under three main categories: antecedents and rationale of reform, the broad perspective of market embeddedness, and the policy-making and regulatory institutional perspective of market embeddedness. The tables reflect the main conclusions from the data analysis, which lay the foundation for the discussion that follows.

Antecedents and Rationale of Reform

This first findings category summarises some key issues which influenced the choice of the model of reform in Uganda's electricity sector. It captures some of the debates that transpired in the pre-reform years, around 1995 to 1999, leading to a sector strategic plan.[2] The understanding of the political ramifications of these debates and the ensuing plan was an important element in informing the appropriate market entry and embeddedness decisions. The category therefore helps to clarify the broader context that surrounded the reform and to derive its relevance for the ensuing investment decisions. Most importantly, it illuminates important perspectives related to an emerging African interpretation of capitalism.

The findings expose the pre-reform stage as a time of concentrated theorising and debating of the possible approaches to and the potential outcomes of the proposed pro-market reform. The World Bank emerges as an influential actor, given its traditional project funding role in the country's energy sector. While it argued for a full competition model, the government preferred a 'phased' model to allow for gradual adaptation to the reform.

Uganda's experience exemplifies the diverse pressures that new emerging markets have to accommodate in embracing pro-market reform (Bigsten and Durevall 2003). These include considerable uncertainty about the political and socio-economic implications of the impending changes, which tempt governments to seek to retain a substantive level of control (especially over tariffs and end consumer prices).

Putting the pre-reform phase in Uganda in a broader political and institutional context, an academic and analyst in the sector commented:

> *Well, you can locate the changes that took place in the electricity industry right from the late 80s/early 90s. That was a period of huge reform, not only in the electricity industry. Generally in the way all utilities are run. The thinking was that government should get away from business to free resources for other pressing development needs.*[3]

The Ugandan government was hence under pressure to introduce reforms that would free it from paying subsidies to the corresponding sectors, thereby releasing resources for other urgent development needs. However, this was a hard decision for the government to make given the political value of the electricity sector and the natural need to want to retain control (Jamasb 2006; Keating 2009; Mawejje et al. 2012). But it ultimately succumbed to an emerging global trend reflected in pioneer reforms in Chile, the UK and New Zealand, for example (Bacon 1995; Bacon and Besant-Jones 2001).

Another respondent, who had been a manager at the state-owned monopoly (UEB) and later joined the unbundled distribution sector, commented:

> *In the first three years, Umeme (the predominant power distributor) had such goodwill because of the impact of deregulation in the telecom and banking sectors.*[4]

The reform in the electricity sector was therefore an ingredient of wider reforms in the country, not least in response to global ideological shifts and emerging neo-liberal thinking about a multi-polar world order. Positive experiences in the telecommunications and banking sectors raised hope of a replication in the electricity sector. The reforms were also a precondition for multilateral financial assistance, as the same respondent argued:

> *And these reforms were spearheaded by the World Bank. In fact the World Bank provided a lot of funding. I can say the reforms are the baby of the World Bank.*[5]

As further evidence of how much the World Bank was involved in laying the foundation for the reforms, below is quoted an exchange between the bank and the relevant government ministry shortly before reform (Ministry of Natural Resources 1997).

> *Senior World Bank Official: Our view is that the proposed government objectives of improving efficiency and the delivery of services in the power sector on a sustainable basis, and expanding access of the population to the electricity supply at reasonable prices, can be more effectively met through fostering competition rather than relying on regulation.*

Minister:

> *Fundamentally, we agree. However, although the MNR*[6] *is committed to the development of a competitive power market in Uganda in the long run, it is keenly aware that the need for improved efficiency and delivery of services in Uganda is an immediate one. Therefore, the MNR recognizes that it cannot institute a plan of immediate full competition. It is for this reason that the MNR has adopted what it terms as a phased approach and why it has maintained the flexibility to review progress at each stage of the implementation programme.*

The strong push by the bank also had the side effect of making it seem like it was in charge rather than the government. An image of inadequate regard for contingent realities in developing countries while administering borrowing conditionality led to some political resistance to the bank's proposals. But the proposals were ultimately accepted out of desperation and lack of funding alternatives (Pender 2001; Linaweaver 2003).

Political Market Embeddedness: The Broad Perspective

Following Sun et al. (2010), the research takes political market embeddedness to mean a '*firm's social embeddedness, with special reference to political actors and institutions*'. It accordingly manifests itself both at an interpersonal managerial level and at an inter-organisational level. The insights about political market embeddedness constitute the major thrust of the corporate political perspectives that inform the discussion. The most important issues that emerged in the research were ultimately captured under the following four main sub-categories, in order of importance:

1. stakeholder engagement
2. local embeddedness
3. social and political capital
4. understanding Africa

The key conclusions and insights under each of these sub-categories are summarised in Tables 4.3 and 4.4 below. Examples of supporting evidence are also given, representing the large volume of data that was gathered under each category.

Stakeholder engagement and social and political capital. Stakeholder engagement and social and political capital are integrated in the same row of the table (see Table 4.3 below) because they synergized in explaining the political rationale for approaching intra-African FDI.

For Pisu/Energy Global, the complementarity between the two partners was most evident in the stakeholder engagement and social and political capital factors. The capability to politically leverage the internationality of Energy Global and the localness of Pisu to produce an integrated multidimensional approach to the diversity of stakeholders stands out as a paramount feature of the project.

Frinam, on the other hand, began to expose a strong continental orientation. Benefitting from its mother country's newfound strength as a geopolitical and economic heavyweight in Africa, the EMNE deployed Uganda as its latest milestone in crafting a highly politically oriented, Pan-African multi-stakeholdership in the electricity sector. In doing this, it contributed to an emerging resonance for intra-African FDI and cross-border trade.

Table 4.3 Main insights about stakeholder engagement, social and political capital and local embeddedness

Findings perspective	MNE cases		
	Pisu/Energy Global[i,ii]	Frinam[iii,iv]	Avin[v,vi]
Key insights about stakeholder engagement and social/political capital	– Integration of global and local political capabilities and capital to satisfy stakeholders with evolving needs. – Development of advanced capabilities to deal with stakeholder diversity across African investment contexts.	– Leverage of continent-oriented social and political stakeholdership. – Development of new capabilities to respond to resistance from some stakeholders. – Contribution to an emerging acceptance of intra-African FDI and trade.	– Exploitation of historically embedded political stakeholder management capabilities. – Leverage of experience in Uganda for regional internationalisation.
Examples of supporting evidence	*One thing that made it rather complicated is that there were so many stakeholders. With central government it was and is much more straightforward.* [*I006*]	*So we formed what we called Electricity Generators and Distributors Association of Uganda (EGADAU). And it is through EGADAU that we intend to carry out most of the hard-nosed stakeholder interfaces and engagements.* [*I011*]	*The company employs over 7,500 people and has been responsible for the socio-economic development of this rural area. … The Avin rehabilitation is considered by the World Bank and the African Development Bank to be one of their most successful projects on the continent.* [*D026*]
Key insights about local embeddedness	– Adaptation of global political capabilities to the specific requirements of local embeddedness in Uganda.	– Adaptation of continent-oriented political connectedness to the specific requirements of local embeddedness in Uganda.	– Integration of historical embeddedness with new capabilities for an evolving local and regional market.

Examples of supporting evidence	*Information to the communities has been disclosed in a culturally appropriate manner: conduct of meetings/presentations in the local language; preparation and distribution of a project newsletter in the local language; use of local language radio stations to advertise meetings; engagement of local community leaders to assist in the meetings.* [*D005, p. 279*]	*We feel in every part of the community where we work we want to make a meaningful impact and we are in a community where we are making a product that maybe only 15 % of your local community are consuming. Then you have to find a way to cover the other 85 %, through some type of benefit and showing good neighbourliness.* [*I010*]	*Politically, we get that support. We wrote to the president through the local government in Jinja. We have full support.* [*I017,I018*]

Table 4.4 Main insights about understanding Africa

Findings perspective	MNE cases Pisu/Energy Global[viii,ix]	Frinam[x,xi]	Avin[xii,xiii]
Key insights about understanding Africa	– Leverage of Pisu's political understanding of Africa to support the project. – Strategic positioning for new intra-African cross-border investments. – Evolution into a benchmark company for international regulatory agencies about the social and environmental impact dimensions of large investments.	– Leverage of a politically high-profile understanding of Africa. – Strategic positioning for larger continental projects. – Substantial experiences from other African markets. – Emerging institutional shaper role as a first-mover.	– Leverage of historical understanding of Africa at diverse levels. – A long-term perspective in identifying and exploiting strategic investment opportunities. – Pioneer proposal to the Ugandan government to reform the electricity sector.
Examples of supporting evidence	*During the construction phase, the environmental and social team was bigger than the engineering team. … And also we predominantly had Ugandans because you have very many experienced Ugandans in the environmental and social fields. … They understand the local people, the thinking, the culture.* [*I005*]	*Under 'Africa Strategy' Frinam has recognised that they are best suited to electrify Africa because when this Africa Strategy was put together about 60 % of electricity generated in Africa was being generated by Frinam.* [*I010*]	*But we were also approached by the South Sudan government ... So they wanted us to come and re-establish that (sugar) plant. ... But in the process, that is when the war broke out again.* [*I017, I018*]

Avin, finally, embodied the experiences of a historically embedded EMNE and its ability to capture competitive advantage. The capability to leverage its long-standing social and political capital to overcome the resistance to electricity cogeneration in the early years of the reform underlines its strengths in popularizing new areas of investment.

Local embeddedness. Local embeddedness also emerged as a critical factor for all cases (see Table 4.3 above) in engaging with intra-African FDI. In this research, 'local embeddedness' refers to the degree to which a project engages with or is immersed in the hosting community and its political institutions.

In developing a highly localized strategy that culminated in strong co-ownership of the project by the hosting community and the financing of development projects that were proposed by the community, the Pisu/Energy Global project effectively reflected the potential of MNEs to drive change and alleviate poverty at the base of the pyramid. The extent to which the project went on to actively embed individual managers in the hosting communities further illustrates the scale and scope of possibilities for MNE investments to have far-reaching local impact. Such managers can consequently become a crucial link in a growing portfolio of intra-African FDI by sharing their knowledge and supporting ensuing projects. As an example, the project's managers ultimately played a critical role in securing a new project on the Ruzizi River in Central-Southern Africa. More broadly, this points to the need for human resource management strategies that are conducive to intra-African FDI growth by encouraging and rewarding cross-border collaboration and projects.

Conversely, Frinam's stance in approaching local embeddedness seemed to be more nationally oriented rather than oriented towards the local community. Its deployment of managerial influence and the dependency on government hence reflected this national orientation. Finally, Avin embodied the possibilities and challenges of historic embeddedness in a host market. Most importantly, Avin's approach illustrates how the intra-African investment context constitutes an evolving reality and how MNEs can constructively engage with and even shape this evolution.

Understanding Africa. The understanding MNEs have of Africa as a region emerged as one of the major determinants of successful political strategies in favour of intra-African FDI (see Table 4.4 below). Consequently, the joint venture case depended substantially on Pisu's political resourcefulness in the region to support the project. This was reflected, for example, in the appointment of a manager with extensive African experience to lead Pisu's team in the project and to act as the overall project manager. Similarly, the recruitment of a former senior manager at Frinam to become the general manager of the joint project introduced more depth and diversity into the portfolio of capabilities possessed by the firm. At the same time, Frinam also exploited its political connectedness with various African governments as well as its linkages to strategically important pan-African initiatives like NEPAD.[vii] Further, it nurtured special capabilities based on an explicit 'Africa Strategy' to drive intra-African FDI. Finally, Avin represents the experiences of a historically embedded EMNE to cumulatively grow intra-African FDI and diversify its reach. The firm ultimately used Uganda as a base to penetrate neighbouring markets, some of which were substantially hostile to other forms of FDI.

Political Market Embeddedness: The Policy-Making and Regulatory Institutional Perspectives

This category summarises the most important issues that emerged from an institutional perspective surrounding growing intra-African FDI. It deepens the understanding of the political ramifications of embedding an investment in the host market using the institutionally oriented lens.

Discussion

The discussion of the findings can be grouped under two major conceptual aspects: an emerging institutional perspective and new state capitalism. These categories appear to capture some of the most important issues through which CPA is manifesting itself and influencing FDI patterns in Africa.

The Emerging Institutional Perspective

This perspective is examined from the first two of the three institutional dimensions—regulatory, normative and cognitive-cultural—that have been seminally conceptualised in the extant literature (Dimaggio and Powell 1983; Scott 1987, 1995).

The Regulatory Institutional Perspective

The regulatory institutional perspective acknowledges that several African countries are undergoing pro-market institutional reform in an effort to embrace the free market paradigm that has become globally predominant since the end of the Cold War. Uganda has emerged as one of the pioneers of these reforms in Africa (Karekezi and Kimani 2002; Robinson 2007; Keating 2009; Mawejje et al. 2012; World Bank 2012). In introducing pro-market reform to its electricity industry, Uganda simultaneously opened up to the political strategies of firms as they sought to exploit new investment opportunities. The porosity of boundaries between the fragile emerging institutions and the firms they attempted to regulate was fertile ground for antecedent forms of CPA that ultimately informed more sophisticated variants (Weidenbaum 1980; Grant 1998, 2003; Hillman et al. 2004; Lawton et al. 2013).

The Frinam case is one of the richest illustrations of how a highly politically connected firm can develop and implement a strategy to exploit first-mover advantages (Rahman and Bhattacharyya 2003; Frynas et al. 2006; Magnusson et al. 2012) in the course of institutional reform, positioning itself as the benchmark and the official partner for government (Tables 4.1, 4.3 and 4.4). Firms with a clear perception of their strategic objectives in entering these reforming markets and ability to leverage political networks at a continental level seem to reap important benefits from their investments. Frinam has hence not only consolidated its position as the market leader in its home country, but it has systematically built a leading position on the continent by winning concessions for operation and maintenance of power systems in several countries (Mcdonald 2009). The firm has effectively emerged as a continental activist able to strategically combine business and institutional entrepreneurship by using political strategies (Weik 2011; Dieleman and Sachs 2008; Ndikumana and Nannyonjo 2007; Greenwood and Suddaby 2006). Firms that partner with governments at the sensitive early stages of pro-market reform also serve to fill institutional voids as interpreted a situation identified in extant literature (Khanna et al. 2005; Crittenden and Crittenden 2010). In doing this, they are also helping to set the agenda for African governments in addressing these voids and supporting the emerging home-grown MNEs to nurture their competitive advantage (Stal and Cuervo-Cazurra 2011; Khoury and Prasad 2012; Luiz and Ruplal 2013; Zhao et al. 2013).

The Avin case, in contrast, represents a firm with deep historical roots in a particular region of the continent. The firm's experience surpassed the limitations that Frinam had to accommodate by virtue of its home country's history during the years of international diplomatic and economic isolation. Avin hence was able to draw on historically rooted political capabilities in dealing with fragile institutional and political contexts. In this research, the case is described as a historical entrepreneur. Such historical entrepreneurs have shaped the investment patterns on the continent at diverse levels and created the bridge from colonial to post-colonial experiences. The political capabilities they have nurtured are hence closely associated with the emergence of the continent from the shackles of foreign domination into the often violent and uncertain struggles of carving out an independent space (Shaw and Nyang'oro 2000; Wallis 2014). In Avin's case, it recognised the potential of Uganda's electricity industry long before its peers and eventually emerged as the local partner in the first Bujagali project in a joint venture with the US-based AES Corporation (Linaweaver 2003; Maestad 2003; Luwa 2007). It did this by working closely with government to lay the foundation for the reforms that were eventually introduced (see Tables 4.1, 4.3 and 4.4). While it eventually lost out when the first Bujagali project was terminated following AES's decision to exit the African market after the Enron scandal, its pioneering work would richly inform the successor project.

The political and strategic capability of such historically embedded firms is illustrated by the fact that Avin was eventually able to develop the niche electricity cogeneration sector based on biomass and to emerge as a benchmark firm in later years. By starting feasibility studies for the project during its partnership with AES, the firm demonstrated a high level of strategic political anticipation. In spite of weak political and institutional support for the cogeneration sector in the early years, this historical entrepreneur persisted until the Ugandan government eventually saw the need to diversify the electricity supply mix of the country through projects like Avin's. In a sense, Avin was serving as a business incubator (Meru and Struwig 2011, 2015) for a future national and regional market segment.

The Normative Institutional Perspective

In the wake of pro-market reforms, there also emerges a need for norms in the various industries involved. The process of shaping these norms and winning an intra-industry stakeholdership around them is imbued with major corporate political ingredients. In this study, Frinam displayed the most prominent behaviour in this regard. While it was predominantly engaged with shaping the regulatory institutional framework in the early years, changes in the power balance between the legislative and the executive arms of Uganda's government in later years forced it to adjust its focus. This had to do with the fact that its market entry under the direct championship of the executive arm of government and its ensuing privileged status in the reformed sector was challenged by a more assertive parliament in later years. One of the ways through which Frinam sought to counteract this more hostile institutional environment, however subtly, was to invest in the accumulation of political resources and their development into political capabilities (Dahan 2005) for organising the industry players into an umbrella association. This then translated into an opportunity to shape consensus positions and win stakeholdership for favourable norms.

In effect, while Frinam was still predominantly proactively oriented in its political disposition (Hillman et al. 2004) for safeguarding its investment, political environmental and institutional changes culminated in a need for an adaptive element in its political behaviour. This behaviour illustrates how MNEs within Africa are learning to adapt to evolving political and institutional contexts by developing heterogeneous CPA strategies and the associated political capabilities. Such adaptability is projected to be an important driver of cross-border investments within the continent. However, Frinam's experience also demonstrates the risks associated with using discriminative strategies towards arms of governments (Henisz and Zelner 2010), indicating the need for stronger risk mitigation measures.

Avin, on the other hand, shaped norms by emerging as the benchmark firm in a new market segment that was previously not prioritised by government. Its historical embeddedness in the market equipped it with the capabilities for overcoming government resistance in the first years while developing experience with the niche segment. The anticipatory strategy (Oliver and Holzinger 2008) ultimately put it in a strong position to become the undisputed market leader when government finally lifted its opposition. It then emerged not only as a regulatory benchmark, but also as a normative one (Scott 1995, 2001). The strength of the anticipatory strategy was eventually reflected in both the growth of this segment within Uganda and also in the opportunities to penetrate neighbouring regional markets. Firms like Avin that have a deep historical understanding of the continent and the capability for strategic anticipation far beyond their time are positioned to shape emerging intra-African FDI in unprecedented ways. While they can choose to enter into strategic partnerships with advanced market MNEs, just like Avin had previously done with AES for the first Bujagali project and Pisu did in the ensuing project, they are strategically placed to identify investment areas where they can leverage their home-grown strengths to retain their ability to operate independently.

In both institutional perspectives discussed above, Pisu emerges as a historically embedded case that nurtured political capabilities that synthesised local strengths with an international orientation. It was hence able to enter into a high-profile joint venture with an advanced market firm and make itself attractive for other cross-border projects in the region. In this study, such a firm is seen as a global realist reflecting EMNEs with substantial scope for engaging internationally.

The Emerging African Version of Capitalism

Beyond the institutionally oriented issues raised above, there is a deeper-reaching picture emerging all over Africa that has implications for patterns of investment. This is the interpretation of capitalism as expressed in how the free market economy takes shape (Jackson and Deeg 2008). While market capitalism became the accepted economic *modus operandi* all over the world, including in Africa, following the end of the Cold War, there is evidence that African countries are still immersed in examining what works best for them. Uganda exemplifies the stand-off between governments convinced that they still need a substantive level of involvement in the economy and development partners like the World Bank who would rather see a complete government withdrawal, leaving things to 'free' market forces. Hence, in debating the model that it needed to embrace for its electricity industry reform, Uganda visualised a phased departure from the sector while the World Bank pressed for an immediate full relinquishment. The reservations of the Ugandan government were rooted in deep-seated concerns about the potential political backlash of suddenly removing subsidies to such an important sector of the economy, especially since most citizens saw electricity as a public good (Karekezi and Kimani 2002; Engurait 2005; Mawejje et al. 2012).

In the end, what has emerged is a hybrid model that sees substantive government withdrawal, but also a substantive capability for government to interfere, especially regarding the setting of tariffs. It has also become evident that firms that have recognised the dilemma of African governments in deciding on the right paths within a free market setting are well positioned to present themselves as strategic partners to shape the market. Firms like Frinam that are politically highly disposed and have ambitious pan-African market penetration objectives have emerged as attractive partners in a symbiotic relationship with African governments. It is therefore instructive to note that the unbundling of the former state-owned utility in Uganda was followed by the entry of an otherwise state-owned utility (Frinam) in its home market. This seemed to provide some satisfaction to the Ugandan government that it was not completely handing over a strategic asset to an actor over which it had no control at all. The picture gets replicated over and over again on the continent as governments succumb, on the one hand, to pro-market reforms, but are keen, on the other hand, to identify market entrants with favourable corporate political features. African capitalism is thereby attaining contours that reflect the emergence of a new state capitalism, suggesting an emerging pragmatism about the path of development and the role of the state in these fast-growing emerging markets (Bremmer 2009; Goodstein and

Velamuri 2009; Nölke and Vliegenthart 2009; Li et al. 2014). The emergence of this home-grown version of market capitalism is identified as one of the most important shapers of future intra-African FDI and trade.

Conclusions

In conclusion, this chapter provides an exploratory illumination of how CPA and the associated political capabilities are taking shape in Uganda and, by implication, the rest of Africa. In the context of the pro-market reforms and the broader political changes on the continent, there is some indication of how investment patterns on the continent are being shaped by firms that are ever more politically aware and active. The emerging heterogeneous political capabilities suggest a growing consciousness by firms to better align their classical market strategies with non-market strategies. There is also an indication that a mastery of political capabilities by home-grown EMNEs could position these firms to capture a bigger share of Africa's growing market. Finally, there is a prospect for these firms to play an important role in shaping the African market as one of the last frontiers of large-scale FDI activity.

Appendix

[i] I002, I005, I006, I007, I012, I019, I025, I036, I037, D005, D018–24.

[ii] I005, I006, I007, I019, I025, I029, D005, D009, D010.

[iii] I002, I010, I011, I012, I013, I014, D002, D003, D040.

[iv] I002, I005, I010, I011, I013, I014, D011, D037, D040.

[v] I017, I018, I023, I032, D030, D031, D041.

[vi] I017, I018, I022, I032, I041, D025, D026, D035, D038, D039.

[vii] The New Economic Partnership for African Development (NEPAD) is one of the African Union's core projects: http://www.nepad.org/

[viii] I005, I006, I007, D005, D018–24, D0047, D048, D049.

[ix] I002, I005, I006, I007, I012, I019, I025, D002, D003, D005, D010, D18–24, Bujagali and joint venture partner project websites (accessed several times).

[x]I002, I010, I011, I012, I013, I014, I037, I038, D002, D003, D011, D048.

[xi]I001, I005, I010, I011, I013, I014, I020, I033, I034, I040, D002, D003, D004, D008, D011, D017, Frinam website (accessed several times).

[xii]I017, I018, I022, I023, I032, I041, D013–15, D025, D026.

[xiii]I002, I012, I022, I032, I041, D002, D003, D008, D013–15, D025, D026, Avin website (accessed several times).

Notes

1. This definition, however, is increasingly depicting limitations as a small but growing stream of research, particularly on emerging markets, contends that a proactive search for 'influence' is not always the best approach to CPA strategy
2. D008 (coding for document 8 in the data)
3. I001, I002, I005, I012 (coding for transcripts 1, 2, 5 and 12 in the data)
4. I001,I002, I005, I012,
5. I001, I005, I006, I019, I024, D002, D005,D008
6. Ministry of Natural Resources (responsibility has since been assumed by the Ministry of Energy and Mineral Development)

References

Adeleye, I., Ibeh, K., Kinoti, A., & White, L. (2015). *The changing dynamics of international business in Africa, AIB Sub-Saharan Africa (SSA) Series* (Vol. 1). London: Palgrave Macmillan.

Bacon, R., & Besant-Jones, J. (2001). Global electric power reform, privatization, and liberalization of the electric power industry in developing countries 1. *Annual Review of Energy and the Environment, 26*(1), 331–359.

Bacon, R. W. (1995). Privatization and reform in the global electricity supply industry. *Annual Review of Energy and the Environment, 20*(1), 119–143.

Baines, P. R., & Viney, H. (2010). The unloved relationship? Dynamic capabilities and political-market strategy: A research agenda. *Journal of Public Affairs, 10*(4), 258–264.

Barney, J. (1991). Firm resources and sustained competitive advantage. *Journal of Management, 17*(1), 99.

Bartels, F. L., Alladina, S. N., & Lederer, S. (2009). Foreign direct investment in Sub-Saharan Africa: Motivating factors and policy issues. *Journal of African Business, 10*(2), 141–162.

Baysinger, B. D. (1984). Domain maintenance as an objective of business political activity: An expanded typology. *Academy of Management Review, 9*(2), 248–258.

Bigsten, A., & Durevall, D. (2003). Globalisation and policy effects in Africa. *World Economy, 26*(8), 1119.

Bonardi, J. P. (2011). Corporate political resources and the resource-based view of the firm. *Strategic Organization, 9*(3), 247–255.

Bonardi, J.-P., & Keim, G. D. (2005). Corporate political strategies for widely salient issues. *The Academy of Management Review, 3*, 555–576.

Bremmer, I. (2009). State capitalism comes of age: The recent wave of state intervention in emerging-market countries, a reaction to the current global recession, signals that the free-market tide has receded. *Foreign Affairs-New York, 88*(3), 40–55.

Businge, J. (2014) Universal access to electricity [Online]. *Kampala*. Retrieved August 25, 2014, from http://www.independent.co.ug/news/news/9195-universal-access-to-energy-will-spur-economic-growth-wwf-

Crittenden, V. L., & Crittenden, W. F. (2010). Strategic management in emergingeconomies: A research agenda. *Organizations & Markets in Emerging Economies, 1*(1), 9–23.

Crotty, M. (1998). *Introduction: The research process, The foundations of social research: Meaning and perspective in the research process*. London: Sage Publications.

Cuervo-Cazurra, A. (2006). Who cares about corruption? *Journal of International Business Studies, 37*(6), 807–822.

Cuervo-Cazurra, A. (2008). The multinationalization of developing country mnes: The case of multilatinas. *Journal of International Management, 14*(2), 138–154.

Dahan, N. (2005). *Can there be a resource-based view of politics?*. International Studies of Management & Organization, *35*(2), 8–27.

Daniel, J., Naidoo, V., & Naidu, S. (2003). *The South Africans have arrived: Post-apartheid corporate expansion into Africa*. State of the nation: South Africa, 2004, 368–390.

Dieleman, M., & Sachs, W. M. (2008). Coevolution of institutions and corporations in emerging economies: How the salim group morphed into an institution of suharto's crony regime. *Journal of Management Studies, 45*(7), 1274–1300.

Dimaggio, P. J., & Powell, W. W. (1983). The iron cage revisited: Institutional isomorphism and collective rationality in organizational fields. *American Sociological Review, 48*(2), 147–160.
Doh, J. P., Lawton, T. C., & Rajwani, T. (2012). Advancing nonmarket strategy research: Institutional perspectives in a changing world. *Academy of Management Perspectives, 26*(3), 22–39.
Dyer, W. G., & Wilkins, A. L. (1991). Better stories, not better constructs, to generate better theory: A rejoinder to eisenhardt. *Academy of Management Review, 16*(3), 613–619.
Easterby-Smith, M., Thorpe, R., & Jackson, P. R. (2008). *Management research*. London: Sage.
Eisenhardt, K. M. (1989). Building theories from case study research. *Academy of Management Review, 14*(4), 532–550.
Engurait, S. P. (2005). Power sector reforms in Uganda: Status and achievements. *International Journal of Global Energy Issues, 23*(2), 110–118.
Frynas, J. G., Mellahi, K., & Pigman, G. A. (2006). First mover advantages in international business and firm-specific political resources. *Strategic Management Journal, 4*, 321.
Goodstein, J. D., & Velamuri, S. R. (2009). States, power, legitimacy, and maintaining institutional control: The battle for private sector telecommunication services in Zimbabwe. *Organization Studies, 30*(5), 489–508.
Grant, R. (1998). *Contemporary strategy analysis*. Oxford, UK: Blackwell Publishers Ltd.
Grant, R. M. (2003). Strategic planning in a turbulent environment: Evidence from the oil majors. *Strategic Management Journal, 24*(6), 491.
Greenwood, R., & Suddaby, R. (2006). Institutional entrepreneurship in mature fields: The big five accounting firms. *Academy of Management Journal, 49*(1), 27–48.
Haanyika, C. M. (2006). Rural electrification policy and institutional linkages. *Energy Policy, 34*(17), 2977–2993.
Hammersley, M., & Atkinson, P. (2007). *Ethnography: Principles in practice* (3rd ed.). New York: Routledge.
Helfat, C. E., & Peteraf, M. A. (2003). The dynamic resource-based view: Capability lifecycles. *Strategic Management Journal, 24*(10), 997–1010.
Henisz, W. J., & Zelner, B. A. (2010). The hidden risks in emerging markets. *Harvard Business Review, 88*(4), 88–95.
Hill, C. W., Hwang, P., & Kim, W. C. (1990). An eclectic theory of the choice of international entry mode. *Strategic Management Journal, 11*(2), 117–128.

Hillman, A. J., & Hitt, M. A. (1999). Corporate political strategy formulation: A model of approach, participation, and strategy decisions. *The Academy of Management Review, 4*, 825.
Hillman, A. J., Keim, G. D., & Schuler, D. (2004). Corporate political activity: A review and research agenda. *Journal of Management, 30*(6), 837–857.
Hoskisson, R. E., Eden, L., Lau, C. M., & Wright, M. (2000). Strategy in emerging economies. *Academy of Management Journal, 43*(3), 249–267.
Jackson, D., & Deeg, R. (2008). From comparing capitalisms to the politics of institutional change. *Review of International Political Economy, 15*(4), 680–709.
Jamasb, T. (2006). Between the state and market: Electricity sector reform in developing countries. *Utilities Policy, 14*(1), 14–30.
Karekezi, S., & Kimani, J. (2002). Status of power sector reform in Africa: Impact on the poor. *Energy Policy, 30*(11–12), 923–945.
Keating, M. F. (2009). *Global best practice (s) and electricity sector reform in Uganda*. Coventry: University of Warwick: Centre for the Study of Globalisation and Regionalisation (CSGR).
Khanna, T., Palepu, K. G. & Sinha, J. (2005). Strategies that fit emerging markets. *Harvard Business Review, 83*(6), 4–19.
Khoury, T. A., & Prasad, A. (2012). How do developing country entrepreneurs navigate extreme institutional voids?, *Academy of Management Annual Meeting Proceedings*, 1–1.
Lawton, T., Doh, J. P., & Rajwani, T. (2014). *Aligning for advantage—Competitive strategies for the political and social arenas*. Oxford: Oxford University Press.
Lawton, T., Rajwani, T., & Doh, J. (2013). The antecedents of political capabilities: A study of ownership, cross-border activity and organization at legacy airlines in a deregulatory context. *International Business Review, 22*, 228–242.
Li, M. H., Cui, L., & Lu, J. (2014). Varieties in state capitalism: Outward fdi strategies of central and local state-owned enterprises from emerging economy countries. *Journal of International Business Studies, 45*(8), 980–1004.
Linaweaver, S. (2003). Catching the boomerang: Em, the world bank, and excess accountability: A case study of the bujagali falls hydropower project uganda. *The International Journal of Sustainable Development & World Ecology, 10*(4), 283–301.
Luiz, J. M., & Ruplal, M. (2013). Foreign direct investment, institutional voids, and the internationalization of mining companies into Africa. *Emerging Markets Finance and Trade, 49*(4), 113–129.
Luo, Y. (2004). A coopetition perspective of MNC–Host government relations. *Journal of International Management, 10*(4), 431–451.

Luwa, K. J. (2007). *Power and development: Controversies over the bujagali hydropower porject along the nile river in uganda*. Karlstad University.
Maestad, O. (2003). *The electricity sector in Uganda—Results of development assistance*. Bergen, Norway: Institute for Research in Economics and Business Administration (SNF).
Magnusson, P., Westjohn, S. A., Gordon, G. L., & Aurand, T. W. (2012). Environmental dynamics and first-mover advantages in emerging markets. *Marketing Management Journal, 22*(1), 17–34.
Mawejje, J., Munyambonera, E., & Bategeka, L. (2012). Uganda Electricity Sector Reforms and Institutional Restructuring. *Economic Policy Research Centre Research Series*, 89.
Mcdonald, D. (Ed.) (2009). *Electric capitalism: Recolonising Africa on the power grid*. Cape Town: HSRC Press.
Meru, A. K., & Struwig, M. (2011). An evaluation of the entrepreneurs' perception of business-incubation services in Kenya. *International Journal of Business Administration, 2*(4), 112.
Meru, A. K., & Struwig, M. (2015). Business-incubation process and business development in Kenya: Challenges and recommendations. *Journal of Entrepreneurship and Innovation in Emerging Economies, 1*(1), 1–17.
Miles, M. B., & Huberman, A. M. (1994). *Qualitative data analysis: An expanded sourcebook*. Thousand Oaks, CA: Sage Publications.
Ministry of Natural Resources (1997). *Strategic plan for the Uganda power sector*. Kampala, Uganda: Government of tue Republic of Uganda.
Ndikumana, L., & Nannyonjo, J. (2007). From failed state to good performer? The case of Uganda. In J. K. Boyce & M. O'donnell (Eds.), *Peace and the public purse: Economic policies for postwar statebuilding, Center on International Cooperation Studies in Multilateralism* (pp. 15–54). Lynne Rienner: London.
Nölke, A., & Vliegenthart, A. (2009). Enlarging the varieties of capitalism: The emergence of dependent market economies in east central europe. *World Politics, 61*(04), 670–702.
Oliver, C., & Holzinger, I. (2008). The effectiveness of strategic political management: A dynamic capabilities framework. *Academy of Management Review, 33*(2), 496–520.
Pender, J. (2001). From 'structural adjustment' to 'comprehensive development framework': Conditionality transformed? *Third World Quarterly, 22*(3), 397–411.

Peng, M. W., Wang, D. Y. L., & Yi, J. (2008). An institution-based view of international business strategy: A focus on emerging economies. *Journal of International Business Studies, 39*(5), 920–936.
Prahalad, C. K., & Hamel, G. (1990). The core competence of the corporation. *Harvard Business Review, 3*, 75–91.
Rahman, Z., & Bhattacharyya, S. (2003). Sources of first mover advantages in emerging markets–An indian perspective. *European Business Review, 15*(6), 359–369.
Raman, A. P. (2009). The new frontiers. *Harvard Business Review, 87*(7/8), 130–137.
Robinson, M. (2007). The political economy of governance reforms in Uganda. *Commonwealth & Comparative Politics, 45*(4), 452–474.
Scott, R. W. (2001). *Institutions and organizations*. Thousand Oaks, CA: Sage Publications.
Scott, W. R. (1987). The adolescence of institutional theory. *Administrative Science Quarterly, 32*(4), 493–511.
Scott, W. R. (1995). *Organizations and institutions*. Thousand Oaks, CA: Sage.
Shaw, T. M., & Nyang'oro, J. E. (2000). African renaissance in the new millennium? From anarchy to emerging markets? *African Journal of Political Science/Revue Africaine de Science Politique, 5*(1), 14–28.
Stal, E., & Cuervo-Cazurra, A. (2011). The investment development path and fdi from developing countries: The role of pro-market reforms and institutional voids. *Latin American Business Review, 12*(3), 209–231.
Sun, P., Mellahi, K., & Thun, E. (2010). The dynamic value of mne political embeddedness: The case of the chinese automobile industry. *Journal of International Business Studies, 41*(7), 1161–1182.
Tumwesigye, R., Twebaze, P., Makuregye, N., & Muyambi, E. (2012). *Key issues in Uganda's energy secor*. London: Pro-Biodiversity Conservationists in Uganda (PROBICOU)/International Institute for Environment and Development.
Unctad. (2011). *World investment report 2011. Non-equity modes of international production and development*. New York, USA: United Nations Publications.
Unctad. (2014). *World investment report 2014. Investing in the sdgs: An action plan*. New York, USA: United Nations Publications.
Wallis, W. (2014). *Failure of political systems is biggest threat to African renaissance. Financial Times*, October 05, 2014.
Webb, J. W., Kistruck, G. M., Ireland, R. D., & Ketchen, J. D. J. (2010). The entrepreneurship process in base of the pyramid markets: The case of multinational enterprise/nongovernment organization alliances. *Entrepreneurship: Theory & Practice, 34*(3), 555–581.

Weidenbaum, M. L. (1980). Public policy: No longer a spectator sport for business. *Journal of Business Strategy, 1*(1), 46.
Weik, E. (2011). Institutional entrepreneurship and agency. *Journal for the Theory of Social Behaviour, 41*(4), 466–481.
World Bank. (2012). Uganda: Country brief [Online]. Washington, DC. Retrieved November 16, 2012, from http://www.worldbank.org/en/country/uganda
World Bank. (2014). *Access to electricity* [Online]. Washington, DC. World Bank. Retrieved August 25, 2014, from http://data.worldbank.org/indicator/EG.ELC.ACCS.ZS/countries/UG-ZF-XM?display=graph
Yin, R. (2003). *Case study research: Design and methods*. Thousand Oaks, CA: Sage Publications.
Zhao, M., Tan, J., & Park, S. H. (2013). From voids to sophistication: Institutional environment and MNC CSR crisis in emerging markets. *Journal of Business Ethics, 122*(4), 655–674.

5

Inward Internationalisation of Hotel Services: Evidence from Ghana

Emmanuel Kofi Adjei

Introduction

It is important for companies to understand consumer adoption behaviour, as their investment decisions in technology infrastructure should be driven by consumer acceptance and long-term profitability. The internet offers new opportunities to industries as an alternative marketing tool. According to Rahman (2003), Walsh and Godfrey (2000), Hoffman and Novak (1997) and Peterson et al. (1997), the internet offers opportunities for marketers along with new ways of conducting marketing and approaching consumer markets. Internet marketing makes it easier for customers to make reservations or book rooms of their choice without physically visiting a hotel. While several studies have examined the

E.K. Adjei (✉)
Department of Marketing and Corporate Strategy, Kwame Nkrumah University of Science and Technology, Kumasi, Ashanti, Ghana
e-mail: eadjei.reg@knust.edu.gh

I. Adeleye et al. (eds.), *Africa-to-Africa Internationalization*, AIB Sub-Saharan Africa (SSA) Series, DOI 10.1007/978-3-319-30692-6_5

internationalisation processes of service firms (Freeman and Sandwell 2008; Strom and Mattson 2006), this work seeks to bring to the fore customers' perceptions of inward internationalisation through internet marketing.

Internet marketing provides many advantages to businesses. According to Gregory and Breiter (2001), the establishment of an effective company website puts the company in a competitive position in the global environment. The internet enables the company to build closer relationships with customers (Buhalis and Licasta 2002; Wang et al. 2002). Customers play a key role in every business, and therefore seeking their satisfaction is paramount. Disappointed customers are inclined to switch brands or suppliers and generate adverse publicity that may drive away prospects. The research presented here therefore sought to find out the perceptions of customers regarding inward internationalisation of hotels in Ghana through internet marketing. The findings of this research are important for decision-making in the services sector, for academia and for all stakeholders in the areas of international business and marketing.

The main objective of the study was to examine the perceptions of customers regarding inward internationalisation through internet marketing in Ghana. In seeking to achieve this objective, I focused on three main specific objectives. Firstly, I focused on customers' preferences regarding hotels that have internationalised through internet marketing in Ghana. I learned from customers their preferred online services regarding inwardly internationalised hotels and their preferred medium for booking hotels. Secondly, I focused on the views and expectations of customers regarding hotel websites, including their views on product/service customisation, price customisation, their preferred mode of payment, and how useful they find internet marketing. Lastly, I focused on the challenges faced by customers in dealing with hotels that have inwardly internationalised through internet marketing in Ghana, including online challenges and concerns about using internet marketing.

Internationalisation through internet marketing has become a relatively easy option for positioning business(es) in the global marketplace. It offers new opportunities to firms in terms of winning more customers globally and gaining a competitive advantage. According to Andrews et al. (2007), the increased importance of internet channels can be seen in their contribution to disseminating information, enhancing consumer value, and improving consumer satisfaction, loyalty, retention and overall consumer perceptions, which in turn leads to better profitability and expanded market share. These benefits are especially important to the Ghanaian economy, as the Ghana Tourist Authority has revealed that tourism is now the third-largest foreign exchange earner for the country (Ghana Tourist Authority 2013). Kumasi is a major tourism city in Ghana, with the second-highest number of hotels in the country. Kumasi has a fair representation of all forms of the cultures in and around Ghana. Of the large number of studies on internationalisation and internet marketing, relatively few address developing countries like Ghana. There seems to be limited research in the area of inward internationalisation and internet marketing from the perspective of customers in Ghana. This chapter, therefore, seeks to elucidate customers' perceptions on inward internationalisation of hotel services in Ghana through internet marketing. Findings from this research are vital to the hospitality industry, academia, researchers and hotel customers.

Literature Review

Customers and Internet Marketing

The internet as a marketing tool provides significant opportunities for companies to seek and adopt innovative practices in order to address the increasing demands of customers (Sharma and Aragón-Correa 2005). Competitive advantage is widely seen as the cornerstone of business strategy (Bharadwaj et al. 1993; Greenwald and Kahn 2005; Porter 1980, 1985); hence businesses seek to internationalise, gain more customers and stay competitive. Customer value is usually operationalised as a trade-off between quality (benefit) and cost (price) (Bolton and Drew 1991). During the 1950s, the notion that profitability hinges on satisfying customers took root and gave rise to the managerial school of marketing, which prevails to this day (Harker and Egan 2006).

Customer Satisfaction

Boulding et al. (1993) studied customers' overall satisfaction. Their findings suggest that overall satisfaction is an aggregation of all previous transaction-specific evaluations and is updated after each specific transaction, much like assessments of overall service quality are updated after each transaction. Transaction-specific satisfaction is conceptualised as a customer's evaluation of his or her experience with, and reactions to, a particular product transaction episode or service encounter. It is captures the complex psychological reactions that customers have to a product or service provider's performance for a given time period (Oliver 1997). Cumulative satisfaction is defined as a customer's overall evaluation of a product or service provider to date (Johnson et al. 1995; Johnson and Fornell 1991).

Satisfying customers is important. Disappointed customers are inclined to switch brands or suppliers and generate adverse publicity that may drive prospects away. Delighted customers, in contrast, often become loyal, trusting patrons who eagerly tell others about pleasing products and shopping experiences (Jones and Sasser 1995).

Customer Perception and Retention

Profitability and long-term success in e-retailing depend on customers' perceptions of the shopping experience and e-tailers' follow-up actions. Because of the spatial and temporal separation between buyers and sellers in online markets, exchanges of money and goods are not simultaneous, and customers may not fully trust e-tailers' online offerings and related purchasing processes. For instance, the risk that an item might never be delivered is of particular concern to customers (Smith et al. 2000). Instant comparisons on the web, made possible by powerful search engines, make non-price competitive advantages ever more critical in retaining and attracting customers (Jarvenpaa and Todd 1997; Liu and Arnett 2000). Research has shown that increases in customer retention could result in increased profitability for firms that compete in mature and highly competitive markets, especially service industries such as banking, telecommunications, hospitality and transportation (e.g. Fornell and Wernerfelt 1987; Reichheld and Sasser 1990).

Inward Internationalisation

The inward internationalisation process of service firms involves the movement of foreign consumers to the domestic market where the firm is located. Bjorkman and Kork (1997) define inward internationalisation in a service context as activities related to foreign consumers who come to the firm's premises in the country where the service firm is located. This definition usually applies to consumer services that are location-bound and need to attract foreign consumers to their domestic market in order to provide their service. Such consumer services include tourism, education, transport, health and entertainment. Although some of these companies may decide to open a foreign office or provide the service in a foreign market in the future, the initial stages of the internationalisation process are predominantly focused on servicing foreign consumers in the domestic market (Roberts 1999).

Inward internationalisation requires consumer mobility to a country that is usually unknown to the consumer, instead of firm or service provider mobility to the consumer's market. This implies that the foreign consumer has to travel to a new and uncertain environment and deal with many new elements of the domestic market in addition to consuming the service. Because consumer services involve high levels of contact between service providers from the domestic market and foreign consumers, there is somewhat high probability that problems will arise due to cultural differences and communication errors during the service encounter. In addition, other consumers may also affect a foreign consumer's overall satisfaction with the service encounter due to differences in language and consumption behaviours. In sum, several elements of the domestic environment, as well as the service provider itself and other consumers, may affect the foreign consumer's overall satisfaction with the service.

It is argued that if an inwardly internationalising service firm possesses a number of specific internal resources and/or capabilities to a greater extent, the competitive advantage will be enhanced and internationalisation principles of contingency theory. This line of thinking suggests that the capabilities and resources that drive internationalisation performances are contingent on service type (La et al. 2005; Cicic et al. 2002).

Although there are fundamentals that apply to all service firms that internationalise, inward internationalisation may be distinguished by additional or alternate variables that affect internationalisation performance.

Benefits of Internet Marketing

The use of the internet creates faster and better communication, and the time and cost associated with delivery and postage is also reduced (Gursan 2001). Web users expect information at their fingertips and the highest convenience. Internet marketing allows some individual needs and wants of customers in the hospitality industry to be met through market services such as mass-marketing and mass-customisation (Paraskevas and Buhalis 2002; Ismail and Mills 2001).

Research by Buhalis and Main (1998) identifies a wide range of push and pull factors which determine whether small or medium-sized hospitality organisations utilise information and communication technology (ICT). Push factors are external forces which compel enterprises to utilise ICT so as to avoid potential threats, including education and training, national and regional governments and strategic partners. The pull factors, on the other hand, offer incentives for enterprises to incorporate ICT so as to obtain benefits in their operation. According to Trengove et al. (2011), because online marketing is almost always cheaper and more targeted than traditional approaches, it allows firms to reach customers at a lower price.

Drawbacks of Internet Marketing

According to Trengove et al. (2011), customers tend to be fickle. Customers will not expend a lot of energy to find a firm online. Even worse, if the firm's competitors are easy to find online, the firm's potential customers may happily turn to the competitors. If the firm's details do not come up in a web search, there is a high probability the firm will be ignored.

The drawbacks of internet marketing include the financial cost and the time spent setting up and maintaining the fundamental system (Heung 2003; Van Hoof et al. 1998). Bourgouin (2002) has similarly pointed out that available financial resources are one of the determinants of ICT implementation. The author emphasises the fact that local organisations are limited in their use of ICTs due to the high price of equipment and few resources. Palumbo and Herbig (1998) articulate that security, confidentiality and privacy are issues that need to be taken seriously regarding transacting business using the internet.

Daly (2000) has proposed a framework which shows that utilisation of the internet by those that are connected is influenced by cultural, social and economic factors and can also be influenced by policies. Accordingly, cost is likely to limit the use of the internet in Ghana and other third world countries where charges are high.

Anckar and Walden (2001) present other drawbacks inhibiting small and medium-sized hospitality organisations from fully capitalising on ICT, such as lack of financial resources, lack of ICT knowledge or experience, resistance to change, and low-speed access or low-bandwidth connection to the internet.

The Hospitality Industry in Ghana

According to the Ghana Tourist Board (now the Ghana Tourist Authority), the tourism sector has been growing steadily in Ghana. The number of tourist arrivals and amount of expenditure by tourists has increased steadily, while both public and private investment activity in various tourism sub-sectors has also increased. Ghana is among the top ten tourism destinations in the world, according to Frommer's 2012 list of top destinations (Ghana Tourism Authority Report 2013). Tourism in Ghana has had an annual average growth rate of 20 % in Ghana since 2012. Tourism is now the third largest source of foreign exchange, ranking behind only minerals and cocoa (Ghana Tourism Authority Report 2013).

Between 2005 and the third quarter of 2008, the hotel sector contributed GH¢647,296,664.15 directly to government revenue and GH¢35,011,773.43 to non-governmental/quasi-governmental agencies. During the same period, the restaurant sector contributed GH¢28,129,876.26 directly to government revenue and GH¢1,888,216.42 to non-governmental/quasi-governmental agencies (National Tourism Marketing Strategy for Ghana 2009).

The tourism industry in Ghana is faced with increasing competition from other African countries that are emerging tourism destinations. This issue is exacerbated by the high cost of travel to Ghana, lack of appreciation of tourism's importance by Ghanaian government and society alike, increasing worldwide security concerns about overseas travel, negative associations often associated with Africa (famine, disease, poverty, instability), and the lingering effects of the global financial crisis (National Tourism Marketing Strategy for Ghana 2009).

Research Methodology

Sampling Approach

At the time the research was conducted, there were 448 registered hotels in Ghana's Ashanti Region. The 43 hotels in Kumasi formed the population for this study. The study's sample frame, however, consisted of customers from the 34 hotels in Kumasi with active websites. A total of 110 customers were randomly selected from among the users of the 34 hotel websites.

Non-probability sampling was used in this study. Purposive sampling was adopted in selecting hotels in Kumasi with active internet websites. A stratified method was used to ensure participation of all categories of hotels (1-star, 2-star, 3-star, 4-star and other categories of hotels). Simple random sampling was used in selecting customers who patronised the internationalised hotels in Kumasi.

Data Collection

Data were collected from primary and secondary data sources. A questionnaire was the primary instrument used for data collection. To ensure reliability in the data collection, the questionnaire was pretested with seven customers who patronised internationalised hotels in Kumasi. Pretesting, which helps to ensure clarity, accuracy and appropriateness, guided the researcher in reshaping the final questionnaire to eliminate ambiguity and inconsistencies in this research. The questionnaire was designed mainly to learn about customers' perceptions of inward internationalisation of hotels in Kumasi, Ghana, through internet marketing.

Customers were randomly selected from different hotels depending on their current availability to answer the questionnaire. The researcher sought permission from the various hotels involved, and customers were contacted at the reception desks of the hotels.

Questionnaires were fully explained to respondents in order to deal with any ambiguity. Questionnaires were administered in person by the researcher. Provision was made to ensure flexible responses where necessary. The anonymity of respondents was assured.

Secondary data was collected from websites, research reports, annual reports, journals, books and articles.

Analysis and Findings

Data was analysed using Microsoft Excel and SPSS version 19. Findings are presented in tables and in descriptive and quantitative forms. The study had a response rate of over 90 %. Data was processed in its raw state.

The data was analysed using the relative importance index (RII). Following calculation of the RII (see below), variables were ranked from highest to lowest. RII was used in determining customers' preferred online services and products , preferred sources for looking for hotels, and the challenges they faced when looking for hotels. Other variables were analysed in Excel using simple percentages.

Customers Preferred Online Services and Products

In seeking to discern customers' attitudes toward internet marketing, the researcher sought to ascertain customers' preferred online services and products. Table 5.1 shows a ranking of the preferred online services and products of customers in Kumasi in the Ashanti Region.

Table 5.1 Ranking of online services/products preferred by hotel customers in Kumasi

	Rank						
	1	2	3	4	5		
Services/products	Frequencies (n = 110)and percentages					RII	Rank
Accommodation	100 90.9	10 9.1	–	–	–	98.18	1st
WiFi internet service	10 9.1	40 36.4	50 45.5	10 9.1	–	69.09	2nd
Food services	–	60 54.5	30 27.3	20 18.2	–	67.27	3rd
Health and fitness services	–	–	20 18.2	70 63.6	20 18.2	40.00	4th
Entertainment	–	–	10 9.1	10 9.1	90 81.8	25.45	5th

Formula for calculation of RII:

$$RII = \left\{ \frac{1n5 + 2n4 + 3n3 + 4n2 + 5n1}{5(n1 + n2 + n3 + n4 + n5)} \right\} \times 100$$

where RII = Relative Important Index

$n1$ = Number of respondents who answered "1"
$n2$ = Number of respondents who answered "2"
$n3$ = Number of respondents who answered "3"
$n4$ = Number of respondents who answered "4"
$n5$ = Number of respondents who answered "5"

The data indicates that the most important consideration of customers of the 34 hotels in the study was accommodation, followed by availability of internet services, food services, health and fitness facilities, and entertainment.

Preferred Medium of Looking for Hotels Online

Customers were asked about their preferred medium of searching for hotels when needed. The majority of customers chose the internet as their

Table 5.2 Kumasi hotel customers' preferred sources for looking for hotels

	Rank							
	1	2	3	4	5	6		
Preferred medium	Frequencies (*n* = 110) and percentages						RII	Rank
Internet	70 63.6	20 18.2	–	10 9.1	10 9.1	–	86.36	1st
Directories	–	40 36.4	60 54.5	10 9.1	–	–	71.21	2nd
Recommendations/ referrals	30 27.3	40 36.4	10 9.1	10 9.1	–	20 18.2	71.21	2nd
TV	10 9.1	10 9.1	–	20 18.2	70 63.6	–	46.97	3rd
Magazines	–	–	30 27.3	50 45.5	10 9.1	20 18.2	46.97	3rd
Radio	–	–	10 9.1	10 9.1	20 18.2	70 63.6	24.24	4th

first medium, followed by referral and directories, and then by television and magazines; a minority chose radio (Table 5.2).

The formula for the calculation of RII for customers' preferred medium was slightly different than that for preferred services and products because six different mediums were included on the questionnaire:

$$RII = \left\{ \frac{1n6 + 2n5 + 3n4 + 4n3 + 5n2 + 6n1}{6(n1 + n2 + n3 + n4 + n5 + n6)} \right\} \times 100$$

where $n6$ = Number of respondents who answered "6".

A majority of 86.36 % of respondents preferred using the internet when looking for hotels. The second-most popular media when looking for hotels were directories and referrals.

Challenges Faced by Customers When Looking for Hotels Online

Customers were asked to rank the challenges they faced when looking for hotels online. Their greatest challenge was with the speed of the internet and the length of time required to transact business. In addition they

Table 5.3 Online challenges faced by hotel customers in Kumasi

Challenges faced when looking for hotels online	Rank 1	2	3	4	5	RII	Rank
	Frequencies (*n* = 110) and percentages						
Speed of internet/duration of transaction	70 63.6	20 18.2	20 18.2	–	–	89.09	1st
Slow loading of website due to videos/pictures	40 36.4	60 54.5	–	10 9.1	–	83.64	2nd
Scams/ads	–	10 9.1	60 54.5	10 9.1	30 27.3	49.09	3rd
Pop-ups	–	10 9.1	20 18.2	80 72.7	–	47.27	4th
Language barrier	–	10 9.1	10 9.1	10 9.1	80 72.7	30.91	5th

found the slow loading of websites due to videos or pictures to be a major challenge. Other challenges, such as scams/ads, pop-ups, and language barriers, were also identified, as shown in Table 5.3.

RII for this variable was calculated according to the same formula as for customers' preferred services and products.

According to Reed (2011), the effective use of internet marketing depends on skilful linking of website content with outreach tools. It is therefore necessary for hotels in Kumasi to manage their web content well, but the maintenance and updating of a website comes with a cost. It could mean that hoteliers are trying to avoid the cost of maintaining their websites. The findings are in line with other research which concludes that security is one of the most challenging issues facing the internet-based merchant today. Security is a well-known topic in electronic commerce, and it has been frequently written about by researchers such as Jeong and Lambert (2001), Szymanski and Hise (2000) and Melta and Shah (2001). Shim et al. (2001) also back this idea that online retailers need to build secure websites in order to allay internet users' concerns about purchasing products or engaging in services online because of security concerns.

Customers' Concerns When Looking for Hotels Online

The data revealed that respondents (customers) had some reservations when looking for hotels online; in particular, they were hesitant to give

Table 5.4 Fears of Kumasi hotel customers when looking for hotels online

Fears	Rank 1	2	3	RII	Rank
	Frequencies (n = 110) and percentages				
Giving out of personal details	60	20	30	93.94	1st
	54.5	18.2	27.3		
Scams/website inauthenticity	40	60	10	75.76	2nd
	36.4	54.5	9.1		
Payment system insecurity	10	70	30	48.48	3rd
	9.1	63.6	27.3		

out their personal details; they were also concerned about scams or the inauthenticity of websites and about the security of payment systems (Table 5.4).

These findings agree with those of Palumbo and Herbig (1998) showing that security, confidentiality and privacy are issues that need to be taken seriously regarding transacting business using the internet. A study conducted by TNS Interactive revealed lack of trust in the online payment system as a major factor hindering consumers from shopping online (Global E-Commerce Report 2002). This finding also parallels those of Yee (1988), who found that 38 % of respondents felt that online shopping was not safe, and Suki et al. (2002), who found that 36 % of respondents were reluctant to reveal their credit card details.

Discussion and Implications

The majority of respondents preferred to use the internet when searching for hotels (72.7 %), although some (27.3 %) used other means (Table 5.1). According to the data, the medium of the internet is preferred because consumers can shop at any time and have access to products and services not available in their geographic region. Furthermore, customers are able to access the internet not only from their personal computers but from electronic devices such as personal digital assistants and mobile phones (Kau et al. 2003).

Customers' Views Regarding Hotel Websites

All respondents preferred a website that allows them to send feedback. All respondents also preferred hotel websites with pictures/videos/audio over text-only websites. This suggests that customers prefer interactive websites with pictures or short videos of available products or services more than websites with only words. Websites with visuals help customers better appreciate products and services. However, video and picture files are large and can detrimentally affect the speed of website access.

Customers' Views on Product/Service Customisation

In the process of finding out customers' views about internet marketing, they were asked how they felt when given the opportunity to customise the type of accommodation or other services online. According to the results, 54.5 % appreciated the idea, 27.3 % did not like the idea, and 18.2 % were undecided. This means that a majority of respondents either loved or appreciated the idea of product or service customisation. Customisation helps companies retain customers. It is important to maintain good customer relationships through customisation because winning new customers can be up to five times more expensive than maintaining existing customers (Reichheld and Schefter 2000; Harrison-Walker and Neeley 2004).

Customers' Views on Customisation of Price

Price customisation gives customers the opportunity to choose various options depending on their priorities and budget. In the current study, 54.5 % of respondents said that they felt better when given the opportunity to customise pricing when making hotel reservations online; 27.3 % did not like the idea; and 18.2 % were undecided. According to Paraskevas and Buhalis (2002), internet marketing allows for the individual needs and wants of customers in the hospitality industry to be met through services such as mass-marketing and mass-customisation. These ideas are in agreement with the findings on customisation from the study reported here.

Mode of Payment

Customers were asked what type of payment medium they preferred to use when making payments online for hotel accommodation. The data reveals that 81.8 % preferred making physical payments by cash, while 18.2 % preferred electronic payment. The majority of the respondents were from Ghana and neighbouring countries in West Africa. Most of the respondents who were from West Africa may not have been familiar with electronic payment methods.

This finding confirms customers' reservations regarding making payments online. The security of customers is a priority, and giving out their personal details makes them feel insecure. This finding shows that customers prefer cash over electronic payments in Ghana. This result could possibly be attributed to the fact that the technological infrastructure in Ghana has not yet developed to a level where electronic payments are appreciated.

Usefulness of Internet Marketing to Customers

Customers were asked whether they found internet marketing useful or not. Responses show that 81.8 % found internet marketing to be useful, while 9.1 % thought otherwise and 9.1 % were undecided about the usefulness of internet marketing. According to Dong et al. (2007), ease of use of the internet has a positive effect on consumer buying behaviour and decision-making. The authors argues that ease of use is an antecedent to usefulness. Customers in Ghana find internet marketing useful probably because of the ease of use.

Conclusions and Directions for Future Research

Consumer Preferences

The majority of respondents in this study preferred to use the internet when looking for hotels, followed by referrals and directories, TV and magazines, and then radio. Accommodation was the number-one priority of hotel customers in Ghana, followed by availability of internet or WiFi, food, health and fitness services, and entertainment facilities.

Customers' Views on Websites and Customisation

Respondents preferred websites with audiovisual media and a method for sending feedback. A majority (72.7 %) either loved or appreciated the opportunity for product or service customisation, and 54 % of respondents were in support of price customisation. A majority of respondents preferred paying with cash rather than by electronic payment.

Challenges/Fears of Customers

The major challenge customers faced concerning internet marketing was slow internet connectivity and the long duration of online business transactions. Customers also were challenged by the slow loading of websites due to audiovisual content. Another challenge was the presence of scams or ads. Other challenges were pop-ups and language barriers. The results of the research indicate that customers' major fear with regard to internet marketing is with the giving out of their personal details. Secondly, customers in Ghana are afraid of scams or unauthentic websites. Further, customers in Ghana are afraid of lack of security in making payments online.

Following from the findings of this study, it is recommended that the government of Ghana invest in the communication industry to enrich the rate of internet connectivity, which will eventually boost business operations through internet marketing. Secondly, it is recommended that industries, small and medium-sized enterprises, NGOs, and other institutions support the government regarding the purchase and installation of a strong fibre optic backbone in Ghana. In addition, it is highly recommended that hotels that have inwardly internationalised using internet marketing adopt strong security measures, such as Secure Sockets Layer (SSL), to boost customers' confidence in using their websites for transactions. Furthermore, hotels that have inwardly internationalised should make provision for customers to send feedback through the hotel websites. Last but not the least, customers should also be given the opportunity to customise if they so desire in order to meet their tastes and ensure their retention.

Bibliography

Anckar, B., & Walden, P. (2001). Introducing Web technology in a small peripheral hospitality organisation. *International Journal of Contemporary Hospitality Management, 13*(4/5), 241–250.
Andrews, L., Kiel, G. C., Drennan, J., Veronica Boyle, M., & Weerawardena, J. (2007). Gender perceptions of experimental value in using web-based retail channels. *European Journal of Marketing, 41*(5/6), 640–658.
Bharadwaj, S., Varadarajan, P. R., & Fahy, J. (1993). Sustainable competitive advantage in service industries: A conceptual model and research propositions. *Journal of Marketing, 57*(4), 83–99.
Bjorkman, I., & Kork, S. (1997). Inward international activities in service firms—Illustrated by three Cases from the tourism industry. *International Journal of Service Industry Management, 8*(5), 362.
Bolton, R. N., & Drew, J. H. (1991). A multistage model of customers' assessments of service quality and value. *Journal of Consumer Research, 17*, 375–384.
Boulding, W., Kalra, A., Staelin, R., & Zeithaml, V. A. (1993). A dynamic process model of service quality: From expectations to intentions. *Journal of Marketing Research, 30*, 7–27.
Bourgouin, F. (2002). Information communication technologies and the potential for rural tourism SMME development: The case of the wild coast. *Development Southern Africa, 19* (1 March).
Buhalis, D., & Licasta, M. C. (2002). The future of e-tourism intermediaries. *Journal of Tourism Management, 23*(3), 207–220.
Buhalis, D., & Main, H. (1998). Information technology in peripheral small and medium hospitality enterprises: Strategic analysis and critical factors. *International Journal of Contemporary Hospitality Management, 15*(4), 243–247.
Cicic, M., Patterson, P., & Shoham, A. (2002). Antecedents of international performance: A service firms' perspective. *European Journal of Marketing, 36*(9/10), 1103–1118.

Daly, J. A. (2000). Studying the impacts of the Internet without assuming technological determinism. In D. Nicholas & I. Rowlands (Eds.), *The Internet: Its impact and evaluation. Aslib Proceedings, 52*(8), 285.

Fornell, C., & Wernerfelt, B. (1987). Defensive marketing strategy by customer complaint management. *Journal of Marketing Research, 24*, 337–346.

Freeman, S., & Sandwell, M. (2008). Professional service firms entering emerging markets: The role of network relationships. *The Journal f Services Marketing, 22*(3), 198–212.

Ghana Tourism Authority Report. 2013. Directory of Registered Hotels in Ashanti Region *Global E-commerce Report 2002*, The TNS Interactive. Retrieved 2002, from http://www.tnsofres.com/ger2002/home.cfm

Gregory, S., & Breiter, D. (2001). Levelling the playing field: E-marketing's impact on lodging operations. *Journal of Hospitality & Leisure Marketing, 7*(4), 45–60.

Harker, M. J., & Egan, J. (2006). The past, present, and future of relationship marketing. *Journal of Marketing Management, 22*, 215–242.

Harrison-Walker, L. J., & Neeley, S. E. (2004). Customer relationship building on the Internet in B2B marketing: A proposed typology. *Journal of Marketing Theory and Practice, 12*(1), 19–35.

Heung, V. C. S. (2003). Internet usage by international travellers: Reasons and barriers. *International Journal of Contemporary Hospitality Management, 15*(7), 370–378.

Hoffman, D. L., & Novak, T. P. (1997). A new marketing paradigm for electronic commerce. *The Information Society, 13*(1), 43–54 special issue on electronic commerce.

Ismail, J. A., & Mills, J. E. (2001). Contract disputes in travel and tourism: When the online deal goes bad. *Journal of Travel and Tourism Marketing, 11*(2–3), 63–83.

Jarvenpaa, S. L., & Todd, P. A. (1997). Is there a future for retailing on the internet? In R. A. Peterson (Ed.), *Electronic marketing and the consumer*. Thousand Oaks, CA: Sage Publications.

Johnson, M. D., Anderson, E. W., & Fornell, C. (1995). Rational and adaptive performance expectations in a customer satisfaction framework. *Journal of Consumer Research, 21*, 128–140.

Johnson, M. D., & Fornell, C. (1991). A framework for comparing customer satisfaction across individuals and product categories. *Journal of Economic Psychology, 12*(2), 267–286.

Jones, T. O., & Sasser Jr., W. E. (1995). Why satisfied customers defect. *Harvard Business Review, 73*(6), 88–99.
Kau, A. K., Tang, Y. E., & Ghose, S. (2003). Typology of online consumers. *Journal of Consumer Marketing, 20*(2), 139–156.
La, V. Q., Patterson, P. G., & Styles, C. W. (2005). Determinants of export performance across service types: A conceptual model. *The Journal of Services Marketing, 19*(6), 379–391.
Liu, C., & Arnett, K. P. (2000). Exploring the factors associated with web site success in the context of electronic commerce. *Information and Management, 38*(1), 23–33.
Paraskevas, A., & Buhalis, D. (2002). Outsourcing IT for small hotels: The opportunities and challenges of using application service providers. *Cornell Hotel and Restaurant Administration Quarterly, 43*(2), 27–39.
Peterson, R. A., Balasubramanian, S., & Bronnenberg, B. J. (1997). Exploring the implications of the internet for consumer marketing. *Journal of the Academy of Marketing Science, 25*(4), 329–346.
Porter, M. E., & Strategy, C. (1980). *Techniques for analyzing industries and competitors. Competitive Strategy*. New York: Free
Porter, M. E. (1985). *Competitive advantage*. New York: Free Press/Macmillan.
Rahman, Z. (2003). Internet-based supply chain management: Using internet to revolutionise your business. *International Journal of Information Management, 23*, 493–505.
Reed, J. (2011). *Get up to speed with online marketing: How to use websites, blogs*, social networking and much more. Pearson Education India.
Reichheld, F. F., & Sasser, E. W. (1990). Zero defections: Quality comes to services. *Harvard Business Review, 14*, 495–507.
Reichheld, F. F., & Schefter, P. (2000). E-loyalty: Your secret weapon on the Web. *Harvard Business Review, 78*, 105–113.
Roberts, J. (1999). The internationalisation of business service firms: A stages approach. *The Service Industries Journal, 19*(4), 68–88.
Sharma, S., & Aragón-Correa, J. A. (2005). Corporate environmental strategy and competitive advantage: A review from the past to the future. In S. Sharma & J. A. Aragón-Correa (Eds.), *Environmental strategy and competitive advantage*. Northhampton: Edward Elgar Academic Publishing.
Shim, S., Eastlick, M., & Lotz, S. (2001). Assessing the impact of internet shopping on store shopping among mall shoppers and internet users. *Journal of Shopping Centre Research, 7*(2), 7–43.

Smith, M., Bailey, J., & Brynjolfsson, E. (2000). Understanding digital markets: Review and assessment. In E. Brynjolfsson & B. Kahin (Eds.), *Understanding the digital economy*. Cambridge, MA: MIT Press.

Strom, P., & Mattson, J. (2006). Internationalisation of Japanese professional business service firms. *The Service Industries Journal, 26*(3), 249–265.

Suki, N., Ahamd, M. I., & Thyagarajan, V. (2002). Motivation and concern factors for internet shopping: A Malaysian perspective. *The Electronic Journal for E-commerce Tools and Applications, 1*, 1–18.

Jones, A. T., Malczyk, A., & Beneke, J. (2011). *Internet Marketing: A highly practical guide to every aspect of internet marketing*.

Van Hoof, H., Ruys, H., & Combrink, T. E. (1998). The use of the Internet in the Queensland accommodation industry. *Australian Journal of Hospitality Management, 6*(1), 11–24.

Walsh, J., & Godfrey, S. (2000). The Internet: a new era in customer service. *European Management Journal, 18*(1), 85–92.

Wang, Y., Yu, Q., & Fesenmaier, R. D. (2002). Defining the virtual tourist community: Implication for tourism marketing. *Tourism Management Journal, 23*(4), 407–417.

Yee M. C. (1998). *The potential of electronic commerce via Internet: A case study at University Malaysia Sarawak*. Unpublished Baccalaureate Degree Project Paper, Department of Communication, UKM.

Part III

Cases on Africa-to-Africa Internationalization

6

The Nigerian Beer Wars: SABMiller's Entry into the Nigerian Brewing Space

Nkemdilim Iheanachor and Chris Ogbechie

The Nigerian brewing landscape witnessed intense battles for market share from 1960 to 2010 between Heineken's Nigerian Breweries and Diageo's Guinness. However, the surface of the market was largely unscratched; by 2010, the average Nigerian consumed about 10 litres of beer per annum[1] compared to the global average of 27 litres per annum.[2] Nigerian Breweries and Guinness both achieved annual turnover growth rates of over 15 %[3] between 2005 and 2010, with average annual consumption of beer consistently rising over the period.

The dominance of the two companies was threatened in 2009[4] when SABMiller, Africa's largest brewer, made an inroad into Nigeria, Africa's most populous market. SABMiller insisted that it had come to stay and play across virtually all segments of the market dominated by the oligopoly then running the industry. In response, Heineken, Nigerian Breweries' parent company, significantly increased its production capacity

N. Iheanachor (✉) • C. Ogbechie
Lagos Business School, Pan-Atlantic University, Ajah, Lagos, Nigeria
e-mail: niheanachor@lbs.edu.ng

I. Adeleye et al. (eds.), *Africa-to-Africa Internationalization*, AIB Sub-Saharan Africa (SSA) Series, DOI 10.1007/978-3-319-30692-6_6

by acquiring other breweries. Industry analysts keenly watched the evolution of the market and pondered what initiatives the dominant market players needed to launch to consolidate and retain their leadership position in the Nigerian beer industry. Was the solution a modification of product range or breadth, or should they modify bottling, pricing and branding strategies to capture other segments of the market? How best could they attack the base of the pyramid?[5]

As the beer wars intensified in 2011, Nigerian Breweries and Guinness Nigeria faced new challenges: Could they boost flagging domestic sales? Where would they find new revenue streams? How best could they position themselves to fend off the rising threat of this new entrant? Was their era of sustained growth and profitability coming to an end, or was their knowledge of the market, distribution systems and local terrain going to ensure they retained their dominance over time? What specific capabilities would they require to enlarge their footprint in the base of the pyramid that SABMiller had indicated it would focus on?

Nigerian Beer Industry Developments

Nigeria's annual beer consumption, second only to South Africa on the continent, was estimated to be about 18 million hectolitres in 2010.[6] The market is dominated by Heineken's Nigerian Breweries, with a 70 % market share, and Diageo's Guinness, with over 20 % of the market, leaving SABMiller a share of less than 5 %. Other smaller players made up the rest of the market.[7]

In 2010 SABMiller announced plans to spend over $100 million to build a new brewery in Nigeria as part of its efforts at increasing its presence in Nigeria on a greenfield site at Onitsha in southeast Nigeria. This was in addition to other acquisitions it had made before 2010. The Nigerian beer market grew at an annual rate of 9 %[8] in the years 2000–2010. In response to threats in the market, Heineken acquired controlling interests in five breweries in January 2011 to expand its capacity in Nigeria by nearly a third.[9] The case writer feels that it was uncertain whether Heineken's capacity was the problem, as SABMiller had given a strong indication that it was more interested in the informal market that was dominated by liquors and locally brewed gin. SABMiller's new brewery was expected to have an annual capacity of about 500,000 hectolitres of

Global beer Market Share of production by continent 2003 – 2008						
Continents	2003	2004	2005	2006	2007	2008
Europe	34.9%	34.1%	34.1%	33.4%	33.1%	32.2%
Asia/Middle East	26.9%	28.5%	28.5%	30.0%	31.2%	31.7%
North America	22.2%	21.4%	20.9%	20.0%	19.4%	19.0%
South America	10.2%	10.2%	10.7%	10.6%	10.5%	11.0%
Africa	4.4%	4.4%	4.5%	4.6%	4.7%	5.0%
Australia/Oceania	1.4%	1.3%	1.3%	1.3%	1.2%	1.2%
TOTAL	100%	100%	100%	100%	100%	100%

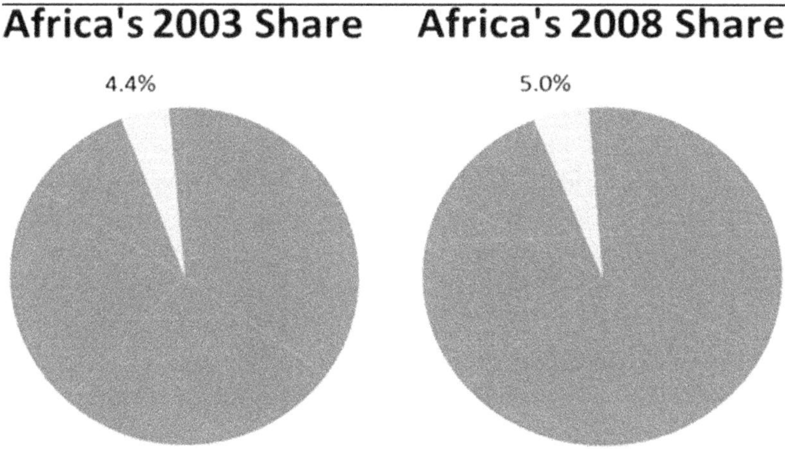

Fig. 6.1 Global beer market. *Source*: Adapted from Vetiva Capital Management, Nigerian Breweries Sector, 2010 research report

beer and malt beverages and to be able to bottle water and other beverages. It was expected to produce local brands like Grand Lager, Eagle and Castle Milk Stout. These brands were traditionally priced lower than the more popular brands of beer from Nigerian Breweries and Guinness (Fig. 6.1).

Dynamics of the Nigerian Beer Industry

The case writer's research revealed that per capita consumption of beer is highly correlated to the level of economic development of a country, with more advanced economies having higher per capita consumption than the level in Nigeria. Growth in consumption figures, however, also depends on cultural and religious beliefs. Islamic regions, for example, generally have lower consumption levels (see Fig. 6.2).

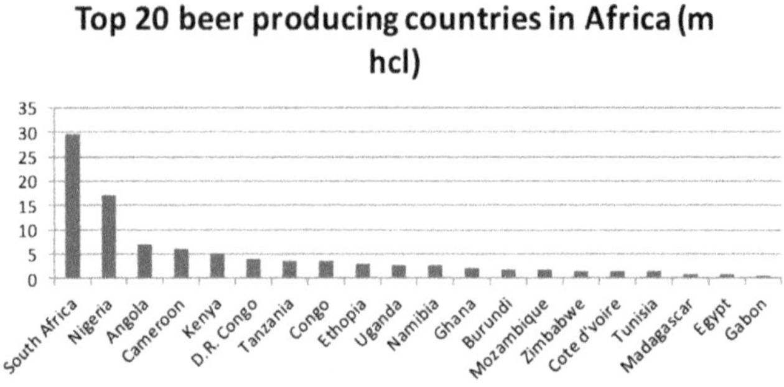

Fig. 6.2 Beer-producing countries in Africa. *Source*: Adapted from FBN Capital Nigerian Breweries Sector Coverage 2010, research report

As of 2010, per capita consumption in Nigeria had risen to about 10 litres from a level of 7.3 litres per capita in 2007, according to local industry sources, although this was still less than half the global average of 27 litres per capita. National beer production was 7.8 million, 8.0 million and 9.5 million hectolitres in 2001, 2002 and 2003, respectively, and rose to a level of 18 million hectolitres in 2010.[10] The growth in beer consumption was fuelled by increased consumer income levels, rising urbanization, and the introduction and popularity of flavoured alcoholic brands. Demand for beer continued to increase with consistent increases in income. The bottom-heavy, youthful demographic of the Nigerian population was also very supportive of the growth witnessed in the industry. Even though each segment of the overall beer market reacted differently to economic cycles, the Nigerian brewing industry was often considered 'recession proof' by some industry analysts. The beer industry contributed approximately 96 % of the Manufacturing Value Added to Nigeria's Gross Domestic Product in 2010,[11] and the two major brewing giants in Nigeria (Nigerian Breweries and Guinness) constituted over 95 % of the total sector capitalization of the Nigerian Stock Exchange as of December 2010.[12] The industry witnessed a compound annual growth rate of 16.46 % between 2004 and 2008.[13]

At the peak of the global financial crisis in 2008, when inflow of foreign direct investment and job losses were at their peak, industry analysts reported that consumers switched from more expensive beers to less expensive varieties. New demand for beer came from some unlikely sources, such as wine and liquor drinkers who had to cut down on their alcohol spending and consumption. In the total market for alcohol-based products, wine and spirits traditionally sit on the more expensive end of the scale. During that period brewers tapped into this trend by offering beers with higher alcohol content.

This resilient and largely inelastic demand profile of some of the industry's products results in volume growth irrespective of the economic climate. Some analysts report that in times of depression consumers drink to drown their fears and anxieties, and in times of excitement they drink to express their joy. Beer consumption is directly linked to individual lifestyles. Though volume consumed is dependent on economic fortunes, the industry continuously plays host to new entrants (new consumers) whose demand compensates for the marginal losses in sales volumes occasioned by declining disposable income. The production and distribution of beer involves three major participants: brewers, retail channels and suppliers.

Brewers

All beers are brewed using a process based on a simple formula. Key to the process is malted grain—mainly barley, though other cereals, such as wheat, rice or sorghum, may be used. There are several steps in the brewing process, including malting, milling, mashing, lautering, fermenting, conditioning, filtering and packaging.

In the 1980s and 1990s, the Nigerian government imposed a ban on the import of barley into Nigeria. Sorghum, the national crop of Nigeria, grows easily in hot climates and poor soils. At the time, Nigeria was Africa's largest sorghum producer (accounting for 35 % of the continent's sorghum production in 2010[14]) and one of the largest producers in the world. The ban on imported barley resulted in increased local sorghum production activity that empowered farmers, distributors and brewers. Although the ban on barley was lifted in 1998,[15] international demand and escalating transportation costs made it impractical for use as a brewing grain in Nigeria. In an effort to establish a reliable supply of sorghum from local farmers, both Heineken and Diageo joined forces with the Common Fund for Commodities, a segment of the United Nations, in the establishment of a cooperative for rural development in Ghana and Sierra Leone.[16]

The two partnered companies were so impressed with the results of the cooperative that in two years Heineken completed the world's largest sorghum malting plant in Aba in the eastern part of Nigeria. Heineken produces beer from sorghum (either wholly or in part) under the names Star Lager and Gulder in Nigeria, Ghana, Sierra Leone, Rwanda and Burundi. Diageo also brews beer with sorghum in Nigeria, Ghana and Sierra Leone.[17]

Brewers manage the raw material procurement and the beer and malt brewing processes, and they move the products through wholesale and retail channels for distribution. A brewer's most significant costs are advertising, promotion, distribution and raw materials. Brewers take the lead in developing and financing most marketing programmes. They invest heavily in trademarks that they use in innovative and sophisticated advertising campaigns. They are also responsible for most trade and consumer promotions. In addition to the provision of marketing support, brewers are also responsible for procurement of major equipment for their key distributors.

Once a fragmented business with many small and local brewers, the landscape of the Nigerian beer industry changed over time into an oligopoly controlled mainly by Guinness and Nigerian Breweries. The brewers maintain cordial relationships with the retail trade to ensure continual brand availability and avoid customer attrition. Cooperative merchandising agreements between brewers and retailers are used to promote beer sales.

The brewing process is highly capital intensive and involves specialized high-speed canning and bottling lines. Canning and bottling lines cost billions of naira, with the cost depending on volume and package type. Among the top brewers in Nigeria, packaging and labour account for a significant portion of direct costs. Brewers invest heavily in trucks and distribution networks to ensure effective market penetration.

Nigerian Breweries and Guinness franchise agreements allow distributors to handle other product brands and categories. The case writer's research revealed that franchise agreements also allow distributors to choose whether or not to market new alcoholic brands introduced by the brewer. There are some restrictions, however, as some distributors cannot carry directly competitive brands. For example, a Guinness distributor cannot sell Nigerian Breweries brand of Amstel Malt, but it could distribute Star if it decided not to carry Gulder. The brewers also have the final say about such issues as retail pricing, new packaging, selling, advertising and promotions in all sales territories.

Suppliers

The majority of Nigerian beer is packaged in bottles and metal cans. Cans are an attractive packaging material because they are durable and light, and they are easily handled, stocked and displayed. Until GZ Industries entered the Nigerian metal can manufacture space in 2010, there was no metal can manufacturing facility in Nigeria, and all cans for use by brewers and carbonated soft drink bottlers were imported. Glass bottles have historically been the main packaging material and were in use for decades before the metal can was introduced to boost home consumption of beer.

Brewers negotiate directly with the major manufacturers and are among the metal can industry's largest customers. Since the can constitutes a significant portion of the total cost of a packaged beer, brewers maintain relationships with local and foreign suppliers.

Retail Channels

The distribution of beer in Nigeria takes place through bars, restaurants, convenience stores, supermarkets, mass merchandisers and other outlets. Cost of distribution is affected by delivery method, distribution infrastructural challenges, delivery frequency, drop size, advertising and marketing.

Beers are among the largest-selling product lines in southern Nigeria. Some industry analysts have stated that northern Nigeria, predominantly inhabited by Muslims, has historically low beer consumption levels owing to the disapproval of alcohol drinking in the Islamic religion. Beer represents a large percentage of a typical Nigerian bar's business and is a big traffic draw. Brewers fight for retail shelf space in emerging formal retail outlets in the major Nigerian cities, like Lagos, Abuja and Port Harcourt, that serve the upper class and emerging middle class. Brewers are also on the lookout for new locations to increase impulse purchases. Historically,

Nigerian Breweries and Guinness have focused on sales through retail outlets and have maintained strong trade channel relationships with their key distributors. The distribution model falls generally into a three-tier system. An interesting aspect of this system is that it requires all alcoholic drinks (there are a few exceptions) to pass through a middleman. The main consequence of the system being set up this way is that the brewers own the primary aspects of the industry: production, distribution and retail.

The three tiers of the system are comprised of:

- Production—The brewers who produce the beer.
- Distribution—Brewers often grant exclusive rights to certain companies licensed as key distributors to distribute their products to different retailers in specific areas. The sophistication of the distribution system now enables the brewer to arrange for finance, technical and marketing support for the distributors. This reduces competition and raises prices since fewer distributors means less incentive to reduce prices.
- Retail—This is the point at which the general consumer can purchase the product, whether at a restaurant, club, bar, supermarket or from a vendor.

Marketing

Brewers defend market share using a combination of price, product quality and promotion, reinforced by distribution models. Market information is usually collected by company sales personnel from wholesalers and retailers and analyzed by marketing department staff, including brand managers and salesmen. Product development activities are in some cases informed by market information and needs. The incentive system in some breweries includes free cartons of beer for salesmen who exceed sales targets.

Legend Extra Stout from Nigerian Breweries was created as a response to Guinness Stout's dominance in the stout market. For some other established products, pricing often follows cost trends. Some newly launched products are priced at a break-even point as a deliberate penetration strategy. Brewers spend time building separate brand identities for various products targeted at the major groups of beer drinkers.

Beer Industry Composition

The Nigerian beer industry is driven essentially by lager, which accounts for about 62 % of beer sector volume.[18] The malt and stout segments account for 24 % and 14 %, respectively.[19] Nigerian Breweries dominates the lager segment with its Star brand, which accounts for over a quarter of sector sales volume. This position is strengthened by its mainstream Gulder brand. Guinness' Harp brand closely follows the leading brands from Nigerian Breweries.

The stout segment of the market, though relatively small with a 14 % sector volume share,[20] sells at a premium of about 40 % over lager brands. The Guinness Stout is believed to be the market leader by some industry analysts. The presence of Nigerian Breweries' Legend Stout has not been very much felt by drinkers of popular stouts. SABMiller's Castle Milk Stout has wrestled some market share from Guinness Stout, though its limited production capacity may not make its impact very significant in the near future.

The malt segment is a fast-growing segment in the Nigerian beer industry. Industry analysts believe there is no clear leader in this segment; the Maltina brand from Nigerian Breweries and Guinness Malt seem to be fighting head-on for market share as their retail prices are the same. In addition to Maltina, Nigerian Breweries also has Amstel Malt, its low-sugar malt drink positioned in the mainstream segment, while Guinness introduced Top Malt in 2009. In recent years the introduction of cans and Tetra Pak packaging has contributed significantly to the growth of this segment. Enhanced advertising and promotions targeted at young consumers have also helped drive segment volume growth.

The Evolution of the Nigerian Beer Industry

The Nigerian beer industry in 2010 was one of the fastest-growing industries in Nigeria. In 2003, beer was produced in all states of the country except Bauchi, Borno, Gongola, Niger and Sokoto, which are in the northern part of the country. There were over 32 breweries producing more than 40 brands of beer.[21]

In the period 1980–1982, brewing was the fastest-growing branch of the manufacturing sector in Nigeria. The volume of production in 1982 was five times greater than in 1970.[22] Even during 1982–1986, when most manufacturing sector branches experienced severe difficulties and production levels fell significantly, the brewing industry continued to grow slowly. Production fell marginally during 1987 and 1988 due to restrictions on the import of barley malt and problems associated with the use of locally produced substitutes. During this period, capacity utilization fell to an all-time low of about 30 %.[23] Increasing success with local substitutes for barley malt improved the capacity utilization rate to about 64 % in 1991.[24]

Bottled lager and stout are beer types commonly produced and consumed in Nigeria. Domestic beer is usually packaged in bottles and not canned. Imported canned beer is fashionable among high-income, upwardly mobile Nigerian beer consumers. However, some industry analysts feel that Nigerian consumers prefer beer with a comparatively higher alcohol content. The alcohol content by volume of the locally produced beer exceeds 5 %, compared to about 4 % for most imported products.

Beers of different brands and from different countries were imported into the country before Nigerian Breweries rolled out its first lager beer in 1949, which happened to be Nigeria's first brewed beer.[25] Soon after Nigerian Breweries started production in Nigeria, a company was formed to import Guinness Extra Stout into the country from Ireland. The popularity of this brand led to the establishment of a Guinness brewery in Lagos in 1962, with production beginning in 1963.[26] Like Nigerian Breweries, Guinness has recorded tremendous growth in production over the years.

Imports and Foreign Competition

The Nigerian import market for lager beer is relatively small; however, it is growing to meet the needs of middle- to high-income groups. An estimated 195,000 hectolitres of bottled beer, valued at more than $35 million, was imported in 2002.[27] Major imported beer brands in Nigeria are Heineken, Becks, Corona, Carlsberg, Budweiser, Castle and Amstel Lager. Heineken beer is the dominant import, accounting for close to 50 % of Nigeria's lager beer imports.[28] Heineken is imported into the country and distributed by its Nigerian partner, Nigerian Breweries. On average, imported lager beers retail at double the price of locally produced beers.

A large portion of imported beer products enter the Nigerian market through cross-border smuggling to evade high import duties. Beer is also imported in mixed containers by several firms holding exclusive distribution rights.

Distribution

There are two broad segments of beer distribution channels in Nigeria: primary and secondary. The primary distribution channel is the segment of the marketing chain controlled directly by the breweries and importers. This distribution model entails direct physical distribution of bottled beer from the breweries and importers to wholesalers. Most breweries and importers use either company-owned trucks or trucks supplied by independent transport companies. The secondary segment of the chain involves product distribution from wholesalers to bulk breakers (in some cases), to retailers, and, ultimately, to consumers. Breweries and importers in Nigeria have developed alliances with wholesalers and key retailers to ensure that products reach consumers at very reasonable prices. Minivans are supplied to key wholesalers on a cost recovery basis to ease product distribution and in some cases to eliminate bulk breakers from the distribution chain. Industry sources estimate beer retailers in the country at approximately 700,000 as of December 2010. Retail outlets include the traditional open markets, beer parlours (pubs) and restaurants. Others include the institutional retailers such as hotels, supermarkets and convenience stores. The traditional open markets account for approximately 60 % of imported beer in the retail trade. Supermarkets and convenience stores account for about 25 %, while restaurants and beer parlours account for the remaining 15 %.[29]

Procurement

The Nigerian brewing industry formerly wholly depended on importation for barley, which was the main raw material for beer production.

However, in 1985 the Federal Government of Nigeria decided to ban the importation of malted barley as part of a large policy aimed at greater economic self-reliance. This development forced the brewing industry to look for local substitutes. The initial use of maize and sorghum caused a drastic change in the taste of the products. As a result, companies like Nigerian Breweries that had already gone into the export market had to withdraw as their products could no longer compete with products in the international market. Both maize and sorghum were supplied locally.

Beer is by far the most popular alcoholic drink in Nigeria and is also an important part of the country's social fabric. A number of international brands are present in the market. Rising disposable income and increased product development by both local and international operators have driven strong growth in this market.

Beer Wars Intensify

In May 2009, after several unsuccessful entry attempts, SABMiller entered the Nigerian market by acquiring the domestic brewer Pabod (30,000-hectolitre capacity).[30] SABMiller's previous attempts to enter the market had been scuttled by the incumbents, who locked up the distribution chains by forbidding their distributors from working for SABMiller, according to local industry sources. SABMiller planned to increase Pabod's capacity to about 250,000 hectolitres by February 2010. In addition to pursuing further acquisitions across Nigeria, SABMiller planned, over the long term, to gain the upper hand on both Nigerian Breweries and Guinness Nigeria in the high-potential and relatively under-penetrated low-cost beer segment. SABMiller estimated the domestically brewed sector in the African markets within which it operated to be worth about US$3 billion.[31] By producing beer using locally sourced inputs, which could potentially bring down the price of lagers by 50–60 %, SABMiller could tap into the low-income segment in Nigeria.

Between 2000 and 2005, Heineken invested $545 million in its Nigerian operations. Heineken subsequently announced that it had strengthened its platform for growth in Nigeria via the acquisition of two holding companies from the Sona Group in 2010.[32] The two acquired businesses had controlling interests in the Sona, IBBI, Benue, Life and Champion breweries in Nigeria. The acquisition provided Heineken with an additional technical capacity of 3.7 million hectolitres,[33] helping to increase the company's capacity and improve the geographic location of its breweries. Some industry analysts believe that the geographic spread of the acquisitions, which are situated in Ota (southwest), Onitsha (southeast) and Kaduna (north-central) Nigeria, broadened the geographic spread of the company and helped improve its penetration. The acquisitions were also expected to give the brewer exposure to the affordable/value segment and strengthen its brand portfolio.

Heineken explored the possibility of consolidating the newly acquired breweries into its existing business structure in Nigeria before the end of 2011.[34] Discussions between Nigerian Breweries and Consolidated Breweries another brewer that in which Heineken had majority stake had begun. The acquired breweries would provide and expand contract brewing services to Nigerian Breweries and Consolidated Breweries until a resolution as to whether they will exist separately or as a single entity is reached. In the interim, Nigerian Breweries will continue to own, brew and support the Goldberg, Williams Dark Ale and Malta Gold brands, as well as various smaller regional brands. The acquired companies will remain independent entities in the meantime and continue business. At the beginning of 2015, some industry analysts believed there was a likelihood of a consolidation of all the breweries under the Nigerian Breweries/Heineken platform.

Guinness announced investments of about N55 billion (US$344 million) during the 2011–2013 period in order to enhance its installed capacity and help maintain its market share.[35] Some industry analysts believe Guinness is more focused on organic growth and less interested in acquisitions.[36]

In the Nigerian beer market, lager beer and malt drinks make up the largest segments. Jointly, these two segments have a combined market share of about 85 %.[37] Nigerian Breweries is the dominant brewer and market leader in mainstream lager, premium lager and malt. Its flagship lager brands, Star and Gulder, continue to enjoy strong market share, while its premium lager, Heineken, continues to show promise. Nigerian Breweries stout brand, Legend Extra Stout, increased its market penetration in 2010.

Highlights of Key Players

Guinness Nigeria

Guinness Nigeria was incorporated in 1950 and listed on the stock exchange in 1965.[38] Guinness was a leading brand of Diageo, the world-famous premium beer manufacturer with a large collection of beverage alcohol brands across the spirits, wine and beer categories. Diageo is a global company trading in over 180 markets around the world.[39] It operates in seven key markets: North America, Europe, Asia Pacific, Latin America, the Caribbean, Africa and the Middle East. Diageo has successfully leveraged top-line growth, innovation and high levels of investment in marketing across its global markets. Diageo's top five markets for Guinness are Great Britain, Nigeria, Ireland, the United States, and Cameroon, while its top brands include Smirnoff, Johnnie Walker, Captain Morgan, Baileys, J&B, Crown Royal and Bushmills whiskeys. Nigerian Guinness was the first Guinness brewery outside the United Kingdom and the third in the world.[40]

Guinness Nigeria engages in brewing, bottling and marketing of foreign extra stout in Nigeria. The company produces five major brands: Guinness Extra Smooth, Gordon's Spark, Harp Lager, Malta Guinness and Smirnoff Ice. Driven by huge growth year on year, Nigeria has become the world's second-biggest market for the beer outside Britain, accounting for 41 % of global volume sales of stout in 2010. Guinness regularly invests in growing production and sales volumes as well as in continued improvement of its operations. Four of the company's premium brands—Guinness Foreign Extra Stout, Guinness Extra Smooth, Harp Larger and Satzenbrau—received a global endorsement from the International Institute for Quality Selection, Brussels, in 2007.[41]

Guinness Nigeria has benefited significantly from Diageo's International Beer Supply process compliance at all its production sites. In 2007, Guinness Lagos and Benin featured in Diageo's League of Excellence Quality Charts, a global quality rating of brewery sites producing Guinness Foreign Extra Stout.[42] In the same vein, Superbrands, one of the world's leading global brand rating agencies operating in 73 countries around the world, has ranked three of Guinness Nigeria's top brands among the top 100 brands in all market categories in Nigeria.[43] Guinness Nigeria had an estimated staff strength of 1700 employees in 2010.[44]

Owing to Guinness Nigeria's popularity, it is considered a Nigerian brand rather than an Irish brand by most Nigerians. Nigeria overtook Ireland to become Guinness' second-biggest market outside the UK in 2009.[45]

Nigerian Breweries

Nigerian Breweries is Nigeria's largest brewer and a subsidiary company of the Europe-based Heineken Holding N.V. group (Heineken owns 54.1 % of Nigerian Breweries shares). Its first brewery was commissioned in Lagos in 1949,[46] and five others were subsequently established in Aba (1957), Kaduna (1963), Ibadan (1982), Enugu (1993) and Ama (2003), providing a geographical spread across the country, albeit with a bias for cities in the southern part of Nigeria.[47] The most recently established is the Ama plant, which the company in 2003 described as the biggest brewery plant in Nigeria and the most modern in the world. The Ama plant gave Nigerian Breweries a distribution advantage in the eastern region market. In addition to Heineken N.V.'s 54.1 % stake in Nigerian Breweries, Heineken N.V. also acquired a 50.05 % controlling stake in Consolidated Breweries in 2004.[48] Consolidated Breweries was in 2003 Nigeria's third-largest brewer, concentrating traditionally on the low-price end of the market. Their principal products are "33" Export Lager and Hi-Malt.[49] However, Consolidated Breweries and Nigerian Breweries have continued to operate as separate entities, focusing on different segments of the beer market. Heineken's acquisition of Consolidated Breweries set the tone for the acquisition of cheaper Nigerian brands by Nigerian Breweries.

Nigerian Breweries had a production capacity of 10 million hectoliters in 2010.[50] Heineken shows considerable commitment to the African market, with its investment in Nigeria its largest outside Europe, and capacity increases and improvement of distribution channels have all been pursued to consolidate its market position. In the first quarter of 2011, Heineken purchased two holding companies from the Sona Group and consequently acquired control of the Sona, IBBI, Benue, Life and Champion breweries. The move helped Heineken add 3.7 million hectoliters to its Nigerian capacity.[51] Heineken's former president for Africa and the Middle East, Mr. Tom de Man, said:

> *This important move reflects Heineken's strategy of increasing our exposure to and growth from developing markets, ... the acquisition will significantly strengthen our platform for future growth.*[52]

Management re-launched the Gulder and Amstel Malt brands in 2009 and 2010, respectively, and introduced the Fayrouz soft drink to Nigeria in order to appeal to Nigeria's large Muslim population. In 2007, the company also commissioned a canning line at its Lagos brewery and launched Heineken, Star and Amstel Malt in can packages. Sales volumes immediately went up by 24.5 %, and the company invested in operations expansion.[53] Nigerian Breweries also plans to establish a new bottling line at its Aba brewery and to undertake structural extensions of its Lagos and Kaduna plants. Nigerian Breweries was listed on the Nigerian Stock Exchange in 1973.[54]

Product Brands

Star Lager, the flagship brand of Nigerian Breweries, was introduced into the Nigerian market in 1949 as the first indigenous beer brand.[55] The beer market had hitherto been dominated exclusively by imported brands. Shortly after its entry into the market, the beer quickly overcame the problems of market acceptance. Star was largely responsible for the growth of the Nigerian indigenous beer industry. The popularity gave other prospective investors courage to consider the establishment of new breweries.

Gulder Lager was introduced in 1970, marketed toward the confident and socially active consumer driven by a desire for success. Gulder was re-launch in a brown 60cl bottle (at the time of re-launch, the only brown bottle in Nigeria). Gulder has a 5.2 % alcohol content and is available in many parts of West Africa, specifically Ghana, Republic of

Benin and Togo,[57] and it is also exported to the United Kingdom and other parts of Europe.

Maltina, Nigeria's premier malt drink, is available in four varieties (Maltina classic, Maltina strawberry, Maltina exotic and Maltina with pineapple). Amstel Malt is also locally brewed. The company delivered its products through 147 key distributors and wholesalers in 2006.[58] Nigerian Breweries does not own the logistics related to the distribution of its products. However, its key distributors are carefully selected to ensure that the company's products are available across Nigeria.[59]

In 2010 Nigerian Breweries ran at about 75 % of capacity (7.5 million hectolitres of approximately 10 million hectolitres installed capacity). Management has announced that it is currently optimizing its facility, which will translate to an additional 20 % capacity (i.e. 12 million hectolitres of estimated installed capacity).[60]

The Entry of SABMiller, Castle and Carlsberg

SABMiller is among the top four global brewers, and it operates on six continents.[61] In 2010 it was the largest brewer in Africa and controlled an 88 % market share of the South African beer market.[62] The company also had a local presence in Tanzania, Zimbabwe and Mozambique.[63] However, the time appeared to be right to change gears, as the brewer identified Nigeria as its next growth frontier. It made a strategic entry in 2008 via the acquisition of 57 % effective interest in Pabod Breweries Limited, using an 80 % effective interest in Voltic Nigeria Limited (a water business) and an interest in Standard Breweries Limited as a launching pad.[64] When SABMiller acquired it, Pabod had a brewing capacity of 250,000 hectolitres, though actual production was about 30,000 hectolitres. SABMiller stated that it would expand Pabod's production capacity to 250,000 hectolitres by 2011.[65] It subsequently announced that it would construct a new greenfield brewery plant in Onitsha in southeast Nigeria with a capacity of 500,000 hectolitres. The plant, completed in September 2012, was part of the company's US$100 million capital expenditures plan over the period 2011–2013.[66] SABMiller has been perceived by industry analysts as being slow in making much-needed investments to expand production capacity.

Carlsberg, the fourth-largest brewer in the world, also made a leveraged entry into the Nigerian market. The company entered a partnership agreement with International Breweries Plc for the production and commercialization of its notable trademarks, Kronenbourg and Wilfort.[67] International Breweries was a small regional player whose core market was in the southwestern part of Nigeria. Carlsberg subsequently acquired a majority stake in International Breweries Plc, one of the fringe players quoted on the Nigerian Stock Exchange, with an installed capacity of about 500,000 hectolitres. Historical performance had been troubled, as evidenced by 11 years of operating losses.[68] It was expected that Carlsberg coming on board and the full optimization of an ongoing capital expenditure programme should set the stage for a turnaround.

While the new entrants were yet to rile up the sector, industry analysts thought that these multiple entries would significantly transform the sector's economics in the long term.[69]

What Next?

Beginning in 2010, growth of beer sales increased significantly across all segments. Since then, Nigerian Breweries and Guinness have invested massively in expanding capacity and acquiring new plants, and sales figures have risen to levels far beyond the expectations of investors (Figs. 6.3, 6.4, 6.5, 6.6, 6.7, 6.8 and 6.9).

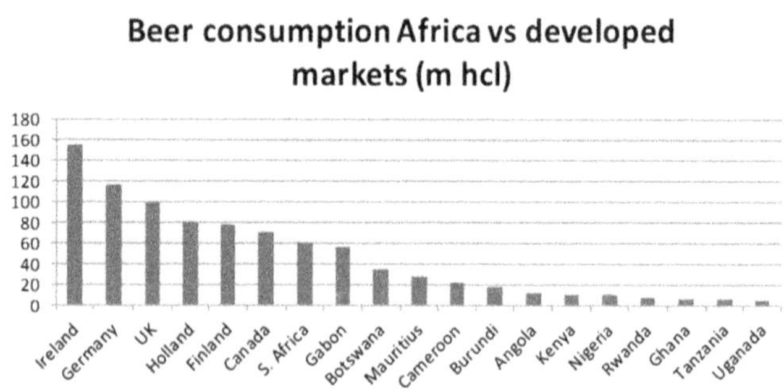

Fig. 6.3 Beer consumption: Africa versus developed markets. *Source*: Adapted from FBN Capital Nigerian Breweries Sector Coverage 2010, research report

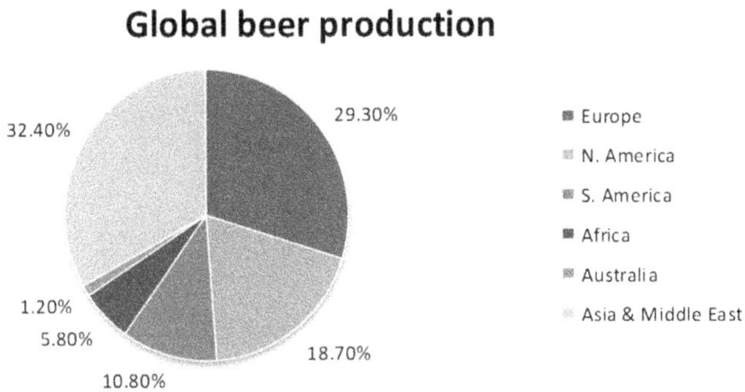

Fig. 6.4 Global beer production. *Source*: Adapted from FBN Capital Nigerian Breweries Sector Coverage 2010, research report

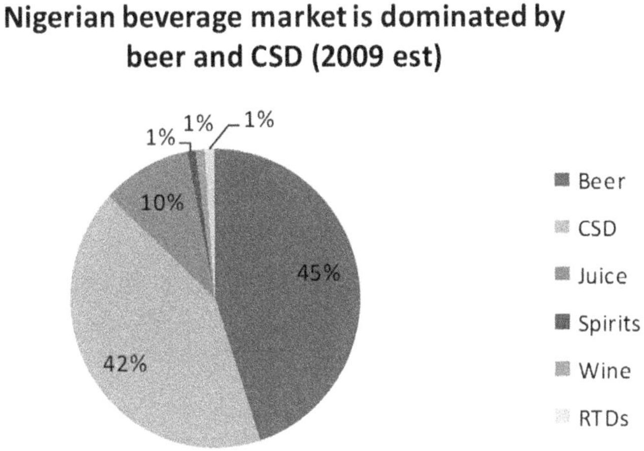

Fig. 6.5 The Nigerian beverage market. *Source*: Adapted from Vetiva Capital Management, Nigerian Breweries Sector, 2010 research report

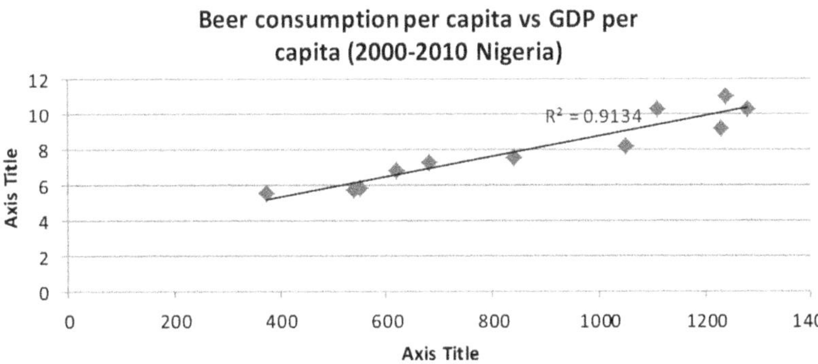

Fig. 6.6 Per capita beer consumption in Nigeria. *Source*: Adapted from FBN Capital Nigerian Breweries Sector Coverage 2010, research report

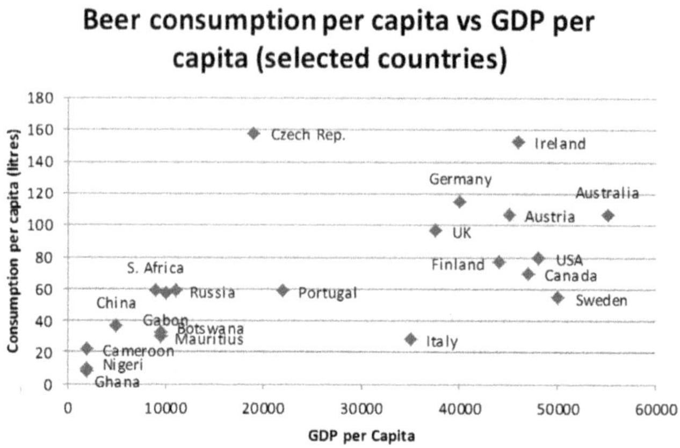

Fig. 6.7 Per capita beer consumption versus GDP per capita in selected countries. *Source*: Adapted from FBN Capital Nigerian Breweries Sector Coverage 2010, research report

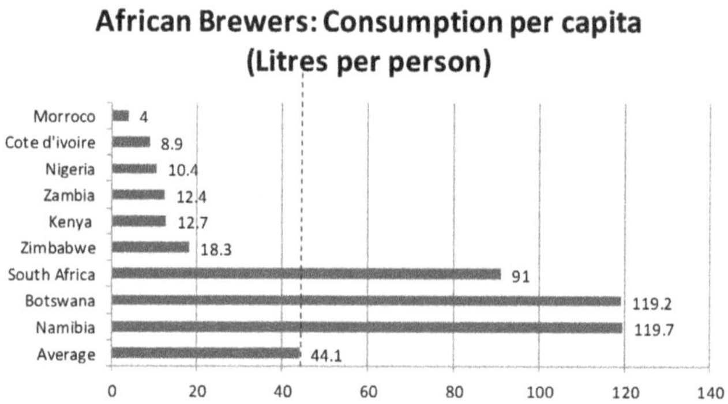

Fig. 6.8 African brewers: Consumption per capita in 2010. *Source*: Adapted from Vetiva Capital Management, Nigerian Breweries Sector, 2010 research report

Was the strategy of remaining a premium player sustainable? Or did the existing incumbents have to figure out how best to tap into the informal liquor market by converting non-beer drinkers into beer drinkers? Was a strategy of expanding their offering of non-alcoholic brands more effective? What best could they do to consolidate their hold on their distribution networks? How easy would it be for the new entrants to create new networks? These were the questions staring the dominant players in the face in the light of the new threats (Tables 6.1, 6.2 and 6.3).

Fig. 6.9 Location of brewery plants in Nigeria in 2010. *Source*: Adapted from Vetiva Capital Management, Nigerian Breweries Sector, 2010 research report

Table 6.1 Beer volume statistics (see Fig. 2)

Beer volume statistics			
Back-of-the-envelope estimates of growth potential			
	Nigeria	**China**	**South Africa**
Population share (%)	2.2	19.8	0.7
Beer volume share (%)	0.8	22.8	1.6
Beer volume share-to-population share	0.34×	1.15×	2.23×
Actual beer PCC (litres) p.a.	**9.71**	**30.94**	**59.83**
Implied estimates			
Potential beer volume share (%)	3.8	33.4	1.2
Implied beer production level (mhl)	68.1	601.1	21.2
Current beer production (mhl)	15.1	401.0	28.0
Production (deficit)/surplus (mhl)	(53.0)	(200.1)	6.8
Implied beer PCC (litres) p.a.	**45.4**	**45.4**	**45.2**
Implied growth (%)	**367.3**	**46.7**	**–24.4**

Source: Adapted from Vetiva Capital Management, Nigerian Breweries Sector, 2010 research report
PCC p.a. – Per Capita Consumption Per Annum; mhl – Million hectoliters

Table 6.2 Financial performance of Guinness 2006–2010

	2006	2007	2008	2009	2010
Market position					
Nigerian beer market size (mhl)	11	12.5	14.5	15	16.42
Beer market volume growth (%)	22.2	13.6	16	3.4	9.4
Population (million)	140	143.85	147.81	151.87	156.05
Beer PCC (litres)	7.86	8.69	9.81	9.88	10.52
Guinness market share (%)	25	24	25	26	28
Guinness volume	2.75	3	3.63	3.9	4.6
Naira Price/mhl	19,510	20,755	19,082	22,859	23,544
Growth (%)					
Volume (%)	22	9	21	8	18
Price/mhl (%)	–7	6	–8	20	3
Turnover (%)	14	16	11	29	23
Core operating profit (%)	5	16	19	23	–2
EBITDA (%)	8	14	18	22	0
PBT (%)	15	29	245	10	0
PAT (%)	53	43	12	14	1
Profitability					
Return on equity (%)	38	40	35	40	42
Return on assets (%)	14	16	16	18	18
Margins					
Gross margin (%)	48	45	49	48	44
EBITDA margin (%)	28	27	29	27	22
EBIT margin (%)	23	23	25	24	19
PBT margin (%)	21	24	27	23	19
Net profit margin (%)	14	17	17	15	13
Per share data					
EPS	6.31	7.19	8.04	9.18	9.31
DPS	4.00	4.50	6.00	7.50	8.25
Sales/share	45.47	42.22	46.90	60.44	74.15

Source: Adapted from Guinness Nigeria Plc. 2010 annual reports and accounts
EBITDA – Earnings Before Interest, Tax, Depreciation and Ammortization,
EBT – Earnings Before Tax, PBT – Profit Before Tax, PAT – Profit After Tax,
EPS – Earnings Per Share, DPS – Dividend Per Share

Table 6.3 Financial performance of Nigerian Breweries (NB) 2007–2009

	2007	2008	2009
Market position			
Nigerian beer market size (mhl)	12.5	14.5	15
Beer market volume growth (%)	13.6	16	3.4
Population (million)	144	148	152
Beer PCC (litres)	8.69	9.81	9.88
NB's market share (%)	56	57	60
NB's volume	7	8.3	9
Price/mhl	15,964	17,600	18,245
Growth			
Volume (%)	16	18	9
Price/mhl (%)	12	10	4
Turnover (%)	29	30	13
Core operating profit (%)	61	35	13
EBITDA (%)	45	31	14
PBT (%)	70	35	10
PAT (%)	74	36	9
Profitability			
Return on equity (%)	48	68	71
Return on assets (%)	23	26	26
Margins			
Gross margin (%)	53	49	46
EBITDA margin (%)	29	29	30
EBIT/sales (%)	24	25	25
PBT/sales (%)	25	26	25
Net profit margin (%)	17	18	17

Source: Adapted from Nigeria Breweries Plc. 2010 annual reports and accounts
EBITDA – Earnings Before Interest, Tax, Depreciation and Ammortization,
EBT – Earnings Before Tax, PBT – Profit Before Tax, PAT – Profit After Tax,
EPS – Earnings Per Share, DPS – Dividend Per Share

Notes

1. http://en.wikipedia.org/wiki/List_of_countries_by_alcohol_consumption accessed on 07/09/2010.
2. Heineken International Website (http://www.heinekeninternational.com accessed on 07/09/2010).
3. Guinness Nigeria 2010 Annual Reports and Accounts; Nigerian Breweries 2010 Annual Reports and Accounts.
4. http://www.developtechnology.co.za/index.php?option=com_content&task=view&id=21848&Itemid=31 accessed on 07/09/2010.

5. The base of the pyramid is the largest but poorest socio-economic group in Nigeria.
6. Vetiva Capital Management Ltd., Nigerian Breweries Sector Research, 2009.
7. FBN Capital Nigerian Breweries Sector Coverage 2010.
8. Vetiva Capital Management Ltd., Nigerian Breweries Sector, 2010.
9. FBN Capital Nigerian Breweries Sector Coverage 2010.
10. Nigerian Bureau of Statistics (http://www.nigerianstat.gov.ng accessed on 06/09/2005).
11. Nigerian Bureau of Statistics (http://www.nigerianstat.gov.ng accessed on 06/09/2010).
12. Nigerian Stock Exchange (http://www.nse.gov.ng accessed on 08/09/2010).
13. Vetiva Capital Management Ltd., Nigerian Breweries Sector, 2010.
14. Analysis of Incentives and Disincentives for Sorghum Production in Nigeria, Food and Agriculture Organization (http://www.fao.org/3/a-at583e.pdf).
15. Oyedoyin, B. O., Adeniyi, A. A., & Ilori, M. O. (2008). The Policy on Local Raw Material Substitution in the Food and Beverage Industry in Southwestern Nigeria. *Journal of Industrial Research and Technology, 2*, 73–86.
16. Sorghum Beer Across Cultures—Beer and Brewing) (http://www.bellaonline.com/articles/art58046.asp accessed on 09/09/2010)).
17. Vetiva Capital Management Ltd., Nigerian Breweries Sector, 2010.
18. FBN Capital Nigerian Breweries Sector Coverage 2010.
19. Vetiva Capital Management Ltd., Nigerian Breweries Sector, 2010.
20. Vetiva Capital Management Ltd., Nigerian Breweries Sector, 2010.
21. Ali, A. N., & Iwuchukwu, C. U. (2015). Socio-Economic Impact of Nigerian Brewery Industry in Kaduna South Local Government Area of Kaduna State, Nigeria. *Mediterranean Journal of Social Sciences*, *6*(6 S4), 59.
22. Malomo, O. (2015). The Nigeria Beer Story. *Int. J. Curr. Microbiol. App. Sci.*, *4*(2), 1037–1052.
23. Malomo, O. (2015). The Nigeria Beer Story. *Int. J. Curr. Microbiol. App. Sci.*, *4*(2), 1037–1052.
24. Brewing—United Nations University (http://archive.unu.edu/unupress/unupbooks/uu34ee/uu34ee0o.htm accessed on 09/08/2014).
25. Nigerian Breweries—New Telegraph's top 100 companies (http://newtelegraphonline.com/new-telegraphs-2014-top-100-companies-in-nigeria-2/) accessed in 12/03/2014.
26. Guinness Website (http://www.guinness-nigeria.com/about/overview/) accessed on 09/08/2014.
27. GAIN Report—Foreign Agricultural Service (http://apps.fas.usda.gov/gainfiles/200307/145985539.pdf) accessed on 09/10/2010.

28. Heineiken NV—Reference for Business (http://www.referenceforbusiness.com/history2/2/**Heineken**-N-V.html) accessed on 09/12/2014.
29. Malomo, O. (2015). The Nigeria Beer Story. *Int. J. Curr. Microbiol. App. Sci.*, *4*(2), 1037–1052.
30. Brewers on the rise—Vetiva Capital Management Ltd, Brewery Sector Coverage 2009.
31. SABMiller's website (http://www.sabmiller.com accessed on 09/10/2011).
32. Heineken Holding N.V. 2010 Full Results.
33. Capital Bancorp Plc, Nigerian Breweries Equity Research Report (http://admin.capitalbancorpng.com/portal_reports/NIGERIAN%20BREWERIES%20PLC.pdf) accessed on 09/12/2013.
34. Capital Bancorp Plc, Nigerian Breweries Equity Research Report (http://admin.capitalbancorpng.com/portal_reports/NIGERIAN%20BREWERIES%20PLC.pdf) accessed on 09/12/2013.
35. Malomo, O. (2015). The Nigeria Beer Story. *Int. J. Curr. Microbiol. App. Sci.*, *4*(2), 1037–1052.
36. Vetiva Capital Management Ltd., Nigerian Breweries Sector, 2010.
37. Malomo, O. (2015). The Nigeria Beer Story. *Int. J. Curr. Microbiol. App. Sci.*, *4*(2), 1037–1052.
38. Guinness Website (http://www.guinness-nigeria.com/about/overview/) accessed on 09/08/2014.
39. http://cpgconnect.ca/company-profiles/company-info/Diageo/441 (accessed on 09/10/2013).
40. Guinness Nigeria's Website (http://www.guinness-nigeria.com) and Guinness 2010 Annual Reports and Accounts.
41. Guinness Nigeria, 2010 Annual Reports and Accounts.
42. Guinness Nigeria, 2007 Annual Reports and Accounts.
43. Guinness Nigeria, 2007 Annual Reports and Accounts.
44. Guinness Nigeria, 2010 Annual Reports and Accounts.
45. http://www.theguardian.com/business/2007/aug/30/9 (accessed on 09/10/2011).
46. Nigerian Breweries 2010 Annual Reports and Accounts; Nigerian Breweries Website (http://www.nbplc.com).
47. Nigerian Breweries Website (http://www.nbplc.com/ourcompany.html#) accessed on 09/10/2011.
48. Heineken Annual Report 2004.
49. http://www.consobrew.com.
50. http://www.corporate-nigeria.com/index/industry/beer-industry.html (accessed on 09/10/2010).

51. http://www.bloomberg.com/news/articles/2011-01-12/heineken-buys-two-sona-companies-to-boost-its-brewery-capacity-in-nigeria (accessed on 09/10/2010).
52. http://www.beveragedaily.com/Manufacturers/Heineken-buys-up-five-Nigerian-breweries (accessed on 09/10/2012).
53. Afrinvest Report on the Non-financials Sector, 2008—(http://naijalowa.com/wp-content/uploads/Afrinvest_Report_on_The_Nigerian_Non-Financials_Sector_(2008)_-_Pt._2.pdf) accessed on 09/10/2010.
54. http://www.africanselect.com/scripts/cgiip.wsc/tradeone/html/quote_and_news.r?pisharetype-id=6095 (accessed on 09/10/2010).
55. http://www.africanselect.com/scripts/cgiip.wsc/tradeone/html/quote_and_news.r?pisharetype-id=6095 (accessed on 09/10/2010).
56. http://www.thedrinkshop.com/products/nlpdetail.php?prodid=4425 (accessed on 09/10/2010).
57. Vetiva Capital Management Ltd., Nigerian Breweries Sector, 2010.
58. Nigerian Breweries 2010 Annual Reports and Accounts.
59. Nigerian Breweries 2010 Annual Reports and Accounts.
60. Nigerian Breweries 2010 Annual Reports and Accounts.
61. http://www.sabmiller.com/about-us/where-we-operate
62. http://www.sabmiller.com/docs/default-source/investor-documents/reports/2010/sustainability/working-for-south-africa-2010.pdf?sfvrsn=4
63. Nigerian Breweries 2010 Annual Reports and Accounts; Nigerian Breweries Website (http://www.nbplc.com).
64. Vetiva Capital Management Ltd., Nigerian Breweries Sector, 2010.
65. Vetiva Capital Management Ltd., Nigerian Breweries Sector, 2010.
66. http://www.southafrica.info/business/trends/global/sabmiller-310812.htm#.VpC8B_krLIU (accessed on 09/12/12).
67. Vetiva Capital Management Ltd., Nigerian Breweries Sector, 2010.
68. Vetiva Capital Management Ltd., Nigerian Breweries Sector, 2010.
69. Vetiva Capital Management Ltd., Nigerian Breweries Sector, 2010.

7

Sasol's Changing Landscape in and with Mozambique

Lyal White and Dianna Games

The Context of Sasol's Transformation Journey in Mozambique

When he first took over the reins at the Sasol Group in 2011 as the chief executive officer, David Constable[1] noticed that instead of operating as one big team, the company's units operated as separate and often competing groups.

> *When I started at Sasol, what surprised me the most was not the apparent lack of a long term game plan, but rather what can best be likened to many teams all playing different sports. I realised early on that when Sasol people speak of "us" and "them", they are often referring to their Sasol colleagues: whether they speak*

Case study researched and written by Dianna Games, CEO of business research and advisory company Africa @ Work and Center for Dynamic Markets (CDM) Fellow at the Gordon Institute of Business Science, and Prof Lyal White, Director of the Centre for Dynamic Markets, Gordon Institute of Business Science (GIBS). The paper was originally produced on behalf of Sasol by GIBS.

L. White (✉) • D. Games
Gordon Institute of Business Sciences, Illovo, Johannesburg, South Africa
e-mail: Whitel@gibs.co.za

I. Adeleye et al. (eds.), *Africa-to-Africa Internationalization*, AIB Sub-Saharan Africa (SSA) Series, DOI 10.1007/978-3-319-30692-6_7

of this notion of the business unit versus "Group" or whether they are referring to the seemingly great divide between certain businesses, or between businesses and the functions. Clearly, this "us" versus "them" notion in the context of a single group of companies is both counter-productive and destructive.

Here, I found individuals and teams of Sasol people doing business with each other and often competing against each other instead of against our competitors in the market place. At Sasol, I found teams confused as to the game they were playing and the opponents they were pitted against. How do we plan to be a great company, if we are not all playing the same game as one team with the same definition of winning?[2]

The One Sasol, One Bottom Line transformation journey was designed to address the rivalry and inefficiency resulting from the bureaucracy, silos and lack of integration Constable noticed when he took over, and to restructure the organisation to align the Sasol organisation to work towards company-wide strategic goals and one bottom line.

A Brief Background to Sasol

Sasol, established in South Africa in 1950 and now one of the country's biggest companies, is a global integrated energy and chemicals organisation. It employs more than 30,000 people in 37 countries ranging from the USA and Germany to Mozambique and South Africa. The company, which is listed on the Johannesburg and New York stock exchanges, develops and commercialises technologies. It is a global leader in the development of liquid fuels, chemicals and energy solutions. It also refines crude oil, mines coal, produces natural gas and extracts shale gas.

Historically, Sasol was a critical resource during the time of the fuel embargoes against South Africa during apartheid. Its first major project was a plant to manufacture fuel from coal, resulting in the emergence of an industrial town named after the company, Sasolburg. Since this strategic positioning in apartheid South Africa, Sasol has developed other world-class technologies. Sasol's giant Secunda Complex, in the South African region of Mpumalanga, is the world's largest producer of fuels and chemicals from coal and gas. Sasol's move into natural gas has been more recent, driven by the gas resources it is exploiting in Mozambique.

Sasol's largest international facility is the Lake Charles Chemical Complex in Louisiana in the USA. The US $8.9 billion facility comprises seven manufacturing units making products used in the cleaning and personal care markets, including soaps, detergents, shampoos and cosmetics, and specialty chemicals used in mild abrasives, thickeners and pharmaceuticals.

Sasol is going ahead with an $8 billion petrochemical complex in the USA, in addition to the existing facility, but it has put on hold a planned $14 billion gas-to-liquids plant at the Lake Charles facility because low oil prices have made the project unviable at this stage.[3]

In terms of Sasol's Africa operations, Mozambique is a priority. The company is increasing its offtake of gas from Mozambique for use in South Africa's energy sector. It is also undertaking a feasibility study in partnership with Mozambique's state oil company and Italian resources multinational Eni on building a large gas-to-liquids plant in northern Mozambique to exploit the large gas resources found recently off the northern coast of Mozambique.[4]

The Mozambique Story

Mozambique, despite discoveries within its national boundaries of what are now known to be among the world's biggest gas deposits, remains one of Africa's poorest and most underdeveloped countries. When colonial rule ended quite suddenly in 1975, most skilled Portuguese workers and professionals rapidly departed, weakening the country and its institutions. The ruling party, Frelimo, established a one-party socialist state. In 1977, a civil war broke out between Frelimo and rebel group, Renamo, which was supported by apartheid South Africa and former Rhodesian military elements. The conflict lasted until 1992, when political changes in South Africa led to declining support for the rebels and a political solution. But the conflict had resulted in the destruction of infrastructure, property and governance across most of the country.

The economy floundered, not just because of the war but also because of weak governance, ineffective socialist economic policies and successive natural disasters. Investment was scarce, leaving the government dependent on external aid. Jobs outside government were also in short supply.

A peace deal signed in the early 1990s, and the successful conclusion of the first multi-party election in 1994 helped the country get back on its feet and move towards a market-driven economy. The government used the concept of mega-projects to boost the country's visibility to and attraction for investors. The first such project was the $2 billion Mozal aluminium smelter, owned jointly by BHP Billiton, Industrial Development Corporation of South Africa and the Mozambique government. Built just outside Maputo, it was launched in 2000 as part of a state-led economic recovery programme. The second mega-project was Sasol's $1.2 billion pipeline to take gas from the fields of central Mozambique to Secunda, in South Africa's industrial heartland. The Mozambican government flagged these projects to showcase the ability of the country to absorb large investments and respond to investor demands. There have been many other sizable resource projects since then.

Mozambicans complain that few benefits have trickled down into the economy from such projects, particularly given incentives for investors. However, this stance discounts the fact that these projects have created thousands of jobs, both temporary and permanent. Sasol's expansion of its Mozambique plant created 600 jobs, along with procurement opportunities for Mozambicans worth $64 million.[5] Companies have injected millions into state coffers in taxes. The oil and gas industry accounts for more than 60 % of the government's total tax take, and Sasol contributes more than half of this.[6]

But Mozambicans are right to be concerned. In spite of high growth rates averaging 8 % for a decade, the country remains one of Africa's poorest, lingering among the bottom 10 countries as measured by the United Nations Human Development Index.[7] Mozambique remains dependent on donor funding for a large chunk of its budget, and most people are employed in subsistence agriculture. The growth has been focused largely on activities in and around the capital and in resource-rich pockets of the country.

The 2012 discovery of massive gas deposits in the Rovuma Basin off the northern coast by international operators has given Mozambique's fortunes a significant boost. It is now the third-largest gas reserve holder in Africa, after Algeria and Nigeria, and one of the top 10 globally. Up to $30 billion in initial investment is expected from the public and private sectors into the development of facilities to produce up to 20 million tons a year of liquefied natural gas (LNG), starting in 2018, according to state energy company, ENH.[8]

In 2015, the government conducted a new licensing bidding round for the exploration and production concessions for 15 new gas blocks in three offshore and two onshore blocks, including the Pande-Temane area where Sasol already operates.[9] Sasol said two of its three applications were successful.[10]

The government hopes the gas boom will end its donor dependence and enable it to tackle pervasive poverty. In this regard, it has become more assertive about the benefits for locals from the commercial exploitation of natural resources existing. In addition to local content obligations for foreign investors in natural resource sectors, it has recently updated legislation regarding the hydrocarbons industry to maximise benefits from new gas finds. For example, operators will have to be listed on the Mozambique STOCK EXCHANGE, commit to channelling 25 % of gas produced to the domestic market, and let state-owned ENH take the lead in marketing gas production.[11]

Sasol in Mozambique

Sasol was first-to-market in Mozambique's gas sector, starting exploration in the late 1990s to source energy for the growing South African market. It bought an exploration licence for the Pande and Temane gas fields in southern Mozambique, and in 2002 a deal was signed for a $1.2 billion, 865km pipeline to move the gas from the fields to South Africa's industrial heartland. The project, backed by both governments, was co-funded by the World Bank, the European Investment Bank and other institutions.

Sasol owns 50 % of the pipeline company, the Republic of Mozambique Pipeline Investments Company (Rompco), with the remainder held by the Mozambique government (25 %) and South Africa's state gas infrastructure company, IGas. Most of the gas is used by Sasol for power generation and downstream products, and it also sells to local industrial users in South Africa.

The gas partnership was forecast to boost Mozambique's gross domestic product significantly. The country was expected to receive up to $2 billion in royalties and taxes over the project's 25-year lifespan, with South Africa receiving gas for a quarter of a century, based on projected production and consumption rates.[12]

Since Sasol's inception, growing demand has led to the expansion of the company's Mozambique facilities. In 2012, a central processing facility (CPF) was inaugurated by former Mozambican president Armando Guebuza at Sasol's Temane plant. In August 2014, the 175-megawatt Central Térmica de Ressano Garcia (CTRG) power station, a partnership between state hydrocarbons company EDM (51 %) and Sasol (49 %) was inaugurated near the South African border at Ressano Garcia. Gas from the pipeline now provides power for 23 % of the Mozambican population.

CTRG, the country's first permanent, large-scale gas-to-power facility, will help supply a market where demand for power is growing at 14 % annually.[13] The power station represents a significant step for Sasol in terms of its stakeholder engagement in Mozambique as it gives the company an opportunity to highlight the benefits of a successful partnership between the state and a foreign multinational, adding impetus to Sasol's first-mover advantage.

By the end of 2014, Sasol had invested about $3 billion in Mozambique, which includes the development and expansion of the CPF and natural gas fields in southern Mozambique, the pipeline construction and the CTRG power project.

The company has big plans for Mozambique. As mentioned above, it won two out of three concessions applied for in the 2015 fifth licensing round, and it is also developing the Inhassoro oil field near its current gas field, the first area in Mozambique to show signs of oil.[14] It is also looking at a joint venture with Italy's Eni, one of the two international oil majors active in the Rovuma Basin, and the state's ENH to build a 96,000-barrel-per-day gas-to-liquids plant in the future.

The new gas finds mean Sasol will, for the first time in its activity in Mozambique, have competition from other international companies, such as Italy's Eni and the USA's Anadarko, their partners and other new players. Its first-mover advantage is under threat.

It is therefore important for Sasol to highlight and improve its local partnerships to ensure it maintains a positive and visible profile in this changing market. As Constable said, Sasol's progress to date in Mozambique has been made possible through strong partnerships.

"For me, partnerships cut across all levels and all areas of society and business. And successful partnerships depend on having a clear and common goal."[15] Sasol's new strategy allows all parts of the company to contribute to that common goal and use it as a platform from which to engage stakeholders and partners in order to create value for the company in all its enterprises.

The Changing Dynamics of Sasol

It is clear that Sasol's interest in Mozambique's oil and gas sector is a long-term play. Thus, its terms of engagement with the state, with communities, with suppliers and with its own staff are key to ensuring future success in this important market.

The company faces many issues in Mozambique that are not present in its other country operations, and there are a number of specific considerations it needs to take into account in doing business in Mozambique, where context is all-important. These include:

- The economic and social environment, which is linked to the state's changing attitude to the exploitation of its resources;
- Whether it has used first-mover advantage sufficiently in positioning itself for future competition;
- Whether it has prioritised technical considerations over the cultural context of Mozambique in a way that has undermined its first-mover advantage;
- How its local staff add value to the local operations and contribute to the company as a whole;
- Whether its local empowerment measures have gone far enough to underpin its market advantage in Mozambique;
- Whether proximity to the head office in South Africa has been positive or negative for relationships with investors and people in Mozambique, compared with other locations further afield;
- How to manage inevitable tensions between Sasol's world-class corporate governance principles and realities on the ground, especially challenges in this regard experienced by its staff in an underdeveloped market;

- Communication between the different technical units of Sasol and the two Mozambique operations to ensure a streamlined approach without diminishing the need for specific technical and operational lines of reporting.

"One Sasol" in Mozambique

As outlined above, Sasol has restructured its complex organisation to increase efficiencies and bolster the bottom line. The integrated operating model is designed to streamline formerly complex and inefficient administrative and reporting structures whilst inculcating an ethos of empowered accountability among staff by focusing on a common game plan and one bottom line. This matrix structure is not country-focused but instead aligns units according to operational cohesion, allowing for greater sharing of information and increased flexibility.

This section examines the One Sasol concept in terms of the Mozambique operations, where Sasol Exploration and Petroleum International (SEPI) is the lead unit. It examines the issues Sasol has experienced with regard to the Mozambique operation and the leadership competencies required for its success in the specific context of that country.

One Sasol Approach and Mind-Set

"You can't be one Sasol in London and another Sasol in Mozambique." one of Sasol's Mozambican executives maintains, highlighting the challenge faced by this global company in its transformation journey. The fact that the company has disparate operations across so many countries at different levels of development makes it vital that core, standardised company-wide principles and practices are developed and adopted.

New resource discoveries have positioned Mozambique as a key market for Sasol, which has pushed operations up a gear.

In the past, Sasol tended to run Mozambique as a satellite operation of the South African head office in order to avoid the challenges of the local environment. This practice was feasible because the location of the plant was a short charter flight away, but it was not favoured by Mozambicans who felt marginalised from the global organisation. The new One Sasol model is slowly changing this by integrating the country operation with the broader organisation, and more attention is being given to local stakeholder management.

Micro-managing Mozambique from Johannesburg has been a hard habit to break, however. The country's proximity to South Africa has been a double-edged sword. The differences in the countries' development levels, business practices, mind-sets, cultures and economic maturity are stark. Mozambique has typically been regarded by South Africans as a poor and inferior neighbour, a deep-seated view that affects the engagement with local operations. In the early years, this proximity precluded the need to involve the Mozambique office in Maputo in matters outside of stakeholder relations and operational issues. Local managers had little autonomy, and their authority was undermined when they were bypassed by executives flying in and out of the country. In operations further afield, however, the operating model of necessity favours an independent local office with real autonomy to which executives defer when they travel there.

The convenience of Mozambique's proximity, it is suggested, has left Sasol with a legacy issue—a perception that it has exploited Mozambicans without paying sufficient attention to local development and creating tangible benefits for locals from its investment. The beneficiary, in the eyes of many locals, is South Africa, not Mozambique.

Sasol's overly complex corporate structure has been a complicating factor for bilateral relations, making it difficult for Sasol Petroleum Mozambique to engage with the head office. Multiple layers of reporting compromised the running of the office and added to costs. A blueprint for empowerment drawn up a few years ago and the introduction of the One Sasol strategy are changing the situation.

The new structure has collected upstream operations into one unit, SEPI, which is the main line of reporting for the plant management team. The Mozambique country manager in Maputo is responsible for operations, stakeholder engagement and business development. Under the new arrangement, the manager reports directly to SEPI in areas relating to the gas operations but also has functional accountability to other units in the Sasol Group. Several core functions located in the Maputo office, including policy and regulatory affairs, finance and human resources, are now directly linked to head office.

The change has not just been about streamlining operational and communication structures. Drawing the local offices into the global unit and making them actively part of a much bigger entity has given the Mozambicans working in them a greater sense of ownership, which has been a catalyst for greater accountability and performance. The Maputo office now serves all units of Sasol, not just SEPI.

But it is taking time for the mind-set to change. As one Mozambican said: "They have given us the keys to the car, now they need to let us drive it without following to see how we are driving."

Shaping Strategy

Sasol's Mozambique strategy is driven entirely from South Africa, even as it builds capability in the local market. The focus of that strategy has been primarily on diversifying energy sources for South Africa, but with new resource finds the plan is evolving.

Its weakness in the past has been a strategy focus on operational, financial and technical issues related to the development of natural resources. It has not adequately recognised the importance of local empowerment as a core component of building a long-term and sustainable business in another country. This is important for a number of reasons, including the fact that Sasol is exploiting Mozambique's natural resources for its own gain and needs to ensure the sustainability of that operation politically, economically and socially. Building capacity and skills in the local market underpins successful stakeholder engagement, which is particularly necessary as competition in the market grows.

Although the operational side of the business is in the hands of experts, many of the South Africans driving and implementing strategy are not sufficiently familiar with the soft issues in Mozambique, notably local business and political culture. Mozambicans believe they have not achieved real monetary value out of Sasol's presence in Mozambique because of a deal in the company's favour struck by the company on entry. This remains a legacy issue despite more recent advances in local empowerment.

Managing expectations is crucial in a poor, developing country. Mozambique requires a different model from, for example, Germany or the USA. For example, certain types of technology may not be utilised in Mozambique if doing so would result in reduced job numbers; this more people-intensive orientation is part of the company's social investment.

Because of local content regulations in Mozambique, another challenge faced by Sasol is the need to procure a range of non-specialist goods and services from local suppliers. Although it seems reasonable, this requirement does not take into account the fact that the local private sector comprises mostly small and medium enterprises, and there is almost no industrial capacity outside multinational companies and little corporate experience in local companies. The need to build capacity in these companies to do work that could easily be done from South Africa is a challenge going forward that may have implications for costs and for delivery timeframes. But it is a necessary investment in the future.

Driving Accountability and High Performance

Mozambique management is still grappling with the concept of seeing SEPI as part of Sasol Ltd. "When we are asked who the Mozambique office serves, we might think SEPI but we say Sasol," said one manager. The change has required management to reorient the Maputo office to ensure it now serves all units of Sasol as part of a global operation rather than as just a one-country business. This requires a mind-set change.

Previously, problems of onerous bureaucracy and internal processes, self-interest within business units, poor communication and other issues affected the Sasol's Mozambique office, leading to the development of the One Sasol ethos. This, in turn, had implications for its relations with stakeholders, which had to be managed by the local office but often without proper support from the head office. As one interviewee said: "This situation had the potential to affect our engagement with important stakeholders such as contractors and even the government but, these people don't understand or care what Sasol's internal issues are."

A high-level, cross-border steering committee has been established to co-ordinate the activities of the different elements of the operation and discuss the strategic interests of the Mozambique operation. The committee ensures that all parties are aware of what is happening in the country. The country manager has become the "control tower".

The committee is not just about co-ordination and increasing efficiency; it also has decision-making capacity, which allows functional improvements and faster action on issues. This structure aligns the Mozambique operation with the One Sasol approach, with all elements both inside and outside the country focusing on one strategic goal.

These new structures have injected a new energy into the Mozambican operations and are having a positive impact on performance and efficiency.

Customer and Stakeholder Focus

Sasol has to satisfy a range of customers and stakeholders both at home and in Mozambique. Key among these is the government of Mozambique. Keeping the government sweet is important to project sustainability and access to new business opportunities, given that natural resources projects require government participation. As one of the first major foreign stakeholders in the Mozambican economy, Sasol is under particular scrutiny from all elements of that society, but particularly from the state, which seeks greater benefits for the country from its natural resources.

The legacy issues from the initial entry strategy have not disappeared in the wake of Sasol's proactive empowerment programmes. For example, in 2013 the Centre for Public Integrity in Mozambique issued a report indicating that the Pande-Temane gas project had failed to deliver the expected revenues for the government. Sasol, in its defence, said the company had invested heavily in post-war Mozambique at a time when perceptions of political risk were still very high, and it had to pay a premium to do so. The investment deal had cushioned this risk, but it had also been structured to increase benefits for Mozambique exponentially over time as the risk decreased.[16] The historical context of the original investment period is important for Sasol but seemingly of little interest to Mozambicans, who are focused on their specific current benefit from the investment.

It is expected that new companies entering into oil and gas investments in Mozambique will note Sasol's experience, although the context is now rather different. They are negotiating their entry at a time of economic stability and predictable policy with regard to technical, regulatory and empowerment issues. Sasol's ability to build on its first-mover position is critical going forward and will depend on strong and intuitive leadership.

Another challenge for Sasol is that of corporate governance. Sasol is governed in this regard by its listings not only in Johannesburg but also on the New York Stock Exchange. This situation binds its global operations to standards of corporate governance drawn up in developed countries, creating a particular challenge for Sasol's operations in underdeveloped Mozambique, where there is no corporate depth and certainly no local benchmarks for corporate governance.

Giving gifts, paying for officials to travel to the head office, or even simply giving villagers near the plant lifts on the back of company vehicles all flout the best practice principles governing corporate behaviour in the Sasol code of conduct. But these are standard practices in Mozambique, and the inability of managers to follow local business norms, which can include behaviour considered to be corrupt in developed markets, has a knock-on effect on the company's reputation among locals, who may see the company as being arrogant, ungenerous and out of kilter with local norms. The key to managing this lies in strategic and skilful stakeholder management. These are important issues for the leadership in South Africa to understand; while they may seem like soft issues, managing them is critical to the future of Sasol in Mozambique.

The fact that Sasol's main customers—nearly 600 users in South Africa—are now dependent on gas from Mozambique makes it critical that Sasol's leadership understands what is required to keep the operation running at optimal levels. As stated above, this is not just an operational consideration but also one related to stakeholder management.

Another area that may become an issue in future is how Sasol balances its first world administration processes, codes of practice and regulation, taken for granted in South Africa but largely foreign in Mozambique, in working with the local suppliers that it will need to use going forward to fulfil local content obligations. Again, this is a tension between business cultures that needs to be carefully managed.

Fostering Teamwork and Collaboration

The response to the One Sasol concept has been well accepted within the Mozambique operation, but implementation has not been easy because of the difficulty of changing entrenched behaviour and thinking. Some have been shaken out of their comfort zones and had an element of power removed from their functions through the changes. In some cases, it has required giving up individual interests and power bases. Units that had been their own profit centres are now part of a streamlined entity and cannot control their functions as before. Every decision now has to be made in the broader interests of Sasol, not just for the business unit in question.

This has met with some resistance. It has required a level of personal accountability by staff that was not required before; the new structure does not allow people to hide behind others either in making decisions or not making them. In the past it was easy to "pass the buck" within units or make decisions and take actions based only on the direct interests of the unit or, at times, the person. Constant vigilance is required. The walls of the Maputo office are covered with posters containing all the relevant messages and action points of the new ethos to keep people on track.

The Mozambique office prefers to work not just on a system of "punishment" for staff who err, but on a system of giving credit where it is due. Management has introduced a monthly staff meeting at which high performance is recognised and where staff are encouraged to focus on positive solutions to challenges.

Leveraging Diversity and Inclusion

In Sasol, people are of course an integral part of the business, from its own staff in any country of operation to its partners and local communities, particularly given its focus on natural resources. But it has taken time to get it right.

Sasol was the second big investor into Mozambique, and it was able to take advantage of generous investment incentives in negotiations with the government. The context then was to make high-cost investments viable. Local empowerment was not a central issue in early mega-deals as it is now. Notwithstanding the different priorities then and now, there are lingering perceptions that Sasol has exploited, rather than developed, Mozambique. Detractors say Sasol had not sufficiently taken into account the harsh realities of the market in which it hoped to make massive profits—realities of huge poverty, strong socialist tendencies, high political risk and a shattered economy.

However, over time the company has recognised the need to increase its empowerment activities in order to build a sustainable operation while simultaneously achieving its production objectives. "Of course I want SEPI to achieve our stated growth ambition of 250,000 barrels of oil equivalent by 2025 but, I want us to build that from a stable base. I want us to grow in a manner that will enable growth and generate momentum to 2050 and beyond," said Ebbie Haan during his time as managing director of Sasol Petroleum International.[17]

Several years ago, Sasol negotiated a blueprint with the government that included provision for locals in senior positions and 95 % locals in the Mozambique operations by 2015. South African managers dragged their heels on implementing the plan, and it was only in 2014 that Sasol Petroleum appointed a Mozambican to run the gas plant in Inhambane, with a second local manager working beneath him—although the local country manager in Maputo has been in situ for some years. The difficulty of getting work permits and some official harassment of foreigners over visas has given the process new impetus.

Another issue was the fact that Sasol was leaving Mozambicans without access to the gas it was exporting. This too is changing. Sasol, in partnership with state energy company ENH, is now providing several hundred households in Inhambane Province, where the gas plant is situated, with household gas. As stated earlier, Sasol, in partnership with the government, completed in 2014 the gas-to-power station at Ressano Garcia, which will provide 23 % of Mozambique's power needs.

A challenge for the company is complying entirely with the spirit and application requirements of Mozambique's local content regulations in its upstream business. Sourcing the specialist skills, goods and services required is difficult given the severe skills shortage in general, and particularly in technical skills. Local content regulations apply mostly to the non-specialised areas of business, such as construction, logistics, information technology and supply of general goods and services, and there is recognition that the country does not have sufficient specialised skills.

The government is relying on the private sector to address the skills shortage and has done little itself to build local capacity.

Sasol has undertaken to drive industrial growth and local business where it can without compromising international safety and quality standards that apply across its global operations. It has a supplier development programme to fast-track and assist small businesses to build capacity so they can serve, and even compete with, international firms.

It has earmarked spending of $12.4 million for three main skills development projects:

- Developing students in the fields of geology, petroleum, drilling and reservoir engineering in association with the Ministry of Mineral Resources.
- Fast-tracking the development of artisans in Mozambique in partnership with the Mozambican National Institute of Employment and Vocational Training and formalising the practice of training artisans on site. The programme began in 2011, and the first learners, who included school leavers in the Vilancoulos area with good school results in maths, science and English, were given jobs at CPF in 2014.
- Developing a downstream masters programme with a local university in support of the Gas Master Plan.

In collaboration with the main Mozambican university, Eduardo Mondlane, Sasol is also supporting the master's degree programme in Upstream Petroleum Engineering specifically to build teaching capability in this regard and support curriculum development of a masters program in Petroleum Development (downstream). The company is also funding equipment used mostly in the science and engineering faculties. Thirty university bursaries have been awarded, 10 of them for tertiary study in South Africa.

Language has not been a big issue for Sasol because it had originally hired Mozambicans who could speak English and had later trained its workers to speak the language. It had also hired local bilingual managers.

In terms of its contribution to raising operational standards in Mozambique, Sasol maintains the same standards of operation in the country as it does anywhere else in the world despite distinct challenges in doing so. Key among these is safety, where the company has set new standards in Mozambique.

Business Acumen

Although technical and business skills levels in Mozambique are low, there are high levels of entrepreneurial activity that can be tapped and trained for the changing needs of the market. A downside for multinationals coming into Mozambique is that there is little history and depth of corporate activity, particularly outside Maputo. Most of the large companies in Mozambique are foreign owned and located in Maputo.

Inhambane Province, the site of Sasol's plant, is in a location popular with tourists; jobs are more plentiful than in other parts of the country, but they are mostly unskilled. Interestingly though, many Mozambicans have studied and travelled abroad, a consequence of the war and foreign assistance given to the country in its darkest days, and they have an understanding of other parts of the world. A driver for Sasol at the Temane plant, for example, was educated in Germany. This makes it easier for them to buy into the concept of a multinational such as Sasol.

Training of Mozambicans has taken place at the plant itself, in the Maputo office, but also through local and South African technical training institutions and programmes. As listed above, Sasol supports a number of educational initiatives in the belief that Mozambique's future depends on developing a skills base for 2020 and beyond.

Building Partnerships

Sasol has built partnerships with Mozambicans through skills training and capacity building (described above under inclusion and diversity). It has also developed partnerships with its own staff. The employee value proposition is important for the sustainability of the operation because it is becoming more essential now than ever to retain staff who have acquired skills and experience with Sasol and who may be poached by new competitors.

As stated above, in 2015 a Mozambican was running the gas plant for the first time. This is a milestone for the company, which had previously kept the highly specialised and critical facility in the hands of South African managers.

The number of locals employed at the plant has been increasing. By the end of 2014, 116 Mozambicans and 65 expatriates were employed. The number of expatriate permits depends on the total number of workers at a facility. In Sasol's case, the 181 workers at Temane technically allow it about nine expatriate permits, but many maintenance and professional skills positions are on contracts from South Africa.

In order to retain staff, Sasol has had to rethink the benefits it offers. It has provided about 100 houses for staff with supporting infrastructure (water, sewage, recreation facilities, etc.). Only companies registered in Mozambique were allowed to construct the houses, and 75 % of the labour used was local. An onsite clinic is available to staff and their families, and they have access to quality education.

Remuneration structures have also been revised to align more closely with current market practices. A human resources review is being done as part of the One Sasol initiative to align country operations with group principles and human resources structures.

Building partnerships is not only about the operation itself, but also about branding, sharing experiences and assisting people to understand the business imperatives and motivations. Sasol's marketing and branding in Mozambique has been criticised for not successfully positioning the company as being an international local company in the country. The company has also been criticised for not doing enough to sell itself locally and present its achievements.

Conclusion

After more than a decade in Mozambique, Sasol is losing its first-mover advantage at a time of rising competition for lucrative natural resource spoils. This is therefore a critical time for the organisation as it establishes its new operating model globally while aligning itself with new demands and pressures in one of its fastest-growing markets.

Having leadership that understands not just the technical aspects of this business opportunity but also the business and cultural norms of this challenging market is key to success and sustainability. Sasol has come a long way with its localisation programme in Mozambique, but there is still a sense that it has some way to go in terms of really understanding the nuts and bolts of the business culture, the political landscape and how to really benefit from its pioneering and risk-taking advantage in what is becoming a highly competitive landscape.

Notes

1. In 2015, Constable declared he would not renew his contract with Sasol, which expired on 31 May 2016. See Hogg A, 'Sasol CEO David Constable calls it quits', BizNews.com, 8 June 2015, accessed at http://www.biznews.com/briefs/2015/06/08/sasol-ceo-david-constable-calls-it-quits-wont-renew-his-contract/.
2. Towards 2020 and Beyond, Sasol Group Document.
3. Detailed information and background to Sasol can be found on the Sasol Website http://www.sasol.co.za/about-sasol/regional-operating-hubs/southern-africa-operations/secunda-synfuels-operations/overview and http://www.sasolnorthamerica.com/louisiana, as well as at Griggs, T 'Why Sasol is delaying $14B fuel facility—the priciest industrial investment in Louisiana history', The Advocate, 28 January 2015. http://theadvocate.com/news/11451337-123/sasol-delays-14-billion-fuel.
4. Mathews, C, 'Sasol sees a 'new era' in natural gas.' Business Day, 9 September,2014.http://www.bdlive.co.za/business/energy/2014/09/09/sasol-sees-a-new-era-ahead-in-natural-gas.
5. Remarks by Sasol CEO David Constable, Inauguration of the CPF Expansion, Mozambique, 30 May 2012. http://www.sasol.co.za/sites/default/files/ceo_speeches/downloads/David_E_Constable_Address_CPF_Expansion_1338407768522.pdf.
6. Ibid.
7. UN Development Programme, 'Mozambique', Human Development Report 2014. http://hdr.undp.org/sites/all/themes/hdr_theme/country-notes/MOZ.pdf.
8. Mucari M, 'Mozambique sees $30bn investment for 2018 liquefied natural gas (LNG) exports startup', Reuters, 21 August 2014.
9. Instituto Nacionale de Petroleo Mozambique website accessed at http://www.inp-mz.com/.
10. 'Sasol, Partners Awarded On-and offshore Blocks in Mozambique's 5th Licensing Bid Round', Reuters, 30 October 2015.

11. Mucari M, Op. Cit.
12. Madamombe I, "Pipeline benefits Mozambique, South Africa', Africa Renewal, October 2007.
13. 'Sasol, EDM inaugurate new gas-to-power plant in Mozambique', Media Centre, Sasol website, 28 August 2014.
14. Hayman A, 'Mozambique's president leads the charge for exploration and development', drillinginfo website, 8 August 2013. http://info.drillinginfo.com/africa-oil-and-gas-mozambique-president-oil/.
15. Remarks by Sasol CEO, Op. Cit.
16. Sasol Petroleum International, aSPIre magazine, Volume 8, April 2014.
17. 'From the Top', Message from the Managing Director, aSPIre magazine, Sasol Petroleum International, Volume 8, April 2014. http://www.biznews.com/briefs/2015/06/08/sasol-ceo-david-constable-calls-it-quits-wont-renew-his-contract/.

Bibliography

Constable, D. (2012). Remarks by Sasol CEO David constable, inauguration of the CPF expansion, mozambique. *Sasol*. Retrieved May 30, from http://www.sasol.co.za/sites/default/files/ceo_speeches/downloads/David_E_Constable_Address_CPF_Expansion_1338407768522.pdf

Griggs, T. (2015). Why Sasol is delaying $14B fuel facility—The priciest industrial investment in Louisiana history. *The Advocate*. Retrieved January 28, from http://theadvocate.com/news/11451337-123/sasol-delays-14-billion-fuel

Hayman, A. (2013). Africa oil and gas: Mozambique's president leads the charge for exploration and development. *drilling info*. Retrieved August 8, from http://info.drillinginfo.com/africa-oil-and-gas-mozambique-president-oil

Hogg, A. (2015). Sasol CEO David Constable calls it quits, won't renew his contract. *BizNews*. Retrieved June 8, from http://www.biznews.com/briefs/2015/06/08/sasol-ceo-david-constable-calls-it-quits-wont-renew-his-contract

Matthews, C. (2014). Sasol sees a 'new era' ahead in natural gas. *Business Day*. Retrieved September 09, from http://www.bdlive.co.za/business/energy/2014/09/09/sasol-sees-a-new-era-ahead-in-natural-gas

The Institute of National Petroleum of Mozambique. n.d. Mozambique 5th licensing round. http://www.inp-mz.com

United Nations Development Programme. (2015). Human Development Report 2015: Work for human development. http://hdr.undp.org/sites/all/themes/hdr_theme/country-notes/MOZ.pdf

8

NGN Telecoms Re-Entry into Kenya: The Power of Perseverance

Amanda Bowen, Stephanie Townsend, José Barreira, and Claire Beswick

In September 2014, Calum McCracken, chief executive officer (CEO) of Next Generation Network Telecommunications (Pty) Ltd (NGN Telecoms), a South Africa–based telecommunications company, met with his partners to discuss making another attempt to enter the Kenyan market. Doing business in Kenya had proved to be far more challenging than in any other country in which the company had worked thus far. Among other challenges, the company had to deal with fraud and negotiate from scratch with a new telecommunications operator. A struggle to renew its Communications Commission of Kenya[1] (CCK) licence ended without success. No licence meant no trading, and the company eventually had to withdraw from the country.

A. Bowen • S. Townsend • J. Barreira • C. Beswick (✉)
Wits Business School, Parktown, Johannesburg, South Africa
e-mail: claire.beswick@wits.ac.za

I. Adeleye et al. (eds.), *Africa-to-Africa Internationalization*, AIB Sub-Saharan Africa (SSA) Series, DOI 10.1007/978-3-319-30692-6_8

Years had passed since the company's first entry into Kenya, but McCracken felt the time was right for another attempt. What should the partners consider to avoid the challenges of the past?

NGN Telecoms Background

NGN Telecoms provides voice and data value-added technology in South Africa and globally to major mobile and fixed-line telephone operators, which then use this technology to sell products and services to their customers. The company's suite of products includes Fax2Email (see Fig. 8.1); Email2Fax; an interactive voice response (IVR) call-handling system; a non-geographic revenue generating telephone number service, Direct Connect (DiCon); the online shopping malls, Glomail and Toshop; an online radio syndicate with 6.4 million listeners (*www.ballz.co.za*); a mining supply business (NGN Mining); and the Cloud Fax application.

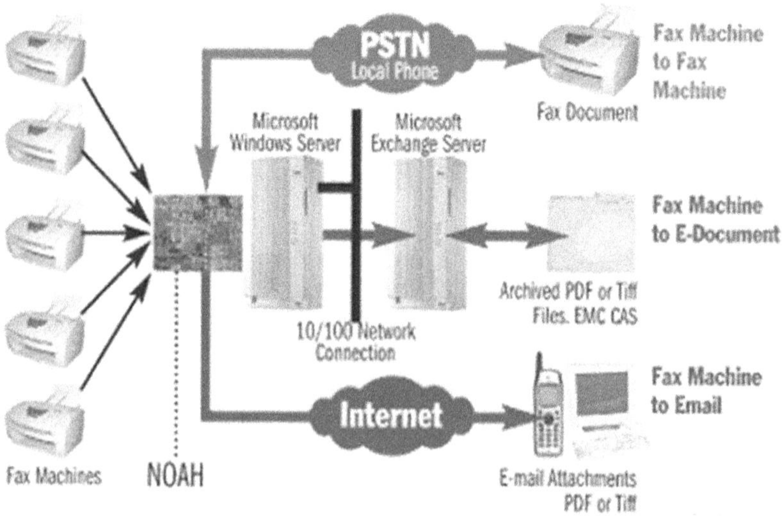

Fig. 8.1 Flow diagram of Fax2Email. *Source*: Courtesy of Naturaldata, available at: http://www.naturaldata.com (accessed 29 August 2014)

In 2014 its Fax2Email service was its most established brand, generating a regular and positive cash flow, and it was also the main product pushed into Africa and countries abroad. The company planned to add value by introducing other suitable add-on products in the future.

By 2014, NGN Telecoms had a presence through partnerships with telecommunication authorities in 19 countries: British Virgin Islands, China, Cyprus, Democratic Republic of the Congo, Indonesia, Lesotho, Malawi, Malta, Mauritius, Mozambique, Rumania, Russia, Saudi Arabia, South Africa, Tanzania, UK, USA (Miami), Zambia and Zimbabwe.

NGN Telecoms had its origins in SafikaTel, an operating company of the black-owned investment holding company, Safika Holdings (Pty) Ltd. In 2008, McCracken, as CEO and deputy chairman, Vuli Cuba, as chairman of the board, and Justin Webb, as chief information officer, became joint shareholders and changed the company name from SafikaTel to NGN Telecoms. The combined strengths of the "golden triangle," as the three were referred to within the company, helped build the company to what it had become by 2014—a market leader in telephony value-added services with a 95 % share in the South African market. In 2012, the company's Fax2Email product reached a milestone of one million fax minutes per day in South Africa. At that point, the partners decided to start diversifying the product line to create other revenue streams.

McCracken, Cuba and Webb had a unique relationship, which they believed was central to their success. McCracken explained: "We work very harmoniously together, because everybody knows what they do well and trusts each other to do it to the best of their ability. When we do strategic planning, Justin and I always go to 'our father' [Cuba], sit down with him and he would give strategic advice. He has been there, done it, all the way from a township in Springs, to being the success that he is today." Because of his business acumen, Cuba focused on giving strategic guidance and managing risk. In addition, his political connections and business relationships served NGN Telecoms well over the years.

As a top information technology (IT) developer, Webb brought invaluable technical expertise to the table, while McCracken lightheartedly referred to himself as the "general dogsbody and operational guy." In reality, McCracken had good marketing and sales skills and was quick to spot opportunities; although he pointed out that it was very difficult to execute a vision without the input of others.

Business Model and Strategy

NGN Telecoms business model was initially similar to a multilevel network marketing model. The top level comprised the company's shareholders in private companies, known as platform partners. Each platform partner had their own agents on a level below who, in turn, had sub-agents below them. By 2014, NGN Telecoms had bought out 80 % of the levels. NGN Telecoms generated revenue by taking a percentage of the fee that the telecommunications service providers charged users for services that required NGN Telecoms technology. Thus, for example, if a telecommunications service provider used NGN Telecoms technology to provide fax-to-email services or for a phone-in competition, the service provider would charge a fee to the user of those services and pay NGN Telecoms a proportion of that fee. Each level in the NGN Telecoms network would get its share of that revenue. Profits were maximised by selling high volumes.

Describing the company's strategy, McCracken said, "We generally look where we want to be in value-added telephony in five years, but always keep an open mind. During those five years, we often reconsider and adapt our direction, even back up a little, and then move forward again. But at the end of the term we end up in the general area wherever the highest revenue opportunity sits."

NGN Telecoms Early Days

McCracken was an inveterate entrepreneur. He was first exposed to the multilevel marketing model when he was only 14 years old and started selling products for Riviera Foods, a food production company that sold biscuits, chips, popcorn and other snacks through home-selling agents. He became Riviera's top-selling agent, earning about R200,000 (US$18 000) in 2014 terms. When his father, who was a director of Riviera, refused to pay him more than R200 (US$18) because he thought it would look inappropriate for his son to be taking home such a lot of money, McCracken left home and stayed with another family for two or three years until he completed school.

McCracken landed in the value-added telephony business by chance through Mark Hutchinson, an acquaintance who had started a scratch card business called Ithuba Scratch-and-Win. Hutchinson convinced a friend, at the time the CEO of mobile telecommunications company MTN, to allocate cellular numbers for use in competitions and to share with him and his partners the revenue generated when people called in to enter the competitions. McCracken's job was to convince CNA, the book, games, toys and electronics retailer for whom he was working as a regional manager at the time, to put competition scratch cards in all of its stores. When customers purchased a cellphone contract, they would also receive a scratch card with a unique number they could call to enter a competition and win a prize. The CNA board agreed. The one million scratch cards sold in CNA stores generated one million phone calls—every person phoned in to enter the competition.

Hutchinson introduced McCracken to Cuba, who was at that stage the CEO of Safika Holdings, a company of which he was the founder. In 1998, Safika Holdings secured a license with South Africa's fixed-line telecommunications service provider, Telkom, to deliver value-added services using Telkom's 086 number range. The business model included the creation of content attractive to the public, such as phone-in competitions channelled through the 086 numbers to generate traffic. The traffic generated revenue for Telkom, and Safika Holdings shared in that revenue. The more time a customer spent on the telephone line, the higher the revenue for both parties.

The contract was not generating the required revenue for either party, however, and Hutchinson suggested McCracken set up a meeting with Cuba. At that point, McCracken had already met and worked with Webb, a highly experienced interactive voice developer, formerly with IBM. For his part, Webb had connections with Safika through Safika's IT subsidiary, SafikaTel. Webb and McCracken initially met with Moss Ngoasheng, an executive at Safika Holdings. Ngoasheng then called Cuba in to the meeting. Cuba noted: "We listened to McCracken's story and like entrepreneurs do, something, a gut feel came to me. I had no idea who this guy was, but you know what, his explanation of this thing was impressive. Fortunately I understand IT so I could quickly pick up the validity of what he was saying."

Cuba asked McCracken to come in as the manager of SafikaTel with a 30 % shareholding. Cuba committed Safika Holdings to investing heavily in the SafikaTel business, but the investments would be in the form of a loan to McCracken, who would have to pay back the loan from SafikaTel turnover. McCracken accepted the terms, and Webb came in with him on a full-time basis. They moved into a small office that used to be a storeroom in the basement of the Safika Holdings building, but they were allowed to use the boardroom upstairs. As McCracken pointed out, this way they could fool people into thinking they had nice offices.

The two of them committed to making the business work, and McCracken would often promise customers a service that did not yet exist. Webb described the situation: "Calum is very good at selling, and he could convince people that we could do massive things and then I had to make it work. I remember one meeting, once or twice I had to kick him under the table, but generally we said we can do it and find a way, or use the fake-it-till-you-make-it scenario."

Business improved slowly, but the loan account still lurking in the background worried McCracken: "We got ourselves quite quickly to break-even. We hit cash break-even quite quickly, but the loan account kept growing." By 2006, the loan had grown to a massive R10 million.

McCracken and Webb had tried out about eight products with little success. It was failure upon failure. One night they were thinking of ways to make an annuity income (securing a steady income of fixed payments over time) and their old fax machine went off. "We ignored it," McCracken recalled, "but the fax machine went off again and again. By the fourth time, Justin [Webb] said, 'Cal, imagine if we could take a bite out of every fax minute.'" The two knew instinctively they were onto something good, and after some negotiation they set up a deal to provide fax-to-email services to the 320,000 clients of MWEB, an internet service provider based in Cape Town. They used Telkom as the provider of actual fax numbers and Internet Solutions to provide the technology that digitised fax data and forwarded it to an email address.

After some initial hitches, the service became hugely popular. "We watched the Fax2Email service traffic going from nothing to 5000 users, to 10,000 users, to 20,000, to 50,000. The people just loved the product. Suddenly, nobody's fighting with me anymore, because this thing is pumping money. Still today, they do three million minutes a month. It was only one bulk mailer ever, no other advertising on the product," laughed McCracken.

McCracken realised that at last they were winning. In addition, three months prior to securing the fax-to-email contract with MWEB, SafikaTel won the tender to run the phone-in voting for the reality show *Idols*. "We were onto real cash. We just jumped around. I would go and pitch for anything, for *Big Brother*, for *Idols*, for all the big phone-in stuff. I got the phone call that we had won and we only had a 120,000 port IVR. *Idols* expected millions of calls, so we had to get a bigger IVR system. So we went to Vuli, got the money and got the bigger IVR system. Then we went from nothing and made R1.6 million in 30 days off *Idols*." SafikaTel continued with *Idols* for three years with great success. By 2007, McCracken and Webb had paid off the R10 million loan account and started receiving after-tax dividends of R2.5 million every six months.

Going Global

McCracken wanted to break into the international market with Fax2Email as soon as possible. Locally, the business was growing well and the market was by no means saturated, but he yearned to expand internationally before anybody else caught on to the idea. He especially wanted to be successful the big markets of the European Union, China and Brazil. Although Cuba backed him, other executives in Safika Holdings, who still held 70 % shares in SafikaTel, did not. They suggested it would be more prudent for McCracken to enter neighbouring African countries instead, such as Botswana and Namibia, with which South African had greater cultural ties.

McCracken disagreed. He believed that starting small in the neighbouring countries would give potential competitors in China and the bigger markets time to figure out the technology for themselves. He was convinced that it would be better to take a top-down approach by starting in the big markets and then moving to the smaller markets in Africa.

Cuba supported McCracken: "I understood the potential and that what we had done was the first of its kind in the whole world. That if we are successful in South Africa, we can export it everywhere. I did not want to stop him from exercising his entrepreneurship. It is a product that we invested in, how exciting is that? It is a huge international commercial opportunity." This difference of opinion would eventually lead Cuba to dilute his shareholding in Safika Holdings from 20 % to 8 % and to purchase SafikaTel for R265 million. Thus NGN Telecoms was born.

However, going global brought challenges of its own. McCracken first attempted to set up business in the UK without much success. Soon thereafter, he flew to Shanghai to try to find a way to tap into the country's massive market. China Telecom agreed to the proposal, and Webb spent three years in China setting up operations and maintaining the trading business.

Doing business in China was far from easy, with cultural differences being a major challenge. "We switched on in Shanghai and it was just problem after problem," explained McCracken. "The faxes did not want to go through and our local partner was fighting with us, saying our software does not want to work and we are terrible. I said to him, 'It does not make sense. If that was the case it would be everywhere, but it is only here. So I am not 100 % sure the problem sits with us. I think the problem sits on China Telecoms side.'" The partner was adamant, however, that the fault had to be with NGN Telecoms.

McCracken decided to send Webb back to China to find out where the problems lay. Webb hacked into China Telecoms switching system, even though he could have been imprisoned for doing so, and discovered that a voice over internet protocol (VOIP) link in the Chinese switching system was causing the problem. However, the service level agreement that was in place specified that there would be no VOIP switches. McCracken remembered the conversation that ensued between him and his partner in China:

McCracken:	Here is the proof, black on white, here is the problem. And it is on China Telecoms lines.
Local Partner:	How did you get this information? asked the partner.

McCracken:	Justin got it for me, replied McCracken.
Local Partner:	How did Justin get this information? asked the partner.
McCracken:	I don't know, McCracken said. I am not technical. Maybe he knows somebody in China Telecom, I don't know.

The partner scooped up the papers and walked away without saying another word. McCracken waited in Shanghai for another two days but did not hear anything from his partner. When he was just about to leave, his partner contacted him and told him the following: "You come Wednesday to the Chinese Telecom office, you apologise for your bad software, he will then accept your apology and shout at you and then we can carry on with the project."

This incident showed McCracken how important it was for the Chinese not to lose face, and he realised that if he wanted to continue doing business in China he would have to do as his business partner suggested. "There is a point where you say to yourself, out of pride, you know this is really wrong, or you say I want the money, so you go," he explained. So he went to the Chinese Telecom offices and things unfolded exactly as his partner said they would.

It took seven or eight years for NGN Telecoms operations in Shanghai to become profitable, and by 2014 the company had not yet recovered its initial investment of millions of rands. Still, McCracken was committed to staying in China, seeing great potential for his product there.

McCracken continued networking abroad to get a foot in the door in different countries, reasoning that if one country did not work out there was always another to try. NGN Telecoms lost money in some countries, gained some in others, and the hard work started to pay off. The number of minutes started to increase steadily, reaching one million minutes a day in 2012, and the number was still climbing.

The Kenyan Conundrum

The Communications Commission of Kenya (CCK), under Kenya's Ministry of Information and Communication, regulates the telecommunications market in Kenya. Kenyan legislation requires foreign telecommunications to have at least 20 % local ownership within three years of bringing the services into operation.

In 2007, McCracken and Webb started setting up their business in Kenya. They signed an agreement with two local partners, a move that was legally required, registered a company called NGN East Africa in 2008, and obtained the required CCK licence to trade with Telkom Kenya. Trading with Fax2Email commenced, albeit slowly at first as they had to rely on the local partners to promote the product. Business was just beginning to run smoothly when three incidents occurred that changed the whole scenario: NGN East Africa's CCK trading licence came up for renewal; Orange Kenya, the French telecommunications provider which had acquired 51 % (up to 70 % in 2014) of Telkom Kenya's shares in 2008, required NGN Telecoms to renegotiate the contract it had originally signed with Telkom Kenya in 2007; and NGN Telecoms discovered internal fraud in the NGN East Africa office.

When the CCK licence came up for renewal in 2012, Webb and chief operations officer Ingrid Hibbins flew to Nairobi, followed the required process, paid the necessary fees, and received proof of payment. At that point, the two hit a brick wall. Initially, the CCK officials told them they could collect the licence the next day, but one day turned into many, with officials giving various excuses. Eventually, Webb and Hibbins returned to South Africa without the licence but with the assurance that NGN East Africa could continue trading.

In the second half of 2012, Orange Kenya asked NGN Telecoms to renegotiate the contract it had with Telkom Kenya. "That set us back. We had to go back and initiate the whole project with Orange Kenya. It happened five times that we had to go back [to Kenya]. We would just get the guy up to speed with an agreement going three, four months, and then they would call him back to France and send a new guy. Then we had to start all over again, because the contract was changing and being renegotiated every time someone new came in," noted Webb.

The stalling baffled the NGN Telecoms legal representative, who had been involved in the negotiations with Orange Kenya. He recalled that the discussions had gone well and that there was a written agreement in place by 2013. The agreement was never signed, however.

Although NGN East Africa was still able to trade, it started encountering technical challenges when Orange Kenya entered the scene. In the end, Webb had to work side by side with Orange Kenya's equipment suppliers to resolve the issues. "Everything started to fall apart, even when technically it was working in and outbound, it ultimately fell apart contractually," Webb explained.

During that time, NGN Telecoms also became aware of unauthorised withdrawals from its business account. It subsequently terminated its relationship with the local partners on the grounds of dishonest behaviour. As a result, NGN Telecoms closed down NGN East Africa, and Hibbins immediately commenced with the registration of a new, wholly owned company, SunFax.

The final decision to withdraw from Kenya came in 2013, when Webb and Hibbins discovered that certain clauses in the CCK licensing agreement had changed. As a consequence, the existing licence had expired and NGN Telecoms had lost the money paid for the renewal fee. Despite the fact that NGN Telecoms had involved local accountants and attorneys to help in the renewing of the licence, the licence had not been renewed.

At the time, NGN Telecoms decided to cease its attempts to operate in Kenya and to pursue more accommodating territories. McCracken put it thus: "You can't keep flogging the horse. So you start saying, 'Am I going to continue throwing my resources where I am not getting anywhere?' We just said enough is enough."

Reconsidering Kenya

McCracken soon reconsidered, however. He believed there was money to be made in Kenya and that NGN Telecoms should try again. In March 2014, Orange Kenya had informed the government of Kenya, which owned the remaining 30 % of shares in Telkom Kenya, of its intention to sell its 70 % stake in the organisation because the losses it was incurring in the business were too great. The shareholders' agreement permitted Orange to exit after five years, although this was subject to bringing in an equal or larger investor. In the interim, Orange planned to keep the business going on minimum funding and activity.

Moreover, in January 2013, the Progressive Business Forum,[2] representing 50 South African companies, had visited Kenya to strengthen business ties between the two countries. Issues under discussion included non-tariff barriers to trade, visas, taxation, trade licences and protocols. In addition, the South African Department of Trade and Energy had invited businesses to take part in a trade and investment mission to Kenya scheduled for February 2015.

The information and communication technology (ICT) sector, especially mobile technology, constituted an important area of growth and innovation in the Kenyan economy. In its 2013 Kenya Investment Climate Statement, the US Department of State[3] anticipated that the ICT sector could thrive once the government decentralised the provision and maintenance of services to Kenya's 47 county governments after the March 2013 elections. It stated that "Kenya's county governments will require better and faster data services to connect with one another and the national government."

Business Environment

The political violence that followed the 2007 election results[4] had led to the implementation of a new Kenyan constitution, approved by a two-thirds majority in a violence-free referendum. The presidential elections of 2013, in which Uhuru Kenyatta only just avoided a run-off and was elected president, sparked uproar, but not on the scale seen in 2007. Overall, political stability had improved since 2007. A positive outcome was that President Kenyatta vowed to fight corruption.

However, the militant Islamist group Al Shabaab had consistently been carrying out attacks in Kenya since 2011. The most high-profile attack occurred at the Westgate shopping mall in Nairobi on 21 September 2013, where more than 60 people were killed.

By 2014, the general business environment in Kenya had become increasingly volatile, unpredictable and competitive. An article in *Financial Mail* dated 6 February 2014 reported that although there was renewed interest from South African businesses to invest in Kenya, the country was in "dire need of reform across all economic sectors to address regulatory inefficiencies. The country also needs new infrastructure and to tackle its high crime rate."

According to the article, South African businesses in Kenya had "failed as a result of much mistrust between the Kenyan government and South African companies that were trying to set up shop there." The article went on to say that "the mistrust was driven by a lack of understanding of the business cultures of both countries. The aggressiveness of some South Africans led to Kenyans fearing they would dominate in some sectors."

In 2012, the auditing and consulting firm, KPMG, had called corruption in Kenya endemic, but it admitted the situation had improved of late. It also mentioned lengthy business licensing procedures as a barrier to entry in Kenya. Other analysts cited constraints such as high taxes, poor infrastructure, power shortages, the cost of electricity and high data usage costs as some of the main issues impeding internet use.

The Way Forward

McCracken was convinced there were good business opportunities in Kenya, and he was concerned that there was a possibility of competitors entering his market. Thus, time was of the essence. He had to decide quite quickly what he and his partners could do to ensure a successful return to Kenya.

Notes

1. Kenya's industry regulator.
2. The Progressive Business Forum was formed in 2006 with the primary objective of creating an ongoing dialogue between the African National Congress and the business community. [Source: http://www.pbf.org.za/ (accessed 15 September 2014)].
3. This department's mission is "to shape and sustain a peaceful, prosperous, just, and democratic world and foster conditions for stability and

progress for the benefit of the American people and people everywhere." [Source: US Department of State, n.d., 'Department Mission', available http://www.state.gov/s/d/rm/index.htm#mission (accessed 25 September 2015)].

4. The disputed 2007 presidential election sparked a devastating episode of political violence in Kenya, resulting in property damage, approximately 1200 deaths and the displacement of more than 300,000 people. [Source: http://www.irinnews.org/in-depth/76116/68/kenya-s-post-election-crisis (accessed 28 August 2014)].

References

KPMG 2012. Kenya—Country profile. Retrieved August 29, 2014, from https://www.kpmg.com/Africa/en/KPMG-in-Africa/Documents/Kenya.pdf

Mbobo, S. 2014. SA businesses show renewed interest in Kenya. *Financial Mail*, February 6. Retrieved August 25, 2014, from http://www.financialmail.co.za/coverstory/2014/02/06/sa-business-shows-renewed-interest-in-kenya

Mutulu, F. 2014. 'Last call' for orange as France telecom plans exit from Kenya, AFK Insider, 6 June. Retrieved August 29, 2014, from http://afkinsider.com/58874/last-call-orange-france-telecom-plans-exit-kenya

Nojiyeza, S., & Muthoka, J. (2013). Barriers to entry of Kenya's telecommunication industry: Is there a market slice for new entrants? *Journal of Management & Administration, 11*(1), 136–196 .

Townsend, S. 2014a. Interview with Calum McCracken on 27 May, Midrand.

Townsend, S. 2014b. Interview with Calum McCracken on 29 May, Midrand.

Townsend, S. 2014c. Interview with Justin Webb on 29 May 2014, Midrand.

Townsend, S. 2014d. Interview with Vuli Cuba on 29 May, Midrand.

Townsend, S. 2014e. Interview with Howard Nel on 14 July 2014, Midrand.

Townsend, S. 2014f. Interview with Ingrid Hibbins on 14 July 2014, Midrand.

US Department of State. 2013. 2013 Investment climate statement—Kenya. Retrieved from August 29, 2014, from http://www.state.gov/e/eb/rls/othr/ics/2013/204669.htm

9

Equity Bank's Internationalization: Building an African Multinational

Chris Ogbechie and Nkemdilim Iheanachor

As Dr James Mwangi, the managing director and Chief Executive Officer (CEO) of Equity Group Holdings, walked over to the conference room in Equity Centre for a board meeting, he pondered how the bank would eventually enter the sophisticated Nigerian banking industry. The head of the project team charged with the task of developing a concept document for the establishment of the Nigerian subsidiary was Mary Wangari, who was also the director of corporate strategy. She had worked tirelessly with her team to establish possible entry options and evaluate the likelihood of success of each. James had reviewed the document highlighting their findings and recommendations and was set for an extensive debate during the board meeting on how they could best proceed with the Nigerian market entry.

Dr Chris Ogbechie and Nkemdilim Iheanachor prepared this as the basis for class discussion rather than to illustrate either effective or ineffective handling of an administrative situation.

C. Ogbechie (✉) • N. Iheanachor
Lagos Business School, Ajah, Lagos, Nigeria
e-mail: cogbehie@lbs.edu.ng

I. Adeleye et al. (eds.), *Africa-to-Africa Internationalization*, AIB Sub-Saharan Africa (SSA) Series, DOI 10.1007/978-3-319-30692-6_9

With Equity's foray into other markets beginning to show promising results in the existing international locations of Rwanda, South Sudan, Uganda and Tanzania, Equity was now looking at growth opportunities in bigger African markets in fulfilment of the bank's vision to be the champion of socio-economic prosperity of the people of Africa. The Nigerian market was identified as a top priority given its strong fundamentals and similarities to Kenya, Equity's home country.

The decision to establish a Nigerian subsidiary was a bold one given the challenges of doing business in Nigeria. The project team recommended that Equity leverage on its various experiences from operating in other international locations as the Nigerian market would be similar in many ways. They had also established the pros and cons of each of the identified entry options.

The Nigerian banking industry had emerged from two reform phases that left questions about future policy directions and what the minimum regulatory establishment and existence requirements would be for existing players. The structure of the industry had also evolved, with the number of licensed commercial banks in the country decreasing from 89 to 25 at the end of the reforms in 2004. The competition for deposits and loans among Nigerian banks was intense as the licensed banks had well-developed portfolios of savings and loan products aimed at meeting the financial service needs of virtually all segments of the economy. The Central Bank of Nigeria had two major license categories for banks—commercial licenses and microfinance licenses. There were only two non-Nigerian banks with a presence in Nigeria as at December 2013.

The project team had established several entry options: establishment of a brand new commercial bank, acquisition of an existing commercial bank, entering into a partnership or joint venture with an existing commercial bank or establishing a national microfinance bank. Which was the most prudent option? Equity also had to decide on how to position the bank: Was it going to be a national bank or a regional bank? How many branches would they commence with at take-off? How were they going to recruit take-off staff? How would the board members be identified? Would the establishment of the Nigerian subsidiary put a further strain on management resources already stretched by the closure or letting go of 217 branches, 10,260 agents, 584 Automated Teller Machine (ATMs) and 7788 employees in Kenya and other international locations? As James reflected on all these questions, he thought about Equity's position in Kenya and wondered if Equity would succeed in Nigeria, where several other non-Nigerian banks had failed.

About Nigeria

Nigeria is the 10th-largest country and has the largest economy in Africa.[1] It lies on the west coast of Africa, occupies about 923,768 km^2 of land, and borders Niger, Chad, Cameroon and Benin. The country is made up of 774 local governments and 36 states, including the Federal Capital Territory, Abuja.[2] The country is structured into six geopolitical zones: South South, South West, South East, North East, North West and North Central. Nigeria's population was about 160 million people in 2015, about 15 % of Africa's population. It is the most populous country in Africa and the whole black world; one out of every five Africans is Nigerian.[3] Nigeria, the seventh-most populous country in the world, has an age structure in which the largest segment is made up of individuals within the ages of 15 and 64 years (55.9 %), followed by individuals within the ages of 0 and 14 years (40.9 %); people aged 65 years and over represent 3.1 % of the country's population.[4]

Nigeria is a multi-ethnic state with over 250 different ethnic groups. The three largest and most influential ethnic groups in Nigeria are the Hausa, Igbo and Yoruba. Nigeria is roughly split half and half between Muslims and Christians, with a very small minority who practise African traditional religion.[5]

Nigeria's macroeconomic performance was on the upswing between 2000 and 2013. Nigeria's gross domestic product (GDP) of about $369 billion rose to US $567 billion in 2014,[6] a growth rate averaging more than 7 % between 2010 and 2014. Meanwhile, inflation trended downward to less than 10 % during the same period.[7] Substantial oil saving buffers, built before the 2008 global crisis, provided room for the implementation of countercyclical policies that minimized the impact of the crisis on the domestic economy. However, while Nigeria's growth has been among the highest in Sub-Saharan Africa, poverty still remains high.

Nigeria's is a heavily factor-driven economy diversified across agriculture, crude petroleum and natural gas, and wholesale and retail trade, with sectorial contributions to GDP of 39.49 %, 13.54 % and 19.87 % in 2011, respectively.[8]

Nigeria was structured as a federation, a structure inherited from her British colonial rulers. The country's 1999 constitution provides for a bicameral National Assembly consisting of a 360-member House of Representatives and a 109-member Senate.[9] The president and the governors and legislators in both the upper and lower houses are elected by the people for four-year terms. The president heads the executive arm of government, while the judiciary, including all courts (Supreme, Appeal, High and Magistrate) is headed by the Chief Justice of Nigeria.

Despite Nigeria's substantial natural resources, its infrastructure, particularly its road and electricity networks, remains inadequate, presenting a significant obstacle to economic growth. Only about 30 % of the population has access to electricity, and only about 31 % of the road network is paved.[10]

Owing to sectoral reforms, Nigeria has an advanced financial system relative to several other African countries. The cost of finance is still high, and access to medium- to long-term finance is limited. According to the Business Competitiveness Index (BCI) is from the Global Competitiveness Report in 2005 and 2007, Nigeria's level of competitiveness is declining, and the country is less competitive than South Africa and Kenya. After a slight improvement in the overall BCI Index in 2005, both the quality of the national business environment and the competitiveness of company operations and strategy declined yet again in 2007. Inadequate infrastructure, limited access to financing and high levels of corruption have been the key drivers of the decline in competitiveness. However, efficacy of corporate boards and access to the local equity market have improved.

Table 9.1 shows economic growth projections for the 32 largest economies in the world that collectively account for 84 % of global GDP. Nigeria's GDP was projected to rise from 20th in 2014 to ninth in the world in 2050 and to remain the largest in Africa from 2014 to 2050. This comparison further highlights the economic significance of Nigeria in Africa. Figure 9.1 shows Nigeria's rank in the ease of doing business index[11] compared to other Sub-Saharan African countries.

Table 9.1 Economic growth projections for the 32 largest economies in the world

	2014		2030		2050	
PPP rank	Country	GDP at PPP (2014 US$bn)	Country	Projected GDP at PPP (2014 US$bn)	Country	Projected GDP at PPP (2014 US$bn)
1	China	17,632	China	36,112	China	61,079
2	United States	17,416	United States	25,451	India	42,205
3	India	7277	India	17,138	United States	41,384
4	Japan	4788	Japan	6006	Indonesia	12,210
5	Germany	3621	Indonesia	5486	Brazil	9164
6	Russia	3559	Brazil	4996	Mexico	8014
7	Brazil	3073	Russia	4854	Japan	7914
8	France	2587	Germany	4590	Russia	7575
9	Indonesia	2554	Mexico	3985	Nigeria	7345
10	United Kingdom	2435	United Kingdom	3586	Germany	6338
11	Mexico	2143	France	3418	United Kingdom	5744
12	Italy	2066	Saudi Arabia	3212	Saudi Arabia	5488
13	South Korea	1790	South Korea	2818	France	5207
14	Saudi Arabia	1652	Turkey	2714	Turkey	5102
15	Canada	1579	Italy	2591	Pakistan	4253
16	Spain	1534	Nigeria	2566	Egypt	4253
17	Turkey	1512	Canada	2219	South Korea	4142
18	Iran	1284	Spain	2175	Italy	3617
19	Australia	1100	Iran	1914	Canada	3583
20	Nigeria	1058	Egypt	1854	Philippines	3516
21	Thailand	990	Thailand	1847	Thailand	3510
22	Egypt	945	Pakistan	1832	Vietnam	3430
23	Poland	941	Australia	1707	Bangladesh	3367
24	Argentina	927	Malaysia	1554	Malaysia	3327
25	Pakistan	884	Poland	1515	Iran	3224
26	Netherlands	798	Philippines	1508	Spain	3099
27	Malaysia	747	Argentina	1362	South Africa	3026
28	Philippines	695	Vietnam	1313	Australia	2903
29	South Africa	683	Bangladesh	1291	Colombia	2785
30	Colombia	642	Colombia	1255	Argentina	2455
31	Bangladesh	536	South Africa	1249	Poland	2422
32	Vietnam	509	Netherlands	1066	Netherlands	1581

Source: Adapted from The World in 2050 will the shift in economic power continue? PwC UK, February 2015

PPP – Purchasing Power Parity; GDP – Gross Domestic Product

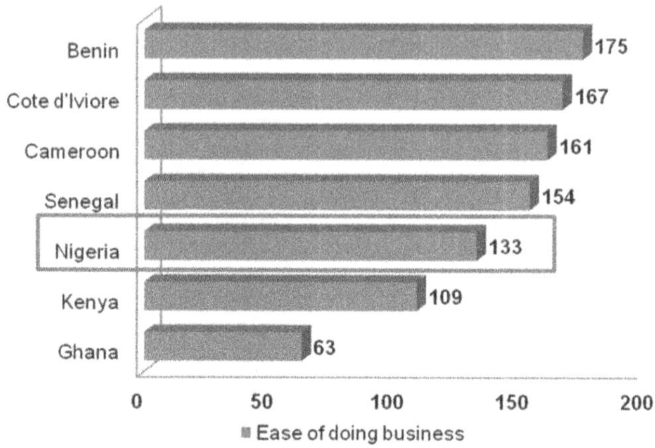

Fig. 9.1 Nigeria's rank in the ease of doing business index. *Source*: Doing Business in a more transparent world report by the International Finance Corporation, World Bank in 2012

Nigeria's Human Development Index (HDI)[12] value for 2012 was 0.471, positioning the country at 153 out of 187 countries and territories and firmly in the low human development category. However, between 2005 and 2012, Nigeria's HDI value increased from 0.434 to 0.471, an increase of 9 %, or an average annual increase of about 1.2 %. The rank of Nigeria's HDI for 2011 based on data available and methods used in 2012 was 154 out of 187 countries. In the 2011 HDI, Nigeria was ranked 156 out of 187 countries. Table 9.2 reviews Nigeria's progress in each of the HDI indicators. Between 1980 and 2012, Nigeria's life expectancy at birth increased by 6.8 years, mean years of schooling increased by 0.2 years and expected years of schooling increased by 2.4 years. Nigeria's gross national income per capita increased by about 34 % between 1980 and 2012.[13]

History of Banking in Nigeria

The first commercial bank in Nigeria, the Bank of British West Africa, was established in 1894 to serve British shipping and trading agencies in Nigeria. Draft legislation for the establishment of the Central Bank of

Table 9.2 Human development statistics for Nigeria as at 2013

	Life expectancy at birth	Expected years of schooling	Mean years of schooling	GNI per capita (2005 PP$)	HDI value
1980	45.5	6.6	-	1571	
1985	45.9	8.4	-	1202	
1990	45.6	6.5	-	1274	
1995	45.1	6.5	-	1303	
2000	46.3	7.9	-	1285	
2005	49.0	9.0	5.0	1540	0.434
2010	51.4	9.0	5.2	1928	0.462
2011	51.9	9.0	5.2	2017	0.467
2012	52.3	9.0	5.2	2102	0.471

Source: Human development report 2013 Nigeria
HDI–Human Development Index

Nigeria (CBN) was presented to the House of Representatives in March 1958. The Act was fully implemented on 1 July 1959 when the CBN commenced full operations.[14] The deregulation of the financial services industry in 1986 following the adoption of the Structural Adjustment Programme led to a rapid increase in the number of banks, from 41 commercial and merchant banks in 1985 to 115 by 1997. Through the liquidation of some banks by the Nigeria Deposit Insurance Corporation (NDIC), with the number of licensed commercial banks in the country decreasing from 89 to 25 at the end of the reforms in 2005.[15] Nigeria benefitted from the largest debt write-off in the history of the Paris Club, reducing its external debt from US $33 billion in 2003 to just US $3.5 billion in 2006.[16]

The Nigerian banking industry serves as the chief medium for financial intermediation in the economy. By 2005, earnings and total assets of the banking sector represented 5.9 % and 49 % of Nigeria's GDP, respectively. Key global banks with varying levels of investment in the sector include Citigroup, Standard Chartered Bank, the State Bank of India and Standard Bank of South Africa. The major offshore institutional investors (debt or equity) include the International Finance Corporation, Kingdom Holding Company of Saudi Arabia and Netherlands Development Finance Company (the Dutch FMO).[17]

To improve the financial base of the country's banking system, in 1997 the Central Bank of Nigeria increased the minimum paid-up capital requirement to N500 million (US$6 million), from N40 million and

N50 million for merchant banks and commercial banks, respectively.[18] The scope of services offered by banks was also expanded with the adoption of universal banking in 2000. The adoption gave banks the freedom to decide which activities they undertook (money, capital market, insurance, clearing house or any combination thereof) as long as they complied with the relevant guidelines.[19]

In January 2001, the minimum paid-up capital for new banks was raised again to N2 billion (US$20 million) from N 500 million to N1 billion (US$7.4 million) that it was raised from N 500 million to, while existing banks were required to raise their capital base to N2 billion (US$15 million) by the end of 2002.[20]

With the number of licensed commercial banks in the country decreasing from 89 to 25 at the end of the reforms in 2004. According to CBN, of the 89 operating banks in Nigeria in 2004, 10 banks accounted for over half of the sector's total assets and deposits, with many of the smaller banks operating at the margin of profitability. The Nigerian economy had a banking sector with credit to the domestic economy at 24 % of GDP, compared to the African average of 87 % and the average in developed countries of 272 %.[21]

Nigeria's Financial Sector

Pre-2004 Characteristics

By 2004, Nigeria's financial system was plagued by various structural problems that hampered its ability to financially intermediate. There was low aggregate banking credit to the domestic economy (about 20 % of GDP), there were various systemic risks as a result of which CBN had to frequently bail out ailing banks, and most banks were grossly undercapitalized and unable to lend to the real sector of the economy. In addition, there was an oligopolistic market structure, with 10 of the 89 existing banks accounting for over 50 % of total banking assets.[22]

Most banks had very weak corporate governance systems, and there was a very low banking population with only one bank branch for every 30,432 Nigerians.[23] The payments system was largely cash-based, and the insurance industry, which was meant to serve as a buffer to banking system risks, was weak. The Nigerian equities market was also very weak, with less than 200 listed companies at the time.

There was an apathy of banks towards small savers, particularly at the grassroots level, which further compounded the problem of low domestic savings. Banks had also abandoned their main role of financial intermediation, resulting in high bank lending rates and crowding out of small savers, who required access to cheap and stable funds that could provide a reliable source of credit to the productive sectors.

In July 2004, the CBN launched a 13-point reform agenda with the broad objective of creating bigger banks with stronger balance sheets, ensuring safe and sound banking practices and enhancing the regulatory capacity to supervise the industry. A key element of the reform program was the increase in the minimum capital base of banks from N2 billion (US$15 million) to N25 billion (US$190 million) by December 2005.[24]

The reform programme was driven by the following factors:

- Small balance sheet size of Nigerian banks compared with their counterparts in emerging economies, which limited their ability to meet the funding requirements of the economy and also hampered their ability to contribute to the growth of the real sector;
- Narrow scale and scope of services provided by Nigerian banks, leading to a loss of business to foreign banks and resulting in low banking penetration and limited retail banking offerings;
- Fragmentation of the industry, with many banks operating as fringe players; and
- Dwindling level of confidence in the banking system as a result of poor corporate governance and sharp practices by some Nigerian banks.[25]

The CBN reforms were intended to strengthen the Nigerian banking system, with the objective of ultimately making Nigeria the financial hub of Africa. At the end of the consolidation exercise, 75 banks were consolidated through mergers and acquisitions into 25 new entities. The remaining 14 banks had their operating licences revoked, preparatory to formal liquidation. The 25 banks comprised 21 public listed banks, 3 foreign-owned banks and 1 locally owned bank. As at 2005, the banks had a consolidated balance sheet size of over N4.5 trillion (US$35 billion) and shareholders' funds of N592 billion (US$4.6 billion).[26]

The consolidation resulted in fresh local investments totalling N350 billion (US$2.7 billion) and US$660 million in foreign direct investment into the industry. There was a significant dilution of ownership of the banks as substantial funds for the enhancement of their capital base was raised from the stock market. This increased the strength of corporate governance in the banks and also increased the number of regulators; the banks became public companies under regulation by the Securities and Exchange Commission and the Nigerian Stock Exchange.[27]

In 2005, following the conclusion of the consolidation exercise of the commercial banks, Central Bank of Nigeria (CBN) launched a new microfinance policy to reverse the prolonged sub-optimal performance of most of the existing 600 community banks. These banks had weak institutional capacity as a result of inadequate capital bases, poor corporate governance, lack of well-defined operations and restrictive regulatory/supervisory requirements.[28] The Nigerian market was also hugely underbanked, with a banking density of one financial institution outlet for every 32,700 inhabitants in urban areas and one outlet for every 57,000 inhabitants in rural areas, translating to less than 2 % of Nigerian households with access to financial services.[29] Aggregate microcredit facilities in Nigeria accounted for about 0.2 % of GDP and less than 1 % of total credit to the economy. The effect of not properly addressing the situation was expected to result in an accentuation of poverty and stunted economic growth.[30]

The new microfinance policy specified two categories of licenses—the unit microfinance bank with a minimum paid-up capital of N25 million and the state microfinance bank with a minimum paid-up capital of N1 billion. At the expiration of the deadline given by CBN for existing community banks to convert to microfinance banks and shore up their paid-up capital, to either N20 million or N1 billion depending on the category of license they sought, over 700 microfinance banks had emerged.[31]

A dramatic change in CBN's regulatory posture was occasioned by the appointment of Mallam Sanusi Lamido Sanusi as the governor of the Central Bank following the expiration of Professor Charles Chukwuma

Soludo's tenure. The Nigerian banking sector witnessed dramatic growth after consolidation. However, neither the industry nor the regulators were sufficiently prepared to sustain and monitor the sector's growth. Prevailing sentiment and economic orthodoxy encouraged this rapid growth while at the same time creating a blind spot to the risks building up in the system.[32]

CBN identified eight main interdependent factors that led to the creation of a fragile financial system after the 2005 consolidation, allowing the tip into distress by the global financial crisis and recession of 2008. The factors were macroeconomic instability caused by large and sudden capital inflows, major failures in corporate governance at banks, lack of investor and consumer sophistication, inadequate disclosure and transparency about financial position of banks, critical gaps in regulatory framework and regulations, uneven supervision and enforcement, unstructured governance and management processes at the CBN/weaknesses within the CBN, and weaknesses in the business environment.[33]

Following an industry-wide stress test carried out by joint examiners from the CBN and NDIC, nine out of the 25 commercial banks were adjudged to be in grave condition, prompting immediate intervention by CBN. Some of the problems identified in the nine banks included: non-performing loans totalling N1.7 trillion, representing 44.38 % of total loans; aggregate provisioning required amounting to N1.3 trillion; capital adequacy ratio ranging between 1.01 % and 7.41 %, which was below the minimum ratio of 10 %; and additional required capital injection of N495.83 billion.[34] The CBN immediately took steps to ameliorate the situation by injecting N620 billion into the nine banks, replacing the chief executives/executive directors of eight of the banks, reaffirming guarantee of the local interbank market to ensure continued liquidity for all banks, and guaranteeing foreign creditors' and correspondent banks' credit lines to ensure confidence and maintain important correspondent banking relationships. The capital injection enabled the nine banks to continue normal business operations and prevented a run on the banks. The Asset Management Corporation of Nigeria was established to stimulate the recovery of the financial system by acquiring non-performing loans from banks and assisting banks in improving their liquidity and capital positions.[35]

Post-2004 Reforms

The end of the banking industry consolidation saw a dramatic transformation in the nature and structure of banking in Nigeria. The minimum share capital of banks was raised by 1150 % from N2 billion ($15 million) to N25 billion ($200 million), and the number of banks shrank from 89 to 25.[36] The CBN adopted a risk-focused and rule-based regulatory framework. The CBN also introduced the electronic Financial Analysis and Surveillance System to facilitate online real-time monitoring of the activities of the Nigerian banks. There was strict enforcement of contingency planning and a strengthening of the corporate governance code of banks stipulating maximum tenures of 10 years for bank CEOs and 12 years for non-executive directors. Banks also enhanced their adoption and use of information technology (IT) in all their operations. The recapitalization of the banking industry saw the emergence and rise of Nigeria's equity market, the conversion of community banks to microfinance banks and the establishment of the Africa Finance Corporation.

At the end of the recapitalization exercise, 75 banks either merged or independently raised fresh capital to establish the 25 consolidated banks, and the NDIC employed a purchase and assumption mechanism for 11 of the 14 banks that failed to meet the minimum capital requirement.[37]

In 2007, a second self-induced wave of bank recapitalization took place in the Nigerian banking industry via a combination of rights issues and public offers by banks in pursuit of their domestic and regional expansion programs. The enhanced capital level of Nigerian banks heightened competition among them that manifested in the form of branch network expansion, new product offerings and investments in IT infrastructure. Six banks—Access Bank, First Bank of Nigeria, Guaranty Trust Bank, United Bank for Africa, First City Monument Bank and Diamond Bank—accessed the capital market and raised a total of US$2 billion through the Global Depository Receipts channel.

Key Outcomes of Nigerian Financial Sector Reforms: Systemic Risk Reduction

The Nigerian banking sector emerged from the turbulence with 25 strong banks with larger capital bases. International rating agencies like Fitch and Standards & Poor's rated Nigerian banks for the first time, and the overall number of bank branches in Nigeria increased from 3200 in 2004 to 3866 in April 2007.

About 919 community/microfinance banks were established (capital requirement about $156,000), and total non-performing loans/total loans decreased from 23 % to about 7 % in 2006. Longer-tenured deposits fuelled the increase in credit to the private sector. More than seven banks had over US$1 billion each in Tier-1 capital by the end of 2007.[38]

Financial Inclusion in Nigeria

Results from EFInA's 2010 financial access survey of Nigeria showed that only 30 % of the adult population had a bank account, equivalent to 25.4 million people. Of the adult population, 67.2 %, equivalent to 56.9 million people, had never been banked. Only 2.8 % of the adult population, equivalent to 2.4 million people, were previously banked. Of the 25.4 million adults who were banked, 23.6 million had savings accounts, 15.9 million had ATM cards and 6.5 million had current accounts. Overall, 30.7 million adults were financially included, while about 39.2 million adults were financially excluded, with no access to formal or informal financial services. When compared to other emerging markets like South Africa, Kenya and Botswana, these results showed that the estimated 46.3 % level of financial exclusion was high and presented opportunities.

The CBN's Cash-Lite Policy

CBN introduced a new policy on January 1, 2012 in Lagos cash-based transactions which stipulated a cash handling charge on daily cash withdrawals exceeding N500,000 for individuals and N3,000,000 for corporate bodies. The new policy on cash-based transactions (withdrawals) in banks was aimed at reducing the amount of physical cash (coins and notes) circulating in the economy and encouraging more electronic transactions (payments for goods, services, transfers, etc.).

The policy was geared towards the development and modernization of Nigeria's payment system in line with the country's Vision 2020 goal of being amongst the top 20 economies by the year 2020. An efficient and modern payment system was positively correlated with economic development and was a key enabler for economic growth. A second aim was to reduce the cost of banking services (including cost of credit) and drive financial inclusion by providing more efficient transaction options and greater reach. Lastly, the policy aimed at improving the effectiveness of monetary policy in managing inflation and driving economic growth.

Equity's History

Equity Bank started operations in 1984 as the Equity Building Society, originally established to provide mortgage financing for Kenyans who were classified as low-income earners.[39] The bank's house-shaped logo was designed to communicate that Equity was an institution desirous of assisting them in building their own homes. The Kenyan government at the time significantly deregulated the economy in a bid to encourage private investment and economic development. The deregulation of the economy provided opportunities for proactive and discerning investors to start formal financial institutions, leading to an increase in the number of financial institutions in Kenya.

At the time Equity commenced its business activities, competition in the financial services industry was fierce among the big industry players, and the potentials were limited as stated. In addition, the mortgage sector was not well developed or well understood. This forced many of the smaller building societies to close shop.[40] Equity, however, managed to survive the onslaught by mobilizing customers and deposits through one-on-one marketing. The bank was at the time operated as an informal family business whose board members were largely friends of the founders. The absence of disciplined processes and controls led to a gradual deterioration of the bank's loan book quality. In the absence of strong board oversight, Equity's financial health worsened. At the same time there was a gradual decline of interest and involvement in the affairs of the building society by three of the five founding owners/directors and a subsequent withdrawal of two of them from the business. This period of apparent board inactivity (1984–1992) resulted in the stagnation of and subsequent decline in the organization's performance. Customer deposits grew by only KSh1 million between 1986 and 1991. In the same period, loans and advances grew by only KSh7 million, from KSh2 million to KSh9 million. Accumulated losses also grew steadily from KSh5 million in 1986 to KSh22 million in 1991.[41]

Indeed, the first eight years of operations were hard for Equity. No staff member received a salary increase. Twenty staff members worked long hours in order to retain clients. Many other institutions were closing as a result of high costs coupled with the continuous loss of customers and increasing levels of loan default.

By December 1993, the Central Bank of Kenya (CBK) declared that Equity was technically insolvent. Equity's non-performing loans made up 54 %[42] of the total loan portfolio and its liquidity ratio stood at 5.4 %, well below the 20 % required by law. The CBK noted that supervision by the board was very poor. Accumulated losses were KSh33 million on a capital base of KSh3 million.[43] Deposits were being used at this time to meet operating expenses. However, limits to its powers meant the CBK could not request the closure of Equity. Only the Registrar of Building Societies, which licensed Equity for business, had the power to close the institution.[44]

At the start of 1994, Equity was technically bankrupt. It had only 17 staff members, who had extremely low morale, a loan portfolio of KSh12 million (54 % of it bad), and a deposit base of KSh25 million. Three main depositors accounted for 84 % of total deposits: the Kenyan Ministry of Water (KSh12 million), James Mwangi (KSh7 million) and the National Health Insurance Fund (NHIF; KSh2 million).[45] The board had not met between 1992 and 1994 and had performed no oversight functions. The company was grinding to a halt with an average annual loss of KSh5–7 million.[46] A court case was instituted by the Ministry of

Water and NHIF, who were seeking to liquidate Equity. James Mwangi, an accounting graduate from the University of Nairobi, was at the time the financial controller of Trade Bank.

When it became clear to James that his life savings in Equity were threatened, he opted to rescue Equity by joining the team. He resigned his job at Trade Bank and accepted a salary of US $300, compared to his salary of $5000 at Trade Bank. James' humble family background and desire to impact the low-income population in Kenya made him look beyond the fact that he had recently married and his wife had just been delivered of their first baby. After his graduation from the University of Nairobi at the top of his class, James had begun his career at Price Waterhouse, but after one month he had moved over to Ernst & Young, where he worked for three years. He then joined Trade Bank, where he rose to the position of group financial controller after three years.

James joined Equity Building Society as finance and operations director, and he, along with then managing director John Mwangi and chairman Peter Munga, constituted the board. Four independent directors were appointed from pre-eminent Kenyan organizations. James converted his KSh7 million deposit with the bank to ordinary shares, making him the majority shareholder, but John Mwangi remained CEO to allow for continuity and contact with the regulatory authorities.

Equity's Turnaround

James Mwangi also doubled as Equity's chief operating officer at the time, and he and the CEO were saddled with the responsibility of saving the company. He tackled this task in steps, starting with trying to raise the morale of staff. He subsequently ensured that the skill levels of Equity's staff in the technical and managerial areas were significantly upgraded. He was also very open to effective delegation of responsibilities to his colleagues. His vision was of a better future that would be achieved by teamwork, hard work and aspiration. According to James: "*We had to fight to save the bank or sink and lose all we had.*"

At the same time, James had to refocus Equity on microfinance since the existing mortgage market that constituted its primary business required more capital and skill than Equity possessed at the time. The mortgage market was also more competitive than microfinance. The process involved a radical transformation of Equity's DNA; it underwent a company-wide visioning process through which the directional beacons were set. There was broad ownership among staff of what the organization would be about and how the audacious goals and objectives were to be achieved. James believed that poor people made transactions like any other group of people; the difference was in the size of the transactions. He believed a business model to deliver financial services to the Kenyan poor could be effectively executed. The training staff members received reinvigorated the Equity team by educating them on the needs and peculiarities of the microfinance market and the enormous benefit their work would bring to Kenyans.

In the early 90s, the political environment changed with the introduction of a multi-party political system that led to more freedom for the people. In addition, the government relaxed its requirement that state employees bank only at government-controlled banks. This change resulted in a flood of new deposits at Equity and other industry players. The board realized that if it wanted to turn Equity around, it needed more resources (capital and non-capital) to bring in new thinking, train staff to meet the dynamic challenges of the environment, and also expand its marketing thrust.

Gradually, a culture of customer service, hard work, dedication and devotion was institutionalized. James saw his main role as that of trainer/coach. He was very firm in institutionalizing the culture. During the initial stages there were strict deadlines, uncompromising customer service, long working hours and other such measures. Later on, he intensified staff training, encouraged on-the-job training and coaching and promoted a participative leadership style, all of which helped to galvanize the workforce.

By 1995, customer deposits had grown to KSh124 million from KSh31 million in 1993. Within the same period, the bank went from a loss of KSh5 million to profits of KSh9.7 million.[47] With the company showing signs of profitability, James successfully approached the International Finance Corporation and European Investment Bank in 1996 to invest in Equity through AfriCap (owned by both entities), and they were given a seat on the board. This international connection helped improve the image of the company and won customers' confidence.

In 1997, with this new focus, the company set a target of a KShs1 billion deposit base by 2000, which was achieved as planned. This burst of performance saw the deposit base of Equity grow by 40–50 % per year between 1995 and 2002. Profit margins also grew strongly. Equity had bounced back. Successes afforded access to international partners, such as the Micro Enterprises Support Programme funded by the European Union and UNDP's United Nations Development Programme MicroStart, followed by Swisscontact and MicroSave, the British Department for International Development and MasterCard.[48]

Remarkable evidence of Equity's recovery was the rating it was issued by the Central Bank of Kenya. Shortly after 1993, its rating moved to marginal, then to fair, and by 2002 it was satisfactory.[49] Capital adequacy was fair and asset quality was satisfactory, as were earnings and liquidity ratios. By 2002, Equity had become a highly profitable institution that operated through 12 branches and 18 mobile units, with 107,000 depositors whose deposits totalled KSh1.6 billion and a loan portfolio of 18,000 borrowers worth KSh1 billion.[50] The activities of the microfinance institution had also become computerized. It had about 190 staff members, 7 directors, and 2367 shareholders. By the end of 2005, Equity had become the biggest bank in Kenya in terms of customer base, 13th-largest by capitalization and 14th-largest in terms of deposit base, and it was rated among the top five banks in the country by the CBK.[51] By 2010, Equity posted a profit before taxes of KSh9.04 billion, a 71 % increase from the previous year.[52] Equity also massively grew its customer base from 4.4 million in December 2009 to 7.8 million by June 2012.[53] This made Equity home to 57 % of all bank accounts in Kenya. Customer deposits also grew from KSh69.8 billion in 2009 to KSh104.4 billion in 2010.[54]

The East African Financial Services Sector

Several East African banks had to some degree adopted a regional business model motivated by factors like client demand, their own corporate structures, or by regional trade corridor opportunities. Two types of factors influenced the internationalization of East African banks—push factors and pull factors. Push factors are circumstances in the home country that explain why banks decide to move beyond the borders of their home countries. Chief among them are declining opportunities in the home jurisdiction and regulatory requirements. Pull factors, in contrast, are opportunities in host countries that made it attractive for a bank to enter the new market. In other words, pull factors are the expected benefits that banks hope to reap by exploring foreign markets.

One of the most powerful push factors that propels bank expansion beyond home markets is (perceived) declining profit opportunities in the home economy, especially relative to opportunities in potential host markets.

The East African banks displayed a fair degree of operational integration not just within East African markets but all the way along the trade corridors to South Sudan and the eastern Democratic Republic of Congo.

Kenya-based banks led the regional integration in the East African Country (EAC) banking sector. About 11 multinational and Kenyan-owned banks used Kenya as a hub to expand their operations into the EAC region.

About four indigenous Kenyan banks had branches within the region. Kenya Commercial Bank (KCB), Equity Bank, Fina Bank and Commercial Bank of Africa had a total of 63 branches outside Kenya (16 in Tanzania, 31 in Uganda and 16 in Rwanda) in 2012. Ugandan and Tanzanian banks had no regional presence and operated exclusively in their home markets.[55]

- Since 2006 KCB had been expanding in the EAC region. It had 164 branches in Kenya and 36 branches in other countries in East Africa—Tanzania (10), Uganda (11), Rwanda (9) and South Sudan (6). KCB's Tanzanian operation was established in 1997 and is the oldest of its regional subsidiaries.
- In March 2009 Commercial Bank of Africa merged with First American Bank's Tanzanian subsidiary, United Bank of Africa (the bank has since been renamed Commercial Bank of Africa–Tanzania).
- Fina Bank began its regional expansion into Rwanda in 2004, and by 2009 it had a presence in Uganda with five established branches. The bank had a total of 11 branches regionally.[56]

A survey conducted by the World Bank Group to gauge the operational integration of banks operating in the EAC revealed that 56 % of the banks interviewed had their operations concentrated mostly in Kenya. Most of the banks surveyed had yet to achieve full integration of their operations in the region, but partial integration had taken place in the areas of information and communications technology, risk management, customer service, and treasury operations.[57]

Two-thirds of the banks surveyed stated that regionalization had facilitated the introduction of financial products and services that would not have been possible in the absence of scale. Establishment of a single licensing regime (which would remove barriers to entry posed by separate capitalization requirements for each subsidiary and enable cross-border branching) was favoured by a majority of the banks as a measure to promote integration.

The major impediments to attaining full integration cited by banks included the lack of a common tax regime, resistance from bank supervisors (particularly supervisors in Tanzania and Uganda, who were averse to banks under their jurisdiction being managed by Kenyan parents), IT connectivity problems (caused by weak physical infrastructure), differing regulatory requirements, restrictions on the mobility of labour, and the existence of differing capital movement polices within the EAC.

Prior to the implementation of a common trading platform, cross-listing of shares in the EAC had already` increased private capital flows within the region. The total market capitalization for cross-listed shares in the EAC region stood at about US$2.88 billion, with 99.84 % taken up by the Nairobi Securities Exchange and 0.16 % shared between the Dar es Salaam Securities Exchange and the Uganda Securities Exchange. All companies cross-listed and traded regionally were from Kenya. As at 2013 there were no cross-listings of companies based in other EAC countries. Kenya defined a local investor as an EAC citizen and allowed foreign participation of up to 75 %. Tanzania allowed foreign participation of up to 60 % of shares in primary or secondary issues. There were restrictions in Uganda and Rwanda.[58]

Unlike Kenya, Tanzania did not allow foreign participation in initial public offerings (IPOs). Rwanda and Uganda required that citizens seek approval from their central bank to buy foreign IPOs. Sale or issue of shares by foreigners was not restricted in Kenya, Uganda or Tanzania, but Rwanda required central bank approval. There were no restrictions for foreigners to buy debt instruments in Kenya, Uganda, Rwanda or Burundi. Tanzania, however, restricted purchase of government bonds but allowed foreign participation for corporate debt instruments.

Participation in EAC stock and bond markets was usually dominated by institutional investors, national pension funds, fund management firms and insurance companies. Information provided by Kenyan investment banks suggested that the participation of Kenyan investors in other EAC markets was about 10 %, whereas that of Ugandan investors in other EAC markets was between 2 and 5 %, and that of Tanzanian investors reached a maximum of only 0.5 %. Due to the lack of restrictions on capital flows from Kenya, a greater number of its retail investors participated in EAC markets. This was in contrast to Tanzania and Uganda, where mainly institutional investors participated.

Several factors resulted in a regionalization of financial markets in the EAC. The signing of the Common Market Protocol and the initiatives of the private sector banks together created a favourable climate for integration, especially between the three original members of the EAC. However, several factors, like the harmonization of legal and regulatory frameworks, the adoption of a single licensing regime, mutual recognition among regulators, absence of a regionally compatible financial infrastructure and homogenous cross-border supervision practices, still constrained the growth and integration of the regional market. To enhance integration of financial markets in the EAC region, the World Bank proposed a Financial Sector Development & Regionalization Project I (FSDRP I), comprising a three-year US$16 million regional technical assistance grant to the EAC to support the move towards a single market in financial services. The project development objective of FSDRP I was to establish the foundation for financial sector integration among EAC partner states.[59]

Equity's Internationalization Experience

Equity's internationalization was driven by the integration of the EAC region, the bank's pursuit of its pan-African strategic intent to be the champion of the socio-economic development of Africa, the bank's vision of increasing accessibility to financial services to the people of Africa, and its salient desire to contribute to the socio-economic prosperity of the people of Africa through provision of inclusive financial services to the unbanked and underbanked. Equity Bank was, however, a late entrant in the cross-border banking business and had to grapple with the challenge of conquering competition in the various international locations. Domestic banks in the target countries already had high market shares established by subsidiaries of South African and Nigerian banks that commenced internationalization before East African banks. Equity's main strength was its unique high-volume, low-margin business model and strong brand in the region

Equity was also desirous of diversifying its country risk, which was increased by the 2007/2008 post-election violence, by generating earnings from other countries. The low levels of financial inclusion in the Sub-Saharan region, with about 88 % of households in the region unbanked, established strong demand for financial services in the region.[60] Equity was already an exceptionally successful bank with a huge capital base. It was a renowned brand riding on the platform of a stable and scalable core banking system. Equity had a strong management team reputed for deploying its products and services through the various established channels and an effective board with strong oversight capabilities that greatly reinforced management's efforts. Underlying macroeconomic fundamentals and projections suggested that East Africa's GDP would continue to grow at an annual rate of not less than 5 % for the next five years.[61]

Equity's Management had initial reservations when James sold the idea of going international, as they felt their rich culture and time-tested business model would be unreplicable across the international subsidiaries. The management team and entire staff eventually gave their full support when they realized that the pan-African vision of Equity was not realizable if they remained in Kenya only. They also saw internationalization as an opportunity for the growth and advancement of their careers as most senior managers in Equity transited to director and CEO positions in the various subsidiaries. Cultural difference problems were resolved by staff induction programmes in Kenya for all newly recruited subsidiary staff members and rotational secondments to the various core head office units to get a better feel for Equity's operations and a better appreciation of the bank's corporate culture.

Equity's internationalization started with the establishment of the Ugandan subsidiary for the following reasons:

- Uganda had larger unbanked and underbanked populations than Kenya.
- There was a relatively lower degree of financial sector sophistication than in Kenya and hence room for the replication of Equity's existing business model.
- Uganda's GDP growth rate averaged 1.75 % between 2006 and 2015, reaching an all-time high of 5.83 % in the first quarter of 2008 and a record low of –2.29 % in the second quarter of 2014.[62]
- Uganda was Kenya's number-one trading partner and had several business ties with Kenya. Many Kenyans studied at Makerere University in Uganda.
- The close relationship between the vision of the acquired institution (Uganda Microfinance Limited) "to become the leading and preferred micro finance service provider in Uganda" and that of Equity Bank "to be the champions of socio-economic prosperity of the people of Africa" provided a good fit between the two organizations.
- The EAC integration and common use of English as an official language in both countries and Equity's customers required a Ugandan branch. Many of Equity's customers expanded their businesses into Uganda.

Project Team

In 2009, when Equity decided to go international, the Regional Expansion Unit within the Projects Management Office constituted a taskforce for the establishment of each subsidiary. This team had members from the information and communications technology, human resources, finance, procurement, legal, systems audit, facilities management, treasury and shared services departments. Most members of the taskforce were based in the head office and were senior members of staff that had spent a minimum of five years with Equity and had a very good grasp of Equity's values, systems and business model. The taskforce centrally co-ordinated and managed all project-type activities in the bank's subsidiaries, and each country expansion had an independent project team and project manager that managed the day-to-day implementation challenges. All project managers reported to the senior program manager in charge of regional expansion.

Staffing

Initially, most subsidiaries had experienced Equity staff seconded to them for the first six months to help build culture, set up systems and address most of the teething and start-up problems. Following the success of this initial approach, Equity instituted a more structured 6- to 12-month induction course in Kenya for new officers recruited from the host countries in order to help them internalize Equity's unique culture and business model. This induction course included classroom lectures and secondments to Equity's business units on a rotational basis. Newly recruited officers were always inducted in Kenya prior to their resumption in their subsidiary locations. Equity encountered language problems in Tanzania and Rwanda as most staff members were not fluent in English. Rwandese were more fluent in French, and Tanzanians were more fluent in Swahili in spite of the fact that English was Tanzania's main language of instruction. Language was not much of a problem in Uganda. To overcome language problems, most customer-facing staff were recruited from the host countries and thoroughly prepared to handle the business.

The dearth of skilled manpower in the various international locations posed serious challenges to Equity. Most countries in the East African region had a deficiency of skilled banking staff. Tanzania had stringent labour laws that prohibited cross-border labour flow. Equity overcame the challenge of skilled manpower in countries like South Sudan by recruiting graduates directly from colleges and training them thoroughly. With the exception of Uganda, where the managing director was recruited from Standard Chartered Bank Ghana, Equity deployed all subsidiary managing directors (experienced senior business and development managers and heads of departments) from Kenya, mainly because they understood well the Equity Bank model and had strongly internalized the organization's culture. However, Equity had to hire locals to fill other top management positions to localize the brand and give the citizens of the country a feeling of ownership. The aim was to eventually phase out expatriates once credible and competent local staff understood the Equity Bank model.

Differences in language, culture, flexibility of work hours, work ethic, lunch hours and national values led Equity to develop a course called "Leading Across Cultures". This course greatly helped new hires in subsidiaries and seconded Equity staff appreciate the various cultural issues they had to navigate in the course of their work in the international locations. Such issues as cultural integration and key imperatives for success in international locations were extensively discussed. The similarities in the work ethic and national management culture of Rwanda and Kenya made the establishment of the Rwandan subsidiary and integration of cultural issues relatively easier. Equity's staff incentive structure was replicated in all international subsidiaries.

Due Diligence

Equity's acquisition of Uganda Microfinance Limited was facilitated by PricewaterhouseCoopers (which was recruited to conduct the due diligence) and FSI Capital Ltd (which was recruited to conduct the detailed credit assessment study). Equity encountered several cultural difference problems arising from differences in the work cultures of the banks and in the national management culture of Ugandans. It also had to grapple with several integration issues. For the establishment of subsequent subsidiaries—South Sudan, Rwanda and Uganda—all the due diligence and country viability studies were carried out by Equity's regional expansion team and the research and product development team. The taskforce used the PESTEL and SWOT analysis in Fig. 9.16 to establish market feasibility. The central banks of the respective countries were very supportive of the bank's initiatives to bring more unbanked individuals into formal banking. Telecom companies in the region also provided connectivity and mobile money services.

The research and product development team worked with the taskforce for each new international subsidiary to conduct comprehensive market research on existing products, customer needs and likely channels in the new country before establishment. They also established likely geographic areas in the country that would be most receptive to Equity and included a branch expansion plan in all the economically viable states of the country. The research team continuously conducted competitor intelligence exercises to establish the nature and character of competition in the various international locations with a view to improving Equity's positioning at all times (Figs. 9.2, 9.3, 9.4, 9.5, 9.6, 9.7, 9.8 and 9.9).

Equity's legal team researched and hired local legal teams if need be to facilitate licensing and other regulatory compliance issues of new subsidiaries. As the home regulator, CBK introduced cross-border supervision and liaised with other country regulators for cross-border regulation under Basel II standards. CBK and the Kenyan Ministry of Finance issued letters of no objection to the target country regulator and Equity Bank for the establishment of any subsidiary. The approvals were obtained after applications for company incorporation, bank license, investment authority registration and tax personal identification number registration were concluded.

With the exception of Uganda, where entry was by the acquisition of Uganda Microfinance, Equity adopted a greenfield entry strategy for the subsidiaries in South Sudan, Rwanda and Tanzania.

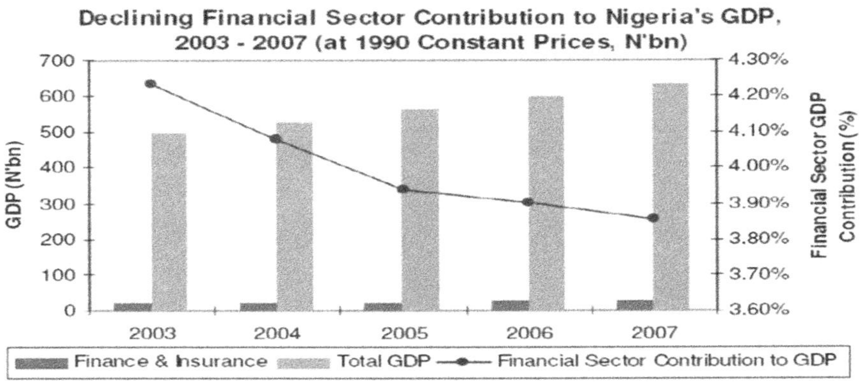

Fig. 9.2 Financial sector's contribution to Nigeria's GDP. *Source*: National Bureau of Statistics

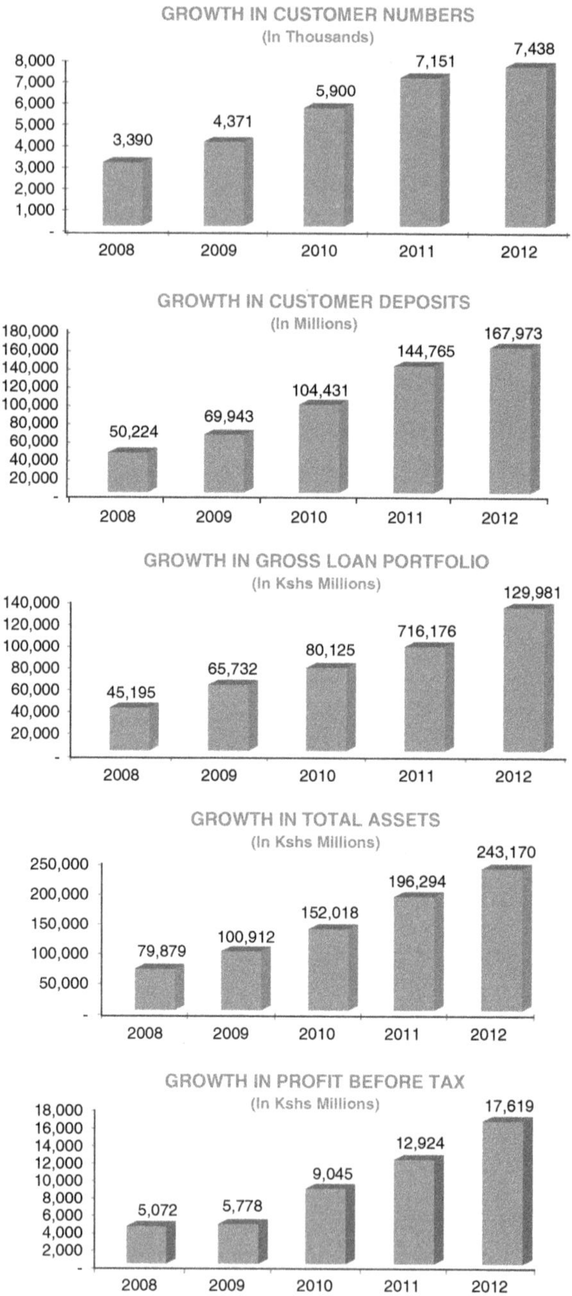

Fig. 9.3 Growth in customer numbers, deposits, gross loan portfolio, total assets and profit before tax. *Source*: Equity Bank Group Annual Reports and Accounts 2012

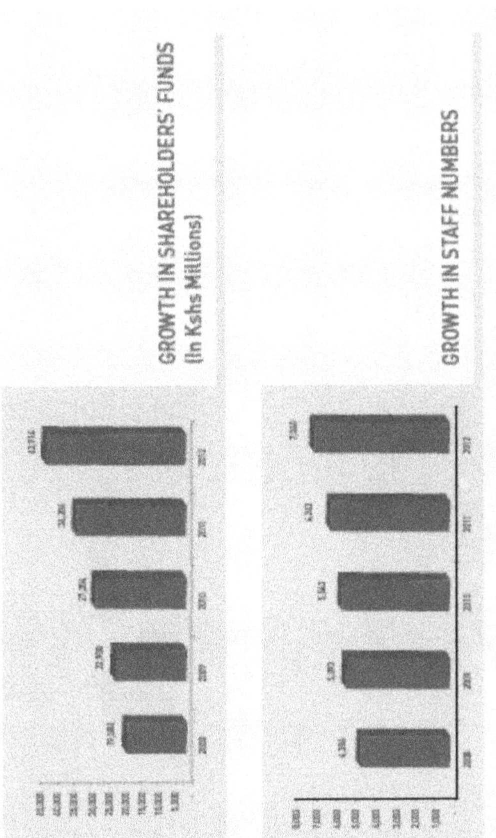

Fig. 9.4 Growth in shareholders' funds and staff numbers. *Source*: Equity Bank Group Annual Reports and Accounts 2012

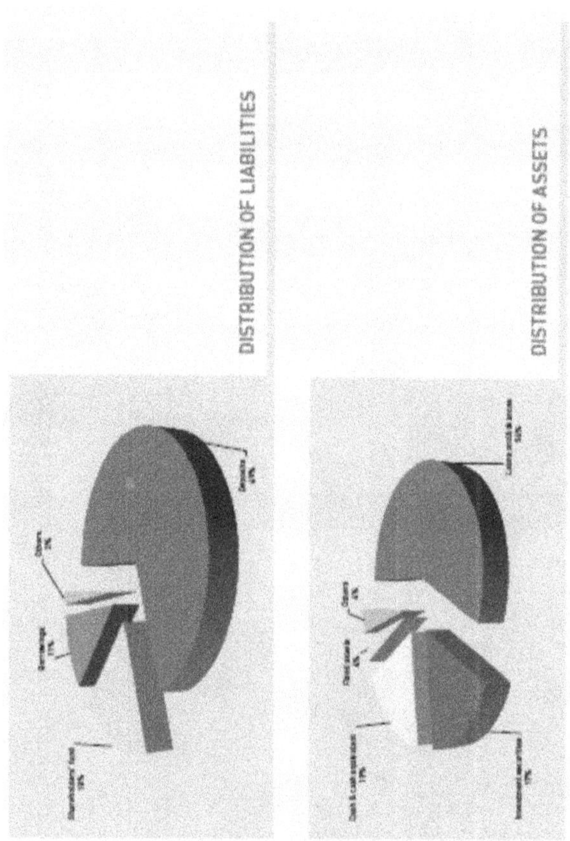

Fig. 9.5 Distribution of liabilities and assets. *Source*: Equity Bank Group Annual Reports and Accounts 2012

Purpose

We exist to transform the lives and livelihoods of our people socially and economically by availing them modern, inclusive financial services that maximize their opportunities

Vision

"…To be the champion of the socio-economic prosperity of the people of Africa.…"

Mission

"…..We offer inclusive, customer-focused financial services that socially and economically empower our clients and other stakeholders….."

Tagline

Your listening caring partner

Positioning

The Listening, Caring Financial Partner.

Motto

"… Growing together in trust…"

Core Values

- Professionalism
- Integrity
- Creativity and Innovation
- Teamwork
- Unity of Purpose
- Respect and dedication to customer care
- Effective Corporate Governance

Fig. 9.6 Equity Bank purpose, vision and mission

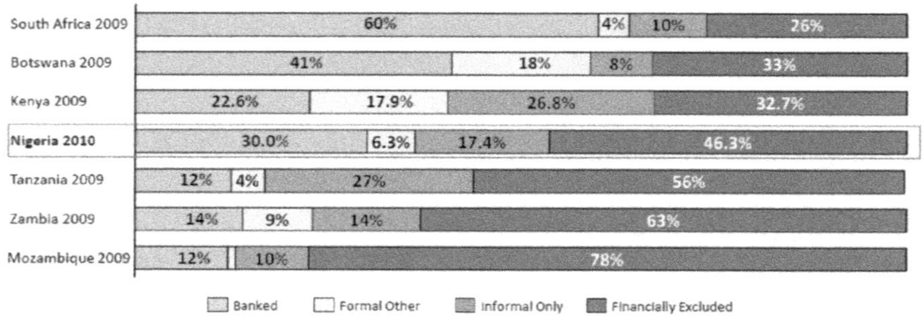

Fig. 9.7 2010 Financial Access Survey. *Source*: Adapted from EFINA's Financial Access Survey 2010—Cross Country Comparisons of Financial Inclusion

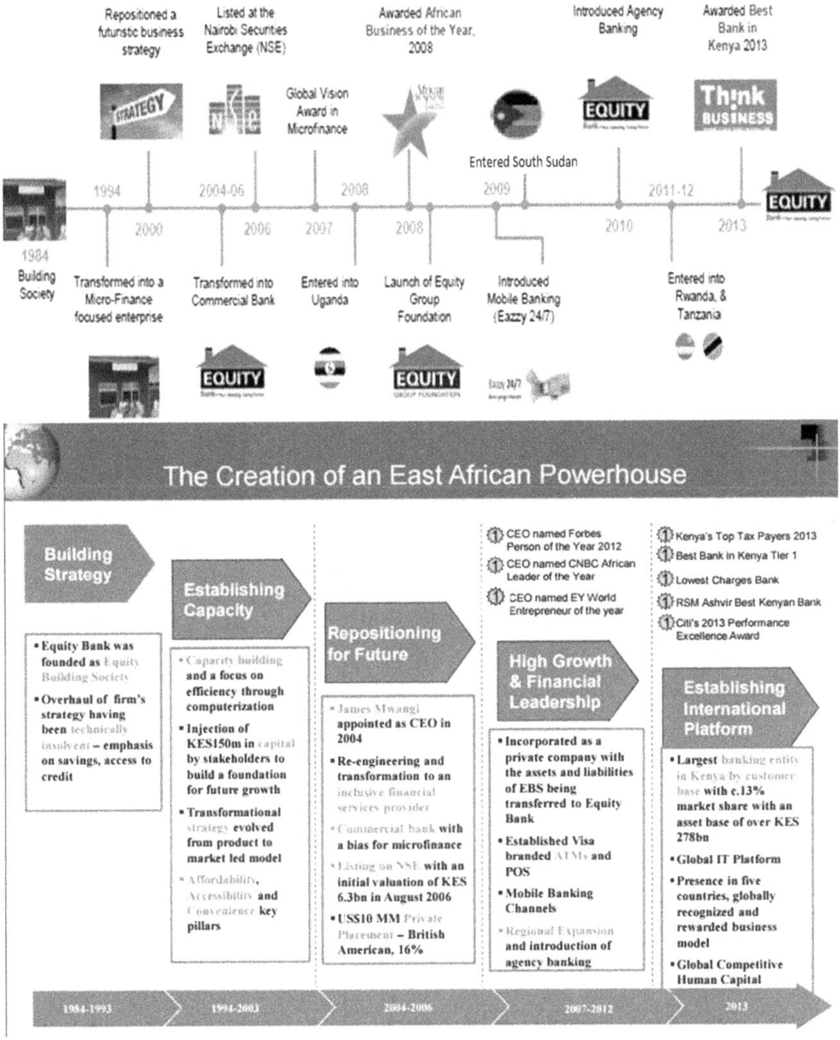

Fig. 9.8 Chronological evolution of Equity Bank. *Source*: Adapted from Equity's 2013 Investor Presentation

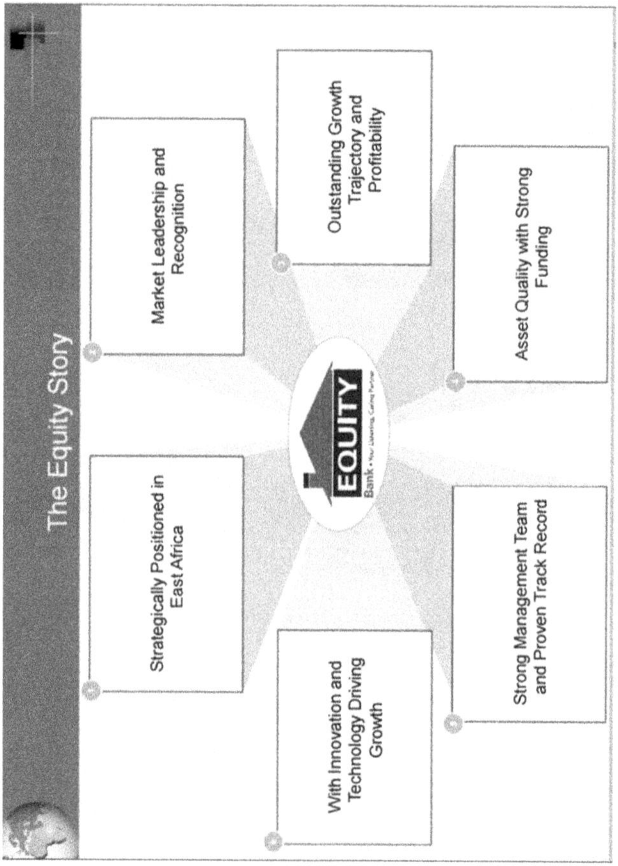

Fig. 9.9 The Equity story. *Source*: Adapted from Equity's 2013 Investor Presentation

Physical and Social Infrastructure

The quality of the physical and social infrastructures in other explored international locations was very similar to the situation in Kenya. Equity leveraged largely on its establishment experience for its Kenyan branches. Lack of a national identification system and land ownership titles in Tanzania affected delivery of credit services. Low gross literacy and financial literacy achievement levels required the bank to offer financial education programmes to its customers. In South Sudan, there was the need for credit guarantee mechanisms to crowd-in lending and effectively reduce the risk of lending. Financial intermediation was made more challenging in South Sudan by political instability; lack of effective treasury bill and bonds money markets; lack of a credit reference bureau; a small formal business sector (few companies registered); lack of a deposit insurance protection fund; and lack of regulatory guidelines for agency banking, mobile banking, and bancassurance. In Uganda there were relatively higher fraud levels as well as lack of regulatory guidelines for agency banking, mobile banking, and bancassurance. Rwanda and Tanzania had young credit reference bureaus.

Demand for Financial Services

There was a relatively high demand for financial services in East Africa as it was estimated that only 12 % of households in the region had access to such services.[63] The low levels of financial penetration and inclusion as well as very low percentages of loans to GDP in East Africa all provided strong evidence of the need for deepening financial services in East Africa.

Equity's skill in converting the unbanked helped it gain scale in every market it entered. This approach reduced time to market in all cases. Some competitor banks imitated Equity's product offerings but were unable to imitate Equity's ability to execute, and customer experience remained one of Equity's advantages.

Barriers to Entry

Most East African countries had relatively high minimum capital requirements. Zambia's high minimum capital requirement of KSh8 billion for a foreign subsidiary posed a difficulty for Equity in the establishment of a Zambian subsidiary.

Delays in processing and issuance of banking licenses in the various host countries hindered Equity's progress and substantially increased set-up time and time to market. In some extreme instances where delays were not anticipated, the Equity head office had to pay the salaries of over 100 staff members for over six months; these staff members were already trained and inducted but could not commence operations because issuance of the license was delayed for six months beyond the expected date.

Kenya was one of the most sophisticated economies in the region, and laws and policies for the conduct of agency banking were already in place. South Sudan had yet to enact an agency banking policy. Rwanda was able to issue guidelines in 2012, while Tanzania issued guidelines in 2013. This situation resulted in stunted growth of customer numbers and reduced profitability of the subsidiaries. A major regulatory hurdle Equity had to overcome was the labour law in Tanzania that restricted movement of labour into Tanzania. Equity sought and obtained the approval of the Bank of Tanzania to hire eight experienced managers to support the establishment of Equity Bank Tanzania. In South Sudan, United States sanctions on banking relations with Sudan (Khartoum) impacted Equity Bank negatively in areas such as delaying approvals for Citibank correspondent banking; SWIFT, Visa, American Express and MasterCard issuance; and customer acquisitions.

Products and Services

Equity at all times retained its microfinance model, which entailed standardized products customized to fit the circumstances of the international subsidiary. Equity typically started each subsidiary with payment products (cards, mobile money and internet payment channels), savings products and microloans. As the operations in a subsidiary gained scale with increased transaction volume and more customers, Equity introduced trade finance and treasury products. Equity had yet (as of 2014) to roll out insurance and investment banking services to customers outside Kenya.

The product development team constantly improved product bundles through market research results that revealed customer touchpoints and customer preferences in the various subsidiaries. Equity early on realized that a one-size-fits-all approach would be inappropriate because the circumstances, needs and peculiarities of each country required some form of customization of Equity's original model. There was also constant information flow between each subsidiary and the research and product development teams to fine tune product offerings and enhance their effectiveness.

Partnerships

Equity worked with the United Nations Capital Development Fund under the MicroLead programme to recognize milestone achievements and deepen financial inclusion and innovation in the subsidiaries. Other notable partners were Swisscontact and the Bill & Melinda Gates Foundation, both of which supported the various financial inclusion and corporate social responsibility initiatives of Equity Group in its various subsidiaries.

Equity's planned to roll out the Equity Foundation in all international subsidiaries to develop and implement the various host country corporate social responsibility (CSR) initiatives. The Equity Foundation also developed CSR programs that extended to other international locations.

Corporate Governance

Each subsidiary's board was well resourced with experienced executive and non-executive directors. Equity Group's board led the process of selection of directors for subsidiaries. Non-executive directors were typically sourced from the host country's reservoir of business and community leaders who had distinguished themselves in their professional careers and proven their integrity. All board members were vetted before appointment, and the vetting took into account professional qualifications, integrity and track record. New board members had to pass the regulator "fit and proper test". Each board was relatively independent and was at liberty in some instances to undertake independent projects without recourse to the head office. An annual self-evaluation exercise of all directors in the subsidiaries was conducted, in line with international best practices. The evaluation focused on the role and responsibility of the board; its structure, composition, functions and processes; information and meetings; and other critical areas. The board structure and all relevant committees at Equity's head office closely resembled the board structure in each subsidiary, with slight customizations in line with the host country's code of corporate governance. Organization structures of the various subsidiaries were customized to meet the needs and circumstances of the host country and also to comply with local labour laws. Each subsidiary sent daily and monthly management and financial reports to Equity's head office. These reports complemented the monthly performance appraisals conducted by both internal and external auditors. Equity had to upgrade its management information systems infrastructure to enable it to monitor and manage the activities of the subsidiaries in real time.

Ownership

All subsidiaries were 100 % owned by Equity. Equity was cross-listed on the Nairobi Securities Exchangwe and the Uganda Securities Exchange. The future plan was to cross-list Equity's shares in established exchanges in countries hosting the international subsidiaries. Equity was instrumental to the injection of foreign direct investment into the different countries that hosted its international subsidiaries, with injection of over US$100 million in Uganda, Tanzania, South Sudan and Rwanda as at December 2013 (Tables 9.2, 9.3, 9.4, 9.5, 9.6, 9.7, 9.8, 9.9, 9.10, 9.11, 9.12, 9.13, 9.14 and 9.15). (Table 9.16 shows total foreign direct investment of Equity Group into all of its subsidiaries in 2013.)

Table 9.3 Macroeconomic indicators for Nigeria

Indicator	1990	1995	2000	2005	2010
GDP (current US$)	28,472,471,051	28,108,826,038	45,983,6000,313	112,248,609,250	193,668,738,107
GDP growth (annual %)	8.20	2.50	5.40	5.40	7.85
GDP, PPP (current international $)	99,836,294,288	127,142,551,468	161,081,163,566	244,642,093,041	377,146,064,036
GDP per capita (current US$)	292	256	372	803	1222
GDP per capita growth (annual %)	5.51	0.11	2.93	2.82	5.17
GDP per capita, PPP (current international $)	1023	1156	1302	1750	2381
Inflation, consumer prices (annual %)	7.36	72.84	6.93	17.86	13.72
Deposit interest rate (%)	19.78	13.53	11.69	10.53	6.52
Lending interest rate (%)	25.30	20.23	21.27	17.95	17.59
Interest rate spread (lending rate minus deposit rate, %)	5.52	6.70	9.58	7.42	11.06
Risk premium on lending (prime rate minus treasury bill rate, %)	0.00	7.73	5.77	10.32	13.74
Domestic credit provided by banking sector (% of GDP)	23.66	23.99	10.09	8.60	36.28
Official exchange rate (LCU per US$, period average)	8.04	21.90	101.70	131.27	150.30

(continued)

Table 9.3 (continued)

Indicator	1990	1995	2000	2005	2010
Exports of goods and services (current US$)	12,365,872,842	12,448,763,502	24,820,549,289	52,237,628,416	76,248,124,979
Imports of goods and services (current US$)	8,202,785,667	11,857,546,902	14,727,556,917	34,849,468,834	51,575,629,421
External balance on goods and services (current US$)	4,163,087,175	591,216,600	10,092,992,373	17,388,159,583	24,672,495,558
External balance on goods and services (% of GDP)	14.62	2.10	21.95	15.49	12.74
Market capitalization of listed companies (% of GDP)	4.81	7.23	9.21	17.24	26.27
External debt stocks, total (DOD, current US$)	33,438,924,000	34,092,471,000	31,354,920,000	22,060,054,000	7,882,519,000
Mobile cellular subscriptions	0	13,000	30,000	18,587,000	87,297,789
Mobile cellular subscriptions (%)	0.00	0.10	0.02	13.29	55.10
Internet users	0		79,261	4,962,548	45,039,711
Internet users (%)	0.00	0.00	0.06	3.55	28.43
Population, total	97,552,057	110,014,688	123,688,536	139,823,340	158,423,182
Rural population	83,116,181	67,218,974	71,120,908	75,224,957	79,528,437

Urban population	34,435,876	42,795,714	52,567,628	64,598,383	78,894,745
Population ages 0–14 (% of total)	44.81	43.94	43.13	42.82	42.81
Population ages 15–64 (% of total)	52.02	52.87	53.64	53.87	53.79
Population ages 65 and above (% of total)	3.16	3.19	3.22	3.31	3.40
Population growth (annual %)	2.51	2.36	2.38	2.48	2.52
Labour force, total	29,932,254	34,290,460	39,388,948	44,768,836	

Source: Adapted from World Bank macroeconomic indicators on Nigeria 1990–2010
GDP – Gross Domestic Product; LCU – Local Currency Unit

Table 9.4 Business growth and performance statistics of Equity Bank Uganda Limited in Ugandan shillings

Year	Dec 2009	Dec 2010	Dec 2011	Dec 2012
Deposits	71,568,612,233	138,882,063,052	167,284,801,451	178,879,223,930
Outstanding loans and advances	82,812,563,951	136,318,592,960	163,849,761,238	197,235,672,896
Total assets (net)	154,740,775,601	204,776,206,544	262,263,465,859	305,300,282,087
Pretax (profit/loss)	(6,978,719,661)	(22,861,827,563)	554,936,464	2,316,480,670
Cost to income ratio (%)	132.35	172.74	97.38	96.0
Return on equity (%)	−23.70	−49.88	2.50	4.13
Return on assets (%)	−7.10	11.68	0.42	0.57

Source: Equity Bank Group Annual Reports and Accounts 2012

Table 9.5 Business growth and performance statistics of Equity Bank South Sudan Limited in South Sudanese pounds

Year	Dec 2009	Dec 2010	Dec 2011	Dec 2012
Deposits	41,371,000	134,750,000	456,832,000	548,268,000
Outstanding loans and advances	5,366,000	21,850,000	61,597,000	135,970,000
Total assets (net)	75,262,000	201,359,000	621,707,000	675,710,000
Pretax (profit/loss)	(1,529,000)	11,540,000	12,827,000	37,882,000
Cost to income ratio	1.499	0.562	0.695	0.55
Return on equity (after tax, %)	−11	39	27	74
Return on assets (after tax, %)	−1.7	5	2.34	5

Source: Equity Bank Group Annual Reports and Accounts 2012

Table 9.6 Business growth and performance statistics of Equity Bank Rwanda Limited in Rwandan francs

Year	Dec 2011	Dec 2012
Deposits	4,341,315,000	15,889,958,000
Outstanding loans and advances	305,231,000	12,485,291,000
Total assets (net)	12,020,961,000	24,196,893,000
Pretax (profit/loss)	(419,096,000)	(1,690,345,000)
Cost to income ratio (%)	349	149
Return on equity (after tax, %)	−37	−34
Return on assets (after tax, %)	−21	−7

Source: Equity Bank Group Annual Reports and Accounts 2012

What Next?

Mary and her team had six months to come up with a market entry strategy document for Nigeria, but they had already submitted a preliminary findings report to the board. This report was going to form the basis for extensive deliberations at the board meeting. As her team began to get more information on the structure of banking in Nigeria, several key questions remained: What market entry strategy should Equity adopt for Nigeria? Was buying an existing bank more prudent, or was a greenfield entry preferable? Was a universal banking license better, or was a state microfinance

Table 9.7 Business growth and performance statistics of Equity Bank Tanzania in Tanzanian shillings

Year	December 2012
Deposits	38,323,905,000
Outstanding loans and advances	24,641,640,000
Total assets	76,218,766,000
Pretax (profit/loss)	(1,406,230,000)
Cost to income ratio (%)	116.90
Return on equity (after tax, %)	−4.43
Return on assets (after tax, %)	−1.50

Source: Equity Bank Group Annual Reports and Accounts 2012

Table 9.8 Equity bank operating segments

Operating segments	
Year	December 2012
Deposits	38,323,905,000
Outstanding loans and advances	24,641,640,000
Total assets	76,218,766,000
Pretax (profit/loss)	(1,406,230,000)
Cost to income ratio (%)	116.90
Return on equity (after tax, %)	−4.43
Return on assets (after tax, %)	−1.50

Source: Equity Bank Group Annual Reports and Accounts 2012

license more appropriate? How was Equity going to raise the required N25 billion required to open shop in Nigeria? What effects would the positioning in the industry have on Equity's brand? The Nigerian banking industry was more sophisticated than the Kenyan banking industry, so the innovation and product development teams would have to work harder to craft value propositions that would excite Nigerians. James stated:

> *The challenge in Nigeria is the banking culture is fairly strong. To operate in Nigeria, one requires a huge capital base in line with regulatory requirement. It's a huge market with a population of about 160 million people. But beyond meeting basic regulatory requirements, you need to open up a very big bank to be able to compete and in order to make business sense.*

Table 9.9 Equity Bank profit and loss as at 31 December 2012

2012						2011					
In millions of Kenyan shillings	Kenya	Uganda	Sudan	Rwanda	Tanzania	Total	Kenya	Uganda	Sudan	Rwanda	Total
Total assets	206,023	9978	19,656	3392	4122	243,170	167,587	9169	17,844	1694	196,294
Net interest income	22,123	985	488	167	201	23,964	15,659	853	(291)	2	16,223
Total operating income	32,181	1443	2425	423	355	36,827	25,642	21,351	1657	20	28,670
Total expenses	15,762	1386	1343	656	432	19,579	13,532	1332	1048	79	15,991
Profit before tax	16,591	57	1082	(233)	(77)	17,420	12,110	19	609	(59)	12,679

Source: Equity Bank Group Annual Reports and Accounts 2012

Table 9.10 Equity bank balance sheet as at 31 December 2012

		Group		Bank	
In millions of Kenyan shillings	Note	2012	2011	2012	2011
Interest income	8	30,848	19,339	28,497	18,376
Interest expense	8	(6884)	(3116)	(6385)	(2815)
Net interest income		23,964	16,223	22,112	15,561
Fee and commission income	9(a)	2301	2349	1809	2034
Net fee and commission income		2301	2349	1809	2034
Net trading income	9(b)	2090	2423	821	1274
Other operating income	10	8472	7675	7133	6598
Operating income before impairment losses		36,827	28,670	31,875	25,467
Net impairment loss on financial assets	11	(1608)	(1630)	(14,561)	(1533)
Operating income after impairment losses		35,219	27,040	30,419	23,934
Personnel expenses	12	(7172)	(6009)	(5905)	(5185)
Operating lease expenses	13	(1213)	(919)	(847)	(687)
Depreciation and amortization	14,15	(2316)	(1745)	(2018)	(1483)
Other operating expenses	16	(7269)	(5688)	(5589)	(4475)
Total operating expenses		(17,970)	(14,361)	(14,359)	(11,830)
Profit before tax and equity income		17,249	12,679	16,060	12,104
Share of profit of associates	17(a)	171	155	–	–
Profit before income tax		17,420	12,834	16,060	12,104
Income tax expense	18	(5340)	(2509)	(5063)	(2330)
Profit for the year		12,080	10,325	10,997	9774
Attributed to: Equity holders of the parent		12,080	10,325	10,997	9774
Earnings per share (basic and diluted)	29	3.26	2.79	2.97	2.64

Source: Equity Bank Group Annual Reports and Accounts 2012

Table 9.11 Equity Bank cash flow statement as at 31 December 2012

		Group		Bank	
In millions of Kenyan shillings	Note	2012	2011	2012	2011
Assets					
Cash and cash equivalents	19	45,134	35,282	35,467	
Loans and advances to customers	20(b)	135,692	113,824	122,410	106,486
Finance lease receivabl	20(c)	–	1	–	–
Investment securities	21	41,101	30,502	32,792	30,199
Amounts due from related parties	22(g)	2	124	983	1094
Other assets	23	7243	5038	6459	4707
Tax recoverable	18	5553	–	–	
Investment in associate	17(a)	1457	1366	1113	1260
Investment in subsidiary companies	17(b)	–	–	8204	6672
Property and equipment	9072	7592	6530	6044	
Prepaid leases	14(c)	292	29	4	4
Intangible assets	15	1415	1352	1123	1076
Goodwill	17(c)	887	887	–	–
Deferred tax assets	820	244	744	239	
Total assets	243,170	196,294	215,829	176,911	
Liabilities					
Deposits from customers	25	167,913	144,165	142,386	125,492
Tax payable	18	2365	487	2258	417
Other liabilities	27	3369	2565	2759	2186
Borrowed funds	26	26,569	14,792	25,755	13,769
Deferred tax liability	24	38	–	–	–
Total liabilities		200,254	162,009	173,158	141,864
Equity					
Share capital	28(a)	1851	1651	1851	1851

(*continued*)

Table 9.11 (continued)

		Group		Bank	
In millions of Kenyan shillings	Note	2012	2011	2012	2011
Share premium	28(b)	12,161	12,151	12,161	12,161
Retained earnings		25,088	17,719	24,308	17,974
Available for sale reserve	28(c)	(732)	(1062)	(732)	(1062)
Loan loss reserve	28(d)	603	521	454	420
Foreign currency translation reserve	28(e)	(603)	(529)	–	–
Revaluation reserve	28(f)	32	34	–	–
Other reserves	28(g)	(113)	(113)	–	–
Proposed dividends	28(h)	4629	3703	4629	3703
Total equity		42,916	34,285	42,671	35,047
Total liabilities and equity		243,170	196,294	215,829	176,911

Source: Equity Bank Group Annual Reports and Accounts 2012

Table 9.12 Loans and advances to customers as at 31 December 2012

		Group		Bank	
In millions of Kenyan shillings	Note	2012	2011	2012	2011
Cash flows from operating activities					
Net profit before taxation		17,420	12,834	16,060	12,104
Adjustments for:					
Depreciation	14	2016	1583	1734	1338
Amortization of intangible assets	15	300	162	284	145
Unrealized exchange (gains)/(losses)		(286)	63	(288)	(67)
Profit on disposal of property and equipment		(4)	(7)	(6)	(3)
Provision for non-performing loans	11	1608	1630	1456	1533
Share of profit of associates	17a	(171)	(155)	–	–
Dividends received	17a	(80)	(49)	–	–
Interest on term borrowings	8	1474	763	1508	806
Operating profit before working capital changes		22,277	16,824	20,748	15,807
Loans and advances		(23,476)	(37,159)	(17,380)	(36,118)
Other assets	(2205)		(1254)	(1495)	(1472)
Finance lease receivable		1	2	–	–
Customer deposits		23,748	39,734	16,893	30,289
Due from related parties		122	(16)	–	144
Other liabilities	804		(151)	573	(73)
Cash generated from operations		21,271	17,980	19,339	9577
Income taxes paid	18	(4002)	(2875)	(3728)	(2747)
Net cash generated from operating activities		17,269	15,105	15,611	6830
Cash flows from investing activities					
Purchase of property, equipment & prepaid leases	14	(3782)	(2225)	(2236)	(1689)
Purchase of intangible assets	15	(363)	(473)	(331)	(467)
Proceeds from sale of property and equipment	14	27	25	22	4
Investment in subsidiaries		–	–	(1532)	(1588)
Dividends received		80	49	–	49

(continued)

Table 9.12 (continued)

		Group		Bank	
In millions of Kenyan shillings	Note	2012	2011	2012	2011
Purchase of investment securities	21	(25,893)	(22,546)	(17,091)	(22,248)
Proceeds from sale of investment securities	21	15,625	23,959	14,829	23,888
Net cash generated from/ (used in) investing activities		14,306	(1211)	(6339)	(2051)
Cash flows from financing activities					
Dividends paid	28(h)	(3703)	(2962)	(3703)	(2962)
Proceeds from long-term borrowings		13,581	8096	13,745	7502
Repayment of long-term borrowings		(1804)	(1267)	(1759)	(1197)
Interest paid on long-term borrowings	8	(1474)	(763)	(1508)	(806)
Net cash flow generated from financing activities		6600	3104	6775	2537
Net increase in cash and cash equivalents		9563	16,998	16,047	7316
Effect of foreign exchange differences	323	(63)	290	67	–
Effect of foreign currency translation reserve on cash and cash equivalents	(34)	(156)	–	–	–
Cash and cash equivalents at the beginning of the year	19	35,282	18,503	19,130	11,747
Cash and cash equivalents at the end of the year	19	45,134	35,282	35,467	19,130

Table 9.13 Chronological evolution of the Nigerian banking industry

Year	Key events
1986	• 36 licensed banks • Inception of structural adjustment program
1990	• Entry of numerous small players • 109 registered banks • Introduction of prudential guidelines
1991	• 120 registered commercial and merchant banks • 45 % devaluation of the Naira • Minimum paid-up capital required for commercial banks: N20 million • Minimum paid-up capital required for merchant banks: N12 million
1992	• 6 banks distressed and taken over by the NDIC
1992 (cont'd)	• Minimum paid-up capital required for commercial banks: N50 million • Minimum paid-up capital required for merchant banks: N40 million • Official inflation at 57 % and yield on 90-day treasury bills at 18 % • 90 % gap between interbank foreign exchange market (official) and bureaux de change exchange rates • Establishment of Nigeria Inter-Bank Settlement System • Exchange rate of N17.3/US$1
1993	• 120 licensed banks: 80 solvent banks, 30 banks considered by CBN to be distressed, 4 banks in liquidation and 6 banks taken over by NDIC • Parallel market premium of 70 % over official exchange rate • Official inflation at 60 %; interbank rates top 100 % • Prime lending rates of commercial and merchant banks at 33 % and 66 %, respectively • Exchange rate of N22/US$1
1994	• 120 licensed banks: 4 banks in liquidation, 6 banks sold to the CBN for N1, 66 solvent banks, 44 financially distressed banks • Official inflation of 57 %; treasury bills issue rate fixed at 14.5 % • Exchange rate of N21.9/US$1

(continued)

Table 9.13 (continued)

Year	Key events
1995	• 115 licensed banks: 12 banks acquired, 43 financially distressed banks, 60 solvent banks • Official inflation of 73 %; lending rates fixed at 21 %; deposit rates range between 12 % and 15 % • Exchange rate of N70/US$1
1998	• 115 licensed banks: 26 banks in liquidation, 89 operational banks in the system comprising 51 commercial banks and 38 merchant banks • Minimum paid-up capital for all banks increased to N500 million with March 1999 set as deadline • Official inflation at 10 %; treasury bills issue rate at 20 %
1999	• New banks required to have minimum paid-up capital of N1 billion • Exchange rate of N95/US$1 • Capital requirement for existing banks remains unchanged at N500 million
2000	• Introduction of universal banking
2001	• 4 new licences and 2 approvals-in-principle issued • 8 banks recapitalized and restructured • minimum paid-up capital requirement increased to N2 billion for new banks; existing banks still have minimum capital requirement of N1 billion
2002	• 90 licensed banks: 79 solvent banks and 11 distressed banks
2003	• 90 licensed banks: 78 solvent banks and 12 distressed banks
July 2004	• Number of licensed banks drops to 89 with the revocation of the licence of Peak Merchant Bank; 11 of the 89 banks are distressed • Minimum capital requirement raised to N25 billion with 31 December 2005 deadline

Source: Agusto & Co. 2005 Industry Report (Banking)
NDIC – Nigeria Deposit Insurance Corporation

Table 9.14 Number of branches and outlets in Equity's international subsidiaries as at December 2013

Business drivers	Kenya	Uganda	S. Sudan	Rwanda	Tanzania	Totals
No. of employees	6484	580	258	278	188	7788
No. of branches	159	31	12	9	6	217
No. of agents	9557	0	0	570	133	10,260
No. of ATMs	516	31	18	12	7	584
No. of customer accounts	7,392,479	513,212	126,392	306,288	68,299	8,406,670

Source: Equity Bank Reports 2013

Table 9.15 PEST criteria grid

Political factors	Social factors
• EAC regional integration • Governance • Legislation and regulations • Country risk ranking	• Cultural differences • Management philosophy of the host country • Literacy level • Poverty level • Employment • Food security • Demographic profile
Technological factors	**Economic factors**
• Telecommunications: Mobile and internet penetration rates • Depth of telecommunication services supply • Mobile money penetration	• GDP per capita and GDP growth • Cost and ease of doing business • Currency exchange rate stability • Cost of capital • Interest rate regime (cr, Dr,interest spread) • Foreign exchange reserves/import cover • Balance of trade, current account deficit • Fiscal Policy and Budget Deficit • Credit rating of the country

Mobile Money Penetration refers to the percentage of adults who use the Mobile Money service compared to the total adult population
PEST – Political, Economic, Social and Technological Factors

Table 9.16 Equity's total foreign direct investment into subsidiary companies

Equity Bank foreign direct investment (FDI) as at 31 December 2013					
Country	Subsidiary	Cumulative capital injected by Equity Bank Group	Central bank or national regulatory authority	Central bank minimum capital/FDI requirement	% Equity Bank FDI above minimum capital
Uganda	Equity Bank Uganda Ltd	US$45,574,713	Bank of Uganda	US$9,601,814 (UGX25 billion)	374.65
South Sudan	Equity Bank South Sudan Ltd	US$29,160,920	Bank of South Sudan	US$3,000,000	872.03
Rwanda	Equity Bank Rwanda Ltd	US$16,988,506	National Bank of Rwanda	US$7,274,176 (RWF5 billion)	133.55
Tanzania	Equity Bank Tanzania Ltd	US$16,459,770	Bank of Tanzania	US$8,978,280 (TSh15 billion)	83.33

UGX – Ugandan Shillings; RWF – Rwandan Francs; TSH – Tanzanian Shillings

Notes

1. Nigerian Bureau of Statistics, Statistical Bulletin, 2011.
2. Nigeria—World Afropedia (http://www.worldafropedia.com/afropedia/Nigeria) Accessed on 22/12/2015.
3. Nigeria—World Afropedia (http://www.worldafropedia.com/afropedia/Nigeria) Accessed on 22/12/2015.
4. Nigeria—Population distribution (http://www.indexmundi.com/nigeria/age_structure.html) Accessed on 22/12/2015.
5. Nigeria—Conservapedia (http://www.conservapedia.com/Nigeria) Accessed on 22/12/2015.
6. Nigeria—http://www.tradingeconomics.com/nigeria/gdp Accessed on 22/12/2015.
7. Nigeria—African Economic Outlook (http://www.africaneconomicoutlook.org/fileadmin/uploads/aeo/2015/CN_data/CN_Long_EN/Nigeria_GB_2015.pdf) Accessed on 22/12/2015.
8. Nigeria Bureau of Statistics, Statistical Bulletin, 2011.
9. Nigeria—US Department of State (http://www.state.gov/outofdate/bgn/nigeria/200317.htm) Accessed on 23/12/2015.
10. CIPRA—State of Nigerian Roads Infrastructure Report 2013.
11. *Doing Business 2012* is the ninth in a series of annual reports investigating the regulations that enhance business activity and those that constrain it by presenting quantitative indicators on business regulation and the protection of property rights. Comparisons can be made across 183 economies.
12. The HDI is a summary measure for assessing long-term progress in three basic dimensions of human development: a long and healthy life, access to knowledge and a decent standard of living.
13. United Nations Human Development Report 2013 of Nigeria.
14. Central Bank of Nigeria History (http://www.cen**bank**.org/About**CBN/history**.asp) Accessed on 23/12/2015.
15. Central Bank of Nigeria Website (http://www.cenbank.org)—Banks performance in the implementation of the SMIES—19 June 2001 to 31 December 2003.
16. Romanus, O. O. External Debt Crisis, Debt Relief and Economic Growth: Lessons from Nigeria.
17. Nigerian Bureau of Statistics—Statistical Bulletin, 2005.
18. Central Bank of Nigeria Records.
19. (https://www.kluwerlawonline.com/abstract.php?id=381639) Accessed on 23/12/2015.
20. Economist Intelligence Unit (EIU) Viewswire, Country Profile—Nigeria—2003.

21. Beyond Banking sector consolidation by C. Soludo (http://www.cenbank.org/out/speeches/2006/govadd29-3-06.pdf) Accessed on 23/12/2015.
22. http://www.cenbank.org/out/speeches/2011/Gov_Banks%20in%20Nigeria%20and%20National%20Economic%20Development_CHC-CIBN-RBC_040611.pdf.
23. http://www.cenbank.org/out/speeches/2011/Gov_Banks%20in%20Nigeria%20and%20National%20Economic%20Development_CHC-CIBN-RBC_040611.pdf.
24. Beyond Banking sector consolidation by C. Soludo (http://www.cenbank.org/out/speeches/2006/govadd29-3-06.pdf) Accessed on 23/12/2015.
25. Beyond Banking sector consolidation by C. Soludo (http://www.cenbank.org/out/speeches/2006/govadd29-3-06.pdf) Accessed on 23/12/2015.
26. Central Bank of Nigeria 2005 Annual Report.
27. Beyond Banking sector consolidation by C. Soludo (http://www.cenbank.org/out/speeches/2006/govadd29-3-06.pdf) Accessed on 23/12/2015.
28. Ebomuche, N. C., Ihugba, O. A., & Bankong, B. (2014). The Impact of Nigeria Microfinance Banks on Poverty Reduction: Imo State Experience.*International Letters of Social and Humanistic Sciences*, (05), 92–113.
29. CBN Statistical Bulletin March 2007 (http://www.cenbank.org/OUT/PUBLICATIONS/BULLION/GOV/2008/BULLJAN-MAR07.PDF).
30. Beyond Banking sector consolidation by C. Soludo (http://www.cenbank.org/out/speeches/2006/govadd29-3-06.pdf) Accessed on 23/12/2015.
31. Beyond Banking sector consolidation by C. Soludo (http://www.cenbank.org/out/speeches/2006/govadd29-3-06.pdf) Accessed on 23/12/2015
32. http://www.cenbank.org/OUT/SPEECHES/2010/THE%20NIGERIAN%20BANKING%20INDUSTRY%20WHAT%20WENT%20WRONG%20AND%20THE%20WAY%20FORWARD_FINAL_260210.PDF.
33. CBN—2009 Financial Stability Report—(http://www.cenbank.org/OUT/2010/PUBLICATIONS/BSD/FINANCIAL%20STABILITY%20FINAL%20TO%20PRINTER%20-%2015102010.PDF).
34. The Nigerian Banking Industry—What went wrong and the way forward—(http://www.cenbank.org/OUT/SPEECHES/2010/THE%20NIGERIAN%20BANKING%20INDUSTRY%20WHAT%20WENT%20WRONG%20AND%20THE%20WAY%20FORWARD_FINAL_260210.PDF) Accessed on 23/12/2013.
35. The Nigerian Banking Industry—What went wrong and the way forward—(http://www.cenbank.org/OUT/SPEECHES/2010/THE%20NIGERIAN%20BANKING%20INDUSTRY%20WHAT%20WENT%20WRONG%20AND%20THE%20WAY%20FORWARD_FINAL_260210.PDF) Accessed on 23/12/2013.

36. http://www.cenbank.org/out/speeches/2011/Gov_Banks%20in%20Nigeria%20and%20National%20Economic%20Development_CHC-CIBN-RBC_040611.pdf.
37. http://www.cenbank.org/out/speeches/2011/Gov_Banks%20in%20Nigeria%20and%20National%20Economic%20Development_CHC-CIBN-RBC_040611.pdf.
38. http://www.cenbank.org/out/speeches/2011/Gov_Banks%20in%20Nigeria%20and%20National%20Economic%20Development_CHC-CIBN-RBC_040611.pdf.
39. Equity Bank Group—Our History (**equitybank**group.com/about/our-history) Accessed on 09/10/2011.
40. Ogbechie, C. (2007). "Equity Bank Ltd.—Kenya" Case study for the purposes of class discussion, Lagos Business School, Lagos.
41. Understanding the Rebirth of Equity Building Society (http://www.microsave.net/files/pdf/Understanding_the_Re_birth_of_Equity_Building_Society_in_Kenya.pdf) Accessed on 09/10/2014.
42. Equity's 2006 Annual Reports.
43. Equity's 2006 Annual Reports.
44. Understanding the Rebirth of Equity Building Society (http://www.microsave.net/files/pdf/Understanding_the_Re_birth_of_Equity_Building_Society_in_Kenya.pdf) Accessed on 09/10/2014.
45. Understanding the Rebirth of Equity Building Society (http://www.microsave.net/files/pdf/Understanding_the_Re_birth_of_Equity_Building_Society_in_Kenya.pdf) Accessed on 09/10/2014.
46. Ogbechie, C. (2007). "Equity Bank Ltd.—Kenya" Case study for the purposes of class discussion, Lagos Business School, Lagos.
47. Understanding the Rebirth of Equity Building Society (http://www.microsave.net/files/pdf/Understanding_the_Re_birth_of_Equity_Building_Society_in_Kenya.pdf) Accessed on 09/10/2014.
48. Ogbechie, C. (2007). "Equity Bank Ltd.—Kenya" Case study for the purposes of class discussion, Lagos Business School, Lagos.
49. Ogbechie, C. (2007). "Equity Bank Ltd.—Kenya" Case study for the purposes of class discussion, Lagos Business School, Lagos.
50. Understanding the Rebirth of Equity Building Society (http://www.microsave.net/files/pdf/Understanding_the_Re_birth_of_Equity_Building_Society_in_Kenya.pdf) Accessed on 09/10/2014.
51. Equity Bank's 2006 Annual Reports and Accounts.
52. Equity Bank's 2010 Annual Reports and Accounts.
53. Equity Bank's 2012 Annual Reports and Accounts.
54. Equity Bank's 2010 Annual Reports and Accounts.
55. Africa Trade Policy Notes—Scaling up financial integration in the EAC region (http://web.worldbank.org/WBSITE/EXTERNAL/COUNTRIES/

AFRICAEXT/EXTAFRREGTOPTRADE/0,,contentMDK:22962171~pagePK:34004173~piPK:34003707~theSitePK:502469,00.html).
56. Africa Trade Policy Notes—Scaling up financial integration in the EAC region (http://web.worldbank.org/WBSITE/EXTERNAL/COUNTRIES/AFRICAEXT/EXTAFRREGTOPTRADE/0,,contentMDK:22962171~pagePK:34004173~piPK:34003707~theSitePK:502469,00.html).
57. Africa Trade Policy Notes—Scaling up financial integration in the EAC region (http://web.worldbank.org/WBSITE/EXTERNAL/COUNTRIES/AFRICAEXT/EXTAFRREGTOPTRADE/0,,contentMDK:22962171~pagePK:34004173~piPK:34003707~theSitePK:502469,00.html).
58. Africa Trade Policy Notes—Scaling up financial integration in the EAC region (http://web.worldbank.org/WBSITE/EXTERNAL/COUNTRIES/AFRICAEXT/EXTAFRREGTOPTRADE/0,,contentMDK:22962171~pagePK:34004173~piPK:34003707~theSitePK:502469,00.html).
59. Africa Trade Policy Notes—Scaling up financial integration in the EAC region (http://web.worldbank.org/WBSITE/EXTERNAL/COUNTRIES/AFRICAEXT/EXTAFRREGTOPTRADE/0,,contentMDK:22962171~pagePK:34004173~piPK:34003707~theSitePK:502469,00.html).
60. 2011 Sub Saharan Africa Regional Snapshot—(https://opportunity.org/content/News/Publications/Knowledge%20Exchange/2011%20Sub-Saharan%20Africa%20Regional%20Snapshot.pdf) Accessed on 09/10/2014.
61. http://www.economist.com/blogs/dailychart/2011/01/daily_chart Accessed on 09/10/2014.
62. GDP growth rate in Uganda is reported by the Uganda Bureau of Statistics.
63. Banking in Africa—European Investment Bank (http://www.eib.org/attachments/efs/economic_report_banking_africa_en.pdf) Accessed on 24/09/2013.

Index[1]

[1] Note: Page number followed by 'n' refers to endnotes.

I. Adeleye et al. (eds.), *Africa-to-Africa Internationalization*, AIB Sub-Saharan Africa (SSA) Series, DOI 10.1007/978-3-319-30692-6

www.ingramcontent.com/pod-product-compliance
Lightning Source LLC
Chambersburg PA
CBHW080003120225
21676CB00016B/236
9783319306919